DATE DUE

On the run, shot-down airmen constantly had to evade German patrols and checkpoints. Artist, Terence Cuneo. (TNA: PRO INF 3/1796)

SHOT DOWN
AND ON THE RUN

**The RCAF and Commonwealth aircrews
who got home from behind enemy lines
1940–1945**

Air Commodore
Graham Pitchfork MBE, BA, FRAeS

Foreword by
Air Chief Marshal
Sir Lewis Hodges KCB, CBE, DSO*, DFC*

THE DUNDURN GROUP

TORONTO

Maps by European Map Graphics, Kingsley, Hampshire
Printer: Transcontinental

National Library of Canada Cataloguing in Publication Data

Pitchfork, Graham
    Shot down and on the run : the RCAF and Commonwealth aircrews who got home from behind enemy lines, 1940-1945 / Graham Pitchfork.

Includes bibliographical references and index.
ISBN 1-55002-483-3

1. Prisoner-of-war escapes — History — 20th century. 2. Airmen — Commonwealth countries — Biography. 3. Airmen — Canada — Biography. 4. World War, 1939-1945 — Prisoners and prisons. I. Title.

D785.P58 2003   940.54'72'0922   C2003-906264-3

1   2   3   4   5   07   06   05   04   03

www.dundurn.com

Jacket illustration: (front) Second World War airman dropping
at night amongst windmills, by Terence Cuneo (TNA: PRO INF 3/1795)

Printed in Canada

Contents

Foreword

Air Chief Marshal Sir Lewis Hodges
KCB, CBE, DSO*, DFC*

FOLLOWING THE OUTBREAK of the Second World War, it did not take too long before RAF and Commonwealth aircrew were operating over enemy territory, with the inevitable consequence that some found themselves behind enemy lines, having been shot down or forced to crash-land. For the great majority, it was the end of the war, and all they had to look forward to was an unknown period of time as a prisoner of the enemy. A relative few managed to evade capture and return home. Their backgrounds and abilities were just as varied as their experiences on the run, but they all shared the common quality of tremendous fortitude, initiative and courage – most would also acknowledge that they enjoyed a certain amount of luck as well. Their stimulating stories are the basis of this book.

There have been many books in the past on escape and evasion. Some have recorded individual experiences while others have related a series of accounts. However, unlike many previous authors, Graham Pitchfork has added a new dimension to the evasions he has chosen to describe. Not only has he spread his net very wide to include accounts from every theatre of the air war, but he has provided a fascinating backdrop to the whole evasion business, thus allowing the reader to have a better appreciation of the exploits of the remarkable men and women who appear in this book. His comprehensive review of how the escape and evasion organization was established, developed and operated, the way aircrew were trained and briefed, and the development and provision of escape aids provides an essential background for a full appreciation of just what evaders were faced with, and how and why they were able to successfully combat the problems they faced.

The evaders, however, provide just half the cast of this deeply researched and fascinating book. As the author makes so abundantly clear, the very great majority of evaders would have achieved nothing without their helpers, many of whom paid the ultimate price for their gallantry and patriotism. Many readers will be aware of the great deeds of the escape lines of Western Europe, but what emerges from this book is how universal was the attitude of oppressed people to freedom and their willingness to help those endeavouring to restore peace and order on their behalf. In addition to the gallant men and women of those established escape lines, we also read of Italian, Polish and Greek partisans, of Norwegian and Danish fishermen, of Senussi Arabs, natives of the hill tribes of Burma, the tribesmen of New Guinea and policemen in Siam. Notwithstanding their very diverse cultures and attitudes, all were prepared to take the greatest risks in order to help airmen evade the enemy. In my own experience, if it had not been for the help I received from the farming communities in both the Occupied and Unoccupied Zones of France, I would not have succeeded in reaching the Pyrenees and eventually crossing into Spain.

Graham Pitchfork has unearthed some remarkable stories of evaders and their helpers, which will remind other generations, and those in the future, of just what the human spirit is capable of, and sacrifices that people are prepared to make, at times of great adversity. This excellent book is a fitting memorial to all those who evaded and to their helpers.

Lewis Hodges.

President
RAF Escaping Society

Preface

WHEN I WAS A SCHOOLBOY IN THE 1950s, the rapid emergence of books relating the personal experiences of those who had fought during the Second World War attracted my attention like a magnet, and I couldn't wait for my weekly visit to the local library to exchange one book for another. One particular selection had a significant appeal – those dealing with escape and evasion. Books such as *The Great Escape, Colditz, Boldness be my Friend, The Wooden Horse, Cockleshell Heroes* and *They have their Exits,* to mention just a few from that decade, seemed to encapsulate all the human experiences and qualities that excited a teenage boy – adventure, excitement, fear and courage.

A lifetime of service in the Royal Air Force has allowed me to take a wider perspective on an aspect of warfare that was ever present to those of us involved in flying operations – the possibility of being shot down, and its consequences. In addition, the opportunity to work alongside some of those who had experience of escape and evasion added to my awareness, and more recently my role as Archivist of the Aircrew Association has allowed me to discuss with some of them the realities of being shot down behind enemy lines. Some of their stories appear later in this book. Notwithstanding this wider perspective achieved over the past 40 years, I still find the pulse races when I recall the daring experiences related in the aforementioned books. However, one aspect strikes me most forcibly – the reader of them could be forgiven for thinking that the escapers and evaders had acted almost entirely alone. The books were, of course, written at a time when certain aspects of their escape to freedom could not be told for security reasons. Indeed, conversations I have enjoyed in recent years with those who were shot down and evaded highlight that many of them were completely unaware that there were numerous 'organizations' instrumental in their successful return. Furthermore, many of their courageous 'helpers' were unseen, while others remained anonymous, and their meetings were often no more than brief acquaintances. With the passage of time, the veil of secrecy on these remarkable organizations, and their even more remarkable people, has been lifted and their stories can be told.

There are now books that are the definitive accounts on escape and evasion, and they have become essential reading to those with any kind of interest in the subject. They provide an important backdrop to this book, and the reader is urged to read them. The definitive account is *MI 9: Escape and Evasion 1939–1945* by M. R. D. Foot and J. M. Langley. Other significant books as background reading are *Saturday at MI 9* by Airey Neave and *Europe Ablaze* by Jorgen Haestrup. There are many others dealing with specific aspects of the escape and evasion scene that can be recommended, and some of them appear in the Bibliography.

The aim of this book is to relate the experiences of RAF and Commonwealth aircrew who were shot down over enemy territory, but successfully avoided capture to eventually return to friendly territory. It does not attempt to include those who escaped from enemy captivity nor does it discuss the significant and fascinating work of MI 9 in support of prisoners of war, their escape committees, and the gathering and passing of intelligence. Of course, once a prisoner had escaped, he naturally became an evader, and his further progress followed the same pattern as those who had avoided capture. Those readers with a particular interest in RAF escapers are strongly recommended to read *Escape from Germany* by Aidan Crawley.

The second aim of this book is to highlight to the reader the scope and scale of the historical documents which are deposited in the National Archives and are available to the general public. With the exception of personal memoirs loaned to me by some of the evaders, and tape recordings I have made during my visits to meet them, all the material for this book has been obtained through documents available at Kew. For a project such as this, there are a number of key documents, and the majority are held in the WO 208 series. Of particular importance are Brigadier Crockatt's *Historical Record of MI 9* (WO 208/3242) and the *MI 9 Bulletin* (WO 208/3268). Crucial for the subject of RAF evasions are the interrogation reports compiled by MI 9 officers following the debriefing of returned evaders, and they are found in numerous volumes in the WO 208 series. The Air Intelligence Branch also conducted debriefings on RAF operational matters, and these are contained in the AIR 40 series and complement the MI 9 reports to provide valuable additional information.

This book contains 29 accounts of individual evasions. I have taken particular care in their selection because there are a number of aspects that I want the narratives to illustrate. First, the wide range of operations and operational theatres where RAF and Commonwealth aircrew flew. Second, to illustrate the remarkable ingenuity and fortitude that men possess when their freedom, sometimes their lives, are at stake. Third, the many diverse ways and methods that were used, or individuals found, to return evaders to friendly territory. Finally, to emphasize the unique and selfless role of the countless number of 'helpers' who risked their lives to assist the evading airmen.

However, before embarking on the individual stories, I believe their significance will be enhanced if they are placed in the wider context of the organization of escape and evasion. Therefore, the book is arranged in four parts. The first part deals with the development of the MI 9 organization and how it adjusted to the changing features of the war. The three remaining parts form the bulk of this book, and they have been divided into the three geographical areas corresponding to the ultimate organization of MI 9 – Western Europe, the Middle East and Mediterranean, and the Far East.

There is one final aim of this book. The generation of men and women who are the subject of *Shot Down and on the Run* are inevitably fading into the past. Thankfully, some remain to remind us of just what the human spirit is capable of when life and freedom are placed in peril. The fortitude, determination, resolve and courage of the evaders and their wonderful helpers shines out from a ghastly war like a beacon. Today's generation, and those that follow, need to be reminded of the sacrifices these warriors and patriots were prepared to make so that others can live in the freedom that was denied to so many of them and their colleagues. This book is dedicated to the memory of all RAF and Commonwealth evaders and their many helpers.

October 2003
Graham Pitchfork
Gloucestershire

Acknowledgements

MANY PEOPLE HAVE helped me in writing this book, and I want to thank them most sincerely for giving me their time, expertise and friendship. First I want to thank Air Chief Marshal Sir Lewis Hodges for agreeing to write the Foreword, and for all his advice given at a time when he had many other important calls on his time. He was one of the early evaders travelling through France before crossing the Pyrenees, and later commanded two Special Duties squadrons – first 161 Squadron at Tempsford, followed by command of 357 Squadron in the Far East. No-one could be better qualified to understand the life of an evader or appreciate the bravery and sacrifices of the 'helpers'. I am most grateful to him.

I have had the pleasure of meeting a number of the evaders whose stories appear in the pages that follow, and others have kindly sent me details and photographs. My thanks go to Norman Bolitho DFC, Larrie Carr, Terry Corkran (Australia), Ray Jackson MC, Charles Keen, 'Mac' McCaig MBE, AFC, Tony Snell DSO, Rowland Williams DFM, and Ken Woodhouse (Canada). Mrs Kitty Cooper and Mrs Jessie Tweed have kindly allowed me to use their late husbands' written memoirs and photographs. Mrs Joanne McHugo helped me with photographs and the story of her late father, Bob Haye. A number of members of the Royal Air Force Escaping Society have given me a great deal of help, in particular Bill Knaggs and Bryan Morgan of the United Kingdom Branch, Ray Brown from Canada and Robert Chester-Master and Murray Adams from Australia. I am grateful to the latter for allowing me to use a few quotations from his book *Against the Odds*. Lionel Lacey-Johnson and Geoffrey Jeudwine have been most helpful and allowed me to quote from their book *Global Warrior*. I also want to thank Ron Stephens, who served on HMT *Tarana* for his inputs and the use of his photographs.

I have received a lot of help from Norway and want to thank Egil Christopherson of the Nordvjofartmuseet in Bergen, and Halvor Sperbund, Bjarne Øvredal and Knut Störe. A number of papers had to be translated from Norwegian, and I thank James and Bella Irvin and Ian Fraser from the Shetlands and Roland Tucker for their help. From Holland I want to record my appreciation to the Royal Netherlands Air Force History Unit, to Jan van den Driesschen and Bob De Graaf. Dutch translations were made by Margreet Walpole and Biny Gregory. 'Nina' Harper (née Mierzwinska) helped me with details about Poland. Finally, my daughter Siobhan translated French papers. My thanks to all of them.

The staff of the Air Historical Branch have once again given me a great deal of help, and I am grateful to the Head of the Branch, Sebastian Cox, and to Graham Day for their assistance. Roger Stanton, the secretary of the Escape Lines Memorial Society and creator of escape and evasion displays at Eden Camp in Yorkshire, has been a great help. My thanks also go to fellow historian Paul Baillie for his help and advice, and to my friends Peter Green and Andy Thomas for their help with photographs.

Special thanks are due to the staff of the National Archives who stimulated the idea to write this book, and who have provided so much expert advice and assistance. Jane Crompton, Sheila Knight, Peter Leek and Kathryn Sleight have borne the brunt of my many requests, and arranged to have documents available for my extensive research. They have also obtained the necessary permissions to use material from the National Archives and photographs from the Imperial War Museum. Whenever I was stuck with a particular aspect of research, William Spencer came to my rescue, invariably producing what I needed in a matter of minutes. Paul Johnson and Hugh Alexander have given me their expert advice on photographs and made all the arrangements for reproducing those used in the book.

Finally, I should like to thank Lisa Kenwright of Indexing Specialists (UK) Ltd for her diligence in preparing the index.

Abbreviations

'A' Force	Deception and Escape Organization (Middle East)
AFC	Air Force Cross
BAAG	British Army Aid Group
BBC	British Broadcasting Corporation
BEF	British Expeditionary Force
BOAC	British Overseas Airways Corporation
CGM	Conspicuous Gallantry Medal
CMF	Central Mediterranean Forces
DDMI	Deputy Director of Military Intelligence
DFC	Distinguished Flying Cross
DFM	Distinguished Flying Medal
DMI	Director of Military Intelligence
DNI	Director of Naval Intelligence
DSC	Distinguished Service Cross
DSM	Distinguished Service Medal
DSO	Distinguished Service Order
E Group	Escape organization (Far East)
Gestapo	*Geheime Staatspolizei*
GSI	General Staff Intelligence
HMT	Her Majesty's Trawler
IFF	Identification Friend or Foe
IS 9	Intelligence School 9 (used as cover for MI 9)
LRDG	Long Range Desert Group
MAAF	Mediterranean Allied Air Forces
MBE	Member of the Order of the British Empire
MC	Military Cross

ME	Middle East
MGB	Motor Gun Boat
MI	Military Intelligence
	MI 1(a) Organization
	MI 5 Security
	MI 6 Intelligence
	MI 9 Escape and evasion
	MI 19 Refugees and enemy prisoners
	MI R Research
MIS – X	Military Intelligence Section – Escape and Evasion (American)
MM	Military Medal
OBE	Officer of the Order of the British Empire
OSS	Office of Strategic Services (American)
OTU	Operational Training Unit
POW	Prisoner of War
RAAF	Royal Australian Air Force
RAF	Royal Air Force
RAFES	Royal Air Force Escaping Society
RCAF	Royal Canadian Air Force
RNR	Royal Naval Reserve
RNVR	Royal Naval Volunteer Reserve
SAS	Special Air Service
SBS	Special Boat Service
SEAC	South-East Asia Command
SIS	Secret Intelligence Service (MI 6)
SOE	Special Operations Executive
USAAF	United States Army Air Force
WEA	Western European Area
WO	Warrant Officer, War Office

PART ONE

The Escape and Evasion Organization

Chapter One

Evasion

THE PRINCIPLES OF WARFARE have changed little over the centuries. The enormous advances made in technology have undoubtedly had a dramatic influence on how wars have been conducted, and have often had a critical bearing on the final outcome. However, certain activities, such as reconnaissance, deception, and espionage, have been part of the battlefield ever since men, tribes and countries fought each other. To these military disciplines, we can add the human desire to avoid capture by the enemy, since such a calamity almost certainly precipitated a period of harsh and unpleasant treatment, probably great privation, and, in many cases, death. Capture also created a loss of the individual's dignity and morale, both of which could recover over a period of time, and even during a period of captivity. However, the most important consequence of being taken prisoner on the battlefield was the loss of the most treasured of human desires – freedom. The counter to these various levels of discomfort and degradation was to evade capture in the first place, and then to spare no effort in attempting to remain free and return to friendly territory.

Prior to the Second World War, battlefields had been the stages for great armies and navies, and where countries were occupied, the civilian population bore their fate with stoicism and resolve. However, the Nazi tyranny that descended on Europe in the 1930s introduced a new dimension, with whole races subjected to slavery or extermination. Suddenly, the dormant characteristic of self-preservation, which exists within all humans when they and their way of life are threatened, generated a ferment of activity as whole populations attempted to evade the onslaught that they faced. Thousands of Jews had to confront the agonizing decision – should they stay and risk death, or flee? With the German occupation of Poland in 1939, thousands of Poles decided to evade, and many fled to fight again with the Allies. As Germany expanded its march across the whole of Europe, countless others chose the same option. Yet more remained to spawn a new phenomenon of organized 'resistance' by forming underground organizations that soon became a major part of the Allies' order of battle.

Although escape and evasion are as old as war itself, the unique situation that faced Europe in the spring of 1940 created a different environment for the would-be escaper and evader. The majority of countries in Europe found themselves under the occupation of brutal tyrannies that attracted little local sympathy or support. There will, of course, always be some who are prepared to collaborate, but the population's attitude in most occupied countries in Europe was in favour of the evader. With the advent of Resistance groups and Underground movements, there was also the scope for coordinating activities to establish escape lines, and the development, control and success of these will be addressed in detail. As the war progressed, the organization for escape and evasion evolved significantly, training and escape aids improved as experience was gained, and successes increased steadily. By the end of the war, almost 8,000 Allied servicemen reached the Allied lines in Western Europe, including Italy. The great majority who returned in North-West Europe were airmen. A terrible price had to be paid by underground escape workers for their valuable work. Over 500 civilians from France, Belgium and Holland were arrested and shot or died in concentration camps, with many others succumbing to their treatment after they had been released.

Circumstances in other theatres were somewhat different, often influenced by huge distances, the terrain, and the weather. From the end of 1941 onwards the inexorable advances of the Japanese in the Far East generated many similar attitudes among those living in the occupied countries, and a number of underground movements and guerrilla groups developed. However, for the evader of European origin or descent, the Far East presented some unique conditions that were very difficult to combat. He stood out among the local population, and there was a huge cultural difference, not least the clash of ideology that dictated that surrender was utterly dishonourable to a Japanese soldier, whereas death in the name of the Emperor was the greatest honour, as exemplified later in the war by the kamikaze pilots. Such a cultural divide created a huge, virtually unmanageable difficulty for those trying to avoid capture.

The knowledge that in battle it was inevitable that men would attempt to avoid capture, and some would succeed, created significant military implications for all sides. The return of evaders and escapers provided a tremendous boost for the morale of others, demonstrating to them that the unthinkable and unknown could be mastered and lead to success and freedom. It also highlighted that those who were properly prepared, both physically and mentally, could achieve success, often against heavy odds. From a military standpoint there were also huge benefits, none more so than the return of highly trained men who could continue to make a valuable contribution to the war effort. This was a major factor for the RAF during the Second World War, when the training of aircrew was both very long and expensive, and the return of those shot down reduced the need to train replacements. Many of them also returned with valuable intelligence – not least much technical data about how and why aircraft had been shot down, and on bomb damage assessment. A significant, but less obvious, benefit was the need for the enemy to use thousands of men in organizations designed to prevent escape and evasion. Everyone in the Allied forces was taught that it was his duty to escape, and the diversion of manpower to cater for prisoners of war (POWs), escapers, evaders, and the underground movements that supported them was a constant problem for enemy forces, and kept many men tied down in non-operational activities away from the battlefield. In this indirect way, those who fell behind enemy lines to end up as POWs or as evaders were still able to play an important part on the way to victory, and those in command of such men were determined that they should appreciate this valuable point.

RAF and Commonwealth aircrew flew over every type of topography, in all the world's climates, and often deep into enemy territory. Each dictated different priorities for the evader. Where survival was merely a case of ingenuity and determination, it was important to start evading immediately on arrival in enemy territory. However, in some environments, notably the jungle and desert, the crucial priority was survival, and the training and issue of escape aids was geared to this essential approach. It was only when survival had been made possible that a downed airman could start to consider evasion.

In most of Europe it was possible for an evader to pass unnoticed among the local population if careful precautions were taken. This allowed a certain amount of flexibility not available to an evader in the Far East or the desert regions where he would be instantly recognizable. Evaders were likely to be less conspicuous in crowds, but then the risk of identity checks was greater. Clearly, some knowledge of the local language would be a significant bonus. The attitude of the occupying power to the local population had a major influence on the help that local people felt able to offer. Understandably, the fear of reprisals and atrocities was a massive disincentive to assist. It is remarkable that so many people across the globe were prepared to risk their lives, and the chapters that follow will highlight the incredible bravery of these people. Sadly, as in any society, there were a few – a very few – who were prepared to collaborate with the enemy, and they were a danger both to the evader and to the helper. The attitude of the enemy also influenced an evader's approach to the problem. Generally speaking, the German and Italian authorities adhered by the Geneva Convention, and accorded a prisoner his proper rights if he could establish his identity. The same could not be said of the Japanese, who treated aircrew in particular as war criminals. Inevitably, these attitudes were a factor that influenced an evader's decision making and actions.

At the outset of the Second World War, the need for a specialist organization to support the activities of POWs, and to establish guidelines for escape and evasion, was recognized by the formation in December 1939 of MI (Military Intelligence) 9. Initially, it was a very minor operation, sustained almost entirely by the force of personality of a very few people. As the war progressed, and evaders started to return, the organization expanded globally, and its development and activities will be discussed in detail later. Great advances were made in gathering intelligence to support the escape organization, making it possible to establish escape 'lines', and to maintain close liaison with them. Returning evaders often provided a wealth of current information on the regions they had passed through. A compre-hensive debriefing system for evaders was created in order to gain a better understanding of the techniques of evasion, where the safest routes existed, and the value of previous advice and escape aids. In turn, these experiences were acted upon to provide better information and escape aids for those who followed. This led to the creation of training establishments where specialists and instructors analysed the reports and disseminated the lessons learned, through bulletins, lectures and briefings. Similarly, agile minds developed more sophisticated and subtle escape and survival aids subsequently issued to aircrew before they flew on operations. All these measures had an impact on the attitude, knowledge and ability of aircrew who later found themselves being evaders, and thus there was an ever-changing approach to evasion. Further dramatic changes occurred when the Allies landed in Italy in July 1943 and in Normandy in June 1944, creating new situations for the evaders to consider and act upon, not least the problem of having to cross battle lines safely.

Having studied very many accounts and personal debriefings of successful evasions, I am clear that there is no blueprint for success, and what is striking is the realization that no two evasions were the same. There are an infinite number of ways people can react, be they evader, helper or traitor. Methods of travel embraced every system known to man. Almost anything could be eaten if it became necessary, including escape maps! There is one factor that had an immense impact on the evader's success or otherwise, and that was luck. It was, perhaps, the one essential ingredient that the evader had no control over. A very careful man could have the misfortune to call at the only farmhouse in the area where there was sympathy for the occupying power. A careless man might be fortunate to pass the only sleeping sentry on duty. Most evaders who made it back would be the first to acknowledge that luck had, at some stage, played a significant part in their success. However, it is the depths of human endurance and courage, allied to boundless ingenuity and an ability to improvise, that have the greatest bearing on the eventual outcome of an attempt to evade capture. In the chapters that follow, all these aspects, and many others, will be in ample evidence.

Chapter Two

The MI 9 Organization

THROUGHOUT THE FIRST WORLD WAR there still existed a somewhat old-fashioned notion that to be captured by the enemy was some kind of disgrace. There was, therefore, little encouragement to escape, although this did not stop some determined men from trying, and some were successful. It was not until 1917 that there was the realization among the military intelligence staff that there was a potentially large untapped source of intelligence material available from returning escapers. To exploit this opportunity the War Office established a small intelligence directorate, known as MI 1(a).

With the end of the 'war to end all wars', little attention was paid to the possibility of other major wars in the foreseeable future, least of all to the need to maintain a support organization for escapers and evaders. However, by late 1938 war was looking very likely, and two staff officers started to give some attention to the need for an organization similar to the old MI 1(a). Captain A. R. Rawlinson, who had been a young officer on the staff of MI 1(a) at the end of the First World War, was mobilized in the summer of 1939 when he was tasked to review arrangements for the interrogation of enemy prisoners, and the support for escape and evasion. The other officer was Major J. C. F. Holland, who had been appointed to a research branch, later named MI R, to study irregular warfare. Among the subjects he reviewed was the need to provide prisoners of war with support for escape attempts, and in October he submitted a detailed paper outlining the organization that would be needed. Others had also started to give attention to the needs of prisoners of war and escapers, including those who had experience of such activities in the First World War, and MI 1(a) arranged a series of conferences to discuss the way forward.

From the outset of these discussions, it was apparent that a joint service approach was necessary, and the Director of Naval Intelligence (DNI) and the Director of Intelligence (D of I) at the Air Ministry were consulted. The outcome of these various initiatives was the establishment on 23 December 1939 of a new section, MI 9, within the Directorate of Military Intelligence (DMI), to combine the work of MI 1(a) with certain aspects of the work of MI R. The brief minute to establish MI 9 was given a very limited circulation to MI 5, MI 6, the naval and air intelligence branches and DMI's two deputies. This significant document, Conduct of Work No. 48, was brief and to the point. It read:

1. A new section of the Intelligence Directorate at the War Office has been formed. It will be called MI 9. It will work in close connection with and act as agent for the Admiralty and Air Ministry.
2. The Section is responsible for:
   a. The preparation and execution of plans for facilitating the escape of British Prisoners of War of all three services in Germany or elsewhere.
   b. Arranging instructions in connection with above.
   c. Making other advance provision as considered necessary.
   d. Collection and dissemination of information obtained from British Prisoners of War.
   e. Advising on counter-escape measures for German Prisoners of War in Great Britain, if requested to do so.
3. MI 9 will be accommodated in Room 424, Metropole Hotel [off Whitehall].

Placed in charge of MI 9 was Major Norman Crockatt DSO, MC, who had served with distinction in the First World War, and who would provide a focused and dynamic leadership for the section for the remainder of the war. It was divided into two halves – one dealing with enemy prisoners, and the other with British and Common-wealth prisoners, escapers and evaders. Rawlinson was put in charge of the section dealing with the enemy prisoners, called initially MI 9(a). MI 9(b) was responsible for all aspects relating to Allied prisoners and evaders. Following the German bombing of London in September 1940, Crockatt moved his organization to a country house

Brigadier Norman Crockatt – the mastermind of the wartime MI 9. (ACR Archives)

at Wilton Park in the Chilterns, where it became known as Camp 20, Beaconsfield.

The work of MI 9 expanded to such an extent that it resulted in the establishment in December 1941 of a Deputy Directorate of Military Intelligence (Prisoners of War) – DDMI (PW) – when MI 9(a) was formed into a new section, MI 19, with Rawlinson remaining in charge, and MI 9(b) became the new MI 9. A further unit, Intelligence School 9 (IS 9), was created to take over the executive work of MI 9 and to form a school to train intelligence officers from all three services who were capable of briefing the men in their units on the intricacies of escape and evasion. Crockatt was promoted to colonel, and subsequently brigadier, to become the Deputy Director of this new organization.

In outlining the objectives of the new MI 9, Crockatt refined the original 'Conduct of Work' to include an important statement that is of particular importance for the subject of this book:

a. To facilitate the return to the United Kingdom of those who succeeded in evading capture in enemy-occupied territory.

He also emphasized the value of getting back service personnel and containing additional enemy manpower on guard duties. Crockatt outlined the methods to be adopted to achieve his objectives as well, and split these into three categories. Two of these became fundamental pillars of the escape and evasion scene, while the third was to devise methods of maintaining the morale of prisoners of war, and does not concern us in this account. The first series of measures was geared to preparing combatants before they went on operations. These included 'preventive training' (instruction in escape and evasion), and the issue and regular updating of a new publication, the *MI 9 Bulletin*, which passed on information on all aspects of escape and evasion, including sanitized reports of successful evasions. Other measures were the technical research and production of escape aids, including special maps, the issue of these aids and 'blood chits', and the preparation of plans for escape and evasion. The second series of measures was geared to obtaining and distributing post-evasion information, which included the interrogation of escapers and evaders, Allied infiltrators and British civilians with specialist knowledge or recent experience in particular countries. The information obtained was embodied in reports and sent to all three services, and much of it was then used for briefing purposes, and the development of new escape aids.

On 1 January 1942 the new MI 9 was reorganized into two sub-sections. MI 9(b) dealt with coordination, distribution of information and liaison with other services, government departments and overseas commands. MI 9(d) was responsible for organizing preventive training to combatants of the three services, the issue of escape and evasion equipment, and the promulgation of information to units at home and MI 9 organizations overseas.

As early as August 1940, MI 9 had established a section in the Middle East and Mediterranean area under the overall command of Colonel Dudley Clarke, and known under various cover names, but most frequently as 'A' Force. In October 1941 MI 9 started work in the Far East, but it was not until the autumn of 1943, when it was known as the 'E' Group, that it became a significant force. Both these organizations will be discussed in more detail in the appropriate parts of this book.

An important development emanating from the rearrangements made in MI 9 in late 1941 was the establishment in January 1942 of Intelligence School 9 (IS 9) responsible for the executive work of MI 9. The school was divided into six sections, of which two are of particular interest for this narrative.

IS 9 (D) had been established in the spring of 1941 for the purpose of assisting evaders and escapers in enemy-occupied Western Europe to avoid capture and to return to the United Kingdom. This was the top-secret section of MI 9, which remained located in Room 900 in the War Office after the rest of MI 9 had moved to Beaconsfield. It was controlled in its activities by the overriding authority of the Special Intelligence Service (SIS), better known as MI 6 – an organization that had offered to establish an escape line to run from Marseille to Spain following the evacuation of the British Expeditionary Force (BEF) in May and June 1940. To establish this escape route they appointed Donald Darling, operating from Portugal in the first instance, and we shall hear more of him later.

Appointed to IS 9 (D) on formation was Captain Jimmy Langley MC of the Coldstream Guards, who had been captured at Dunkirk after being severely wounded. Despite having had his left arm amputated, he made a daring escape to Marseille, from where, after a few months' internment by the Vichy French, he was repatriated to the United Kingdom. Unfit for combat duties, he was offered an appointment in MI 6 to organize escape lines through north-west Europe. Although paid and commanded by MI 6, he was nominally on Crockatt's staff in MI 9, where he served with distinction throughout the war. Joining his staff in May 1942 was Captain Airey Neave DSO, who had also been wounded and captured at Dunkirk before ending up in the infamous prison at Colditz Castle. He made a brilliant escape to reach Switzerland before completing his escape through France and Spain to Gibraltar. He spent the rest of the war with MI 9 organizing and supporting the escape lines.

In the early stages of its existence, IS 9 (D) faced considerable difficulties and apathy towards its work. At the end of the war, Crockatt stated in his report on MI 9 activities:

The oft repeated statement that Nurse Edith Cavell, who apparently worked for SIS, had been discovered through assisting a prisoner of war seemed to dictate the whole attitude of SIS towards the section. They were determined to prevent evaders and escapers from involving them in any way. This attitude may have been correct from their own security aspect, but it was a terrific handicap to those trying to build up an organization.

Jimmy Langley. (ACR Archives)

Crockatt acknowledged that after two years MI 6 had begun to recognize the need for support for IS 9 (D). However, he appreciated that 'this was due to their realization that increased numbers of evaders on the Continent were coming under the orbits of their organizations and endangering their agents.'

The second section of Intelligence School 9 with particular importance to this book was IS 9 (W), responsible for the interrogation of escapers, evaders and repatriated personnel, and for compiling reports for distribution. It soon became apparent that returning escapers and evaders had a great deal of valuable information for various organizations, and the aims of the interrogations were clearly spelled out:

1. To obtain information for MI 9 lectures and the *MI 9 Bulletin*.
2. To obtain information which might be of use to IS 9 (X) in their planning of escapes.
3. To supply information whereby MI 9 could make recommendations for awards to escapers and helpers, settle claims for expenses incurred, and pay compensation.
4. To help IS 9 (D) to keep in touch with the progress of organizations [escape lines] on the Continent.

5. To obtain and make available to the three services and other Government departments information on conditions in enemy and enemy-occupied countries and on military and specialist subjects.

6. To keep MI 5 informed of matters of security interest affecting prisoners of war and evaders and to enable them to interrogate personnel whose cases were regarded as doubtful from the security point of view.

Most returning escapers and evaders were interrogated in London. MI 9 was very conscious of the welfare aspects of those returning, many of whom had been 'on the run' for many months, and others who had suffered particular hardship and gruelling experiences. A standard form was used for the interrogations, designed in such a way that individual annexes could be distributed to appropriate authorities without necessarily disclosing the whole report. The main report contained information on an escape or evasion up to the point where the individual passed into the hands of 'an organization'. No names of persons were mentioned, nor any descriptions given which might have identified helpers. The main report had a fairly wide distribution. Appendix 'A' was classified 'Top Secret' and contained names and addresses of helpers, the nature of the help given and relevant dates. This information was particularly important for IS 9 (D) and, eventually, the sections charged with tracing and rewarding helpers. 'Black list' foreigners were also included in the appendix, which had a very limited circulation. Appendix 'B' contained military intelligence and information and was distributed to the service departments and others that might have an interest. Appendix 'C' was similar to Appendix 'A' and was also classified Top Secret. It continued the narrative after the escaper or evader came under the control of an organization. Names and addresses of helpers, and their descriptions where necessary, were included. Finally, Appendix 'D' gave details of the use and value of the aids box, purse and other escape aids.

These reports had a considerable influence on future policy and the redesign of escape aids. As the number of airmen returning after being shot down and making a successful evasion increased, the reports were of particular value to those responsible for the expanding training organization.

Before leaving the general organization and roles of MI 9, one other section needs to be mentioned. As planning for the invasion of

Normandy, Operation 'Overlord,' commenced in 1943, it was realized that a new section would be required to meet the changing circumstances of the reoccupation of France, and IS 9 (WEA) (Western Europe Area) was established under the command of Jimmy Langley. Some of the established escape lines would no longer be required, and new problems would arise as Allied armies advanced through the occupied countries. In particular, it was expected that many men shot down behind enemy lines after the invasion would remain in hiding to await liberation. The work of IS 9 (WEA) in establishing reception areas for these men behind enemy lines, and the recovery of men following the abortive operation at Arnhem in September 1944, are epic stories deserving of separate accounts.

Finally, it is important to mention the close cooperation that developed with the United States. In many aspects of warfare, the Americans had their own views on how to achieve their aims, very often pursuing their own course of action. As Foot and Langley said in their book *MI 9: Escape and Evasion 1939–1945*:

Escape and evasion provided a body of common predicaments for British and American fighting men, and the Americans, finding a British set-up in working order that was already producing results, were delighted to join in. Most escape and evasion training, inter-service already on the British side, became inter-Allied as well.

The Americans appointed W. Stull Holt to work alongside Crockatt to establish guidelines for American aircrew based on MI 9's experience. Following his report, they set up a very similar organization, called MIS – X, for dealing with escape and evasion within the US Military Intelligence Service (MIS). With British and American aircrew operating in the same skies over Europe, it was manifestly sensible for MI 9 and MIS – X to work in close harmony and to share knowledge on escape lines and evasion techniques. The two men formed a very close relationship, and the success of MIS – X, under the excellent leadership of Lieutenant Colonel Ed Johnston, who also recognized the value of MI 9's experience, was assured. The return of almost 3,500 American airmen from behind enemy lines in north-west Europe speaks volumes for the cooperation and efficiency of the two organizations.

Chapter Three

Preventive Training

WITH THE CREATION and development of MI 9 having been outlined, it is time to review the training organization with specific reference to the specialist training for aircrew. Once the BEF had returned from France in the spring of 1940, almost all operations over Europe were mounted by the aircrew of the Allied air forces, and the scale of these increased dramatically from late 1941, so that much of the preventive training in the early stages of the war was directed towards this requirement. There were significant developments in the training arena throughout the war, and aircrew became far better educated and aware of the skills and knowledge required to successfully evade capture.

During the early stages of the air war, the training programme and advice given to aircrew in the event of landing behind enemy lines was very basic, and a great deal was left to the initiative and ingenuity of the individual. In no previous major war had individuals found themselves alone deep inside occupied and enemy territory, and there was virtually no experience to draw on. At the same time, MI 9 was in the earliest days of its difficult development, and the small staffs were struggling to establish procedures and contacts with organizations in Europe. During 1940 and 1941, instruction in escape had been organized by MI 9(b), in addition to the other duties performed by that sub-section, and was given chiefly by travelling lecturers who visited operational units of the three services. Owing to the large number of personnel – predominantly RAF – who found themselves cut off behind enemy lines, it was decided to expand the teaching to include evasion of capture in addition to escape.

The lectures given to all three services were divided into two categories. A general lecture was given to all officers, warrant officers and sergeants. The object of the lecture was to emphasize the undesirability of being captured, to give instruction in avoiding capture, and to give instruction on conduct in the event of capture. The lecture concluded with a demonstration of certain escape aids issued to the unit. To ensure that a standard lecture was given, a draft specimen lecture for the guidance of lecturing officers was circulated to all units. The lecture took the form of an informal secret talk to an audience of approximately 200 people. As conditions 'in the field' were constantly changing, lectures had to be regularly modified, and these were published in the *MI 9 Bulletin*, which gave up-to-date information on the subject. The second lecture, classified as Top Secret and delivered to a few officers and warrant officers only, dealt with a system of code communication for those who found themselves as prisoners of war.

On the formation of DDMI (PW) in January 1942, and the consequent reorganization of MI 9, MI 9(d) was formed with the specific duties of organizing and coordinating the training of escape and evasion for combatants of all three services, and for the issue of escape aids to units in the United Kingdom and MI 9 organizations overseas. It soon became apparent that the current method of training, which had proved reasonably successful in the early stages of the war, could no longer compete adequately with the vast expansion that had taken place in all three services, in particular the RAF. With the very large number of new RAF squadrons and Operational Training Units (OTU) spread worldwide, and a great increase in operational flying over enemy territory, it became impossible for the small number of MI 9 lecturers to cover these units and return at regular intervals. When lectures could be arranged, prior claims of operations and flying training, leave, sickness and other commitments limited the attendance. By the end of 1941, many aircrew were operating over enemy territory with little or no knowledge of a subject, which was recognized by the authorities as of vital importance.

In September 1941, the RAF started a series of Intelligence Courses at RAF Station 'Z' Harrow, which eventually became known as the 'A' Courses of the RAF Intelligence School. The Air Ministry approached MI 9 with a view to starting an MI 9 course at the school, and although this constituted a radical change in policy regarding MI 9 training, the request was agreed. Instead of the direct approach of MI 9 instructors lecturing to RAF aircrew, the new course was intended to train RAF intelligence officers as instructors in MI 9 subjects. It was hoped that eventually all intelligence officers on operational stations and OTUs would attend the course, but in the meantime, one officer on each RAF station attended the course and was made responsible for instructing the aircrew. The decision to start the special courses did not stop lectures by MI 9 staff direct to aircrew. These continued and were supplemented by lecture tours carried out by successful evaders and escapers, whose experiences, related by the men themselves, proved to be of great value, both from the point of view of morale and in stimulating interest in MI 9 instruction.

The first MI 9 course, known as the 'Special Intelligence Course', and later to be called 'B' Course, opened at Station 'Z' on 5 January 1942, when ten senior intelligence officers from the RAF's No. 6 (Bomber) Group attended. Squadron Leader A. J. Evans MC, the senior RAF officer attached to MI 9, and a successful First World War escaper, was appointed chief instructor of the course and responsible for drawing up the original syllabus. He was assisted in lecturing by visiting lecturers from MI 9 and other departments, while the staff of IS 9 carried out the purely administrative aspects.

The 'B' Course syllabus was drawn up to train instructors on the basis that they should know more than those they taught. Course pupils were 'taken behind the scenes' to a considerable extent, including a visit to MI 9 Headquarters. They also received lectures on specialist subjects, which did not directly concern, and which were not intended to be passed on to, aircrew, but which were considered essential background to prospective instructors. Taking the view that prisoner-of-war camp organizations would deal with new arrivals at the camps, apart from instruction in codes, camp activities were only mentioned briefly for background purposes. The whole stress of the course syllabus was laid on evasion, early escape if caught and prisoner-of-war security. The five-day course ended with a test in the form of a short practice lecture given by each member. The choices given as subjects for the lecture make very interesting reading, as they encapsulate the whole spectrum of the escape and evasion scene. The list is shown in the Appendix.

Twenty-six Special Intelligence Courses had been run at Harrow by September 1942, when the RAF Intelligence School moved to Caen Wood Towers in Highgate, and it was at this time that the course became known as the 'B' Course. From its inception the 'B' Course ran almost continuously until November 1944, and during this period it expanded considerably in both size and scope. Starting as a purely RAF Intelligence Course for ten pupils, it soon became inter-service and eventually also embraced intelligence officers of the US armed forces. In February 1943 Flight Lieutenant H. Hervey MC, who had been attached to MI 9 in the early days, joined as the assistant instructor. In April 1943 a special course was started for selected USAAF aircrew. By the end of the European war, there had been 136 'B' Courses attended by 2,560 pupils. In May 1945 a Far East 'B' Course was started. It was intended only as an introduction to escape, evasion and survival in the Far East, to be supplemented in theatre by more detailed instruction. Captain Bosanquet MM, an escaper from Hong Kong, assisted the newly promoted Squadron Leader Hervey, and they organized 14 weekly courses before the series was brought to an end with No. 150 Course, following the victory over Japan.

MI 9 issued various publications for the education of aircrew. The principal one was the *MI 9 Bulletin*, a secret document, which was the 'bible' of escape and evasion. It contained everything that could be of assistance to service personnel who might find themselves cut off in enemy-occupied territory, or captured by the enemy. It was devised as a textbook and guide to intelligence officers who were required to give instruction. It gave detailed descriptions on conditions in Europe, special features affecting evasion in each country, on escape routes, maps and many other factors relating to escape and evasion. It was regularly amended and updated, as conditions in Europe changed constantly – particularly the advice on underground movements. Short-term or transitory information was sent out under the title of 'Mercury' on the day of receipt, and was issued only to recipients to whom the information would be of immediate value. A similar publication dealing with the Far East, and largely devoted to survival in the jungle, was prepared, but it became available only shortly before the end of the war.

During the basic lectures given to all aircrew on escape and evasion, a number of key principles were given special emphasis. Many will be illustrated in the narratives that follow in later parts of this book. To enable the reader to have a better appreciation of the value and effectiveness of this advice, a brief outline of the basic rules is important.

In international law there is a fundamental difference between an 'escaper' and an 'evader'. As an evader, an individual who reached a neutral country was interned, but as an escaper he was entitled to be repatriated. Hence, all aircrew were told to declare that they were escapers, and they should have a simple story indicating that they had been in the hands of the enemy for a brief time before escaping. By keeping it simple, it was highly unlikely that the authorities would check the story – they very rarely did.

All aircrew were reminded that it was essential that they carry all their escape aids in a safe place so that they did not lose them as a result of baling out of their aircraft or leaving them behind following a crash landing. After crash-landing it was important to destroy the aircraft and all secret documents and equipment before heading away from the crash site as quickly as possible. The crash would inevitably attract the enemy, who would immediately start a search for any survivors, which normally was carried out up to a radius of five miles from the site. Aircrew who baled out during daylight hours were advised to delay opening the parachute since this would give enemy forces on the ground less time to reach the point of landing, and would increase the chances of the falling parachute not being seen. By night or day, the immediate task on landing was to reach cover and bury the parachute. Discovery of the parachute by the enemy would increase the intensity of the search around that area, and could be used as an excuse to punish the local population.

Once safely on the ground, the crews of large aircraft were advised to divide into small parties, with the navigator informing the rest of the crew of their approximate position if at all possible. It was essential to get away from the crash scene immediately by using hedges, ditches and woods as cover, while avoiding crossing roads, to find a secure hiding place well away from the scene, and then to hide up for a few days until the initial search died down. During this time, the evader had to avoid being seen, and to use the time to remove military insignia, except identity tags, and modify his uniform to make it resemble civilian clothing as far as was possible. It was suggested that the evader should wait three days before trying to contact help, during which time he should aim to survive on the rations in his escape aid box. Once the decision to evade had been made, and the evader had adopted the guise of a civilian, he had to make every effort to discard his true identity, in both appearance and behaviour. He needed to adopt in every particular the attributes, clothing and manners of the local inhabitants. In a rural area, it was useful to carry an appropriate farm implement or a bundle of wood. It was imperative to discard all

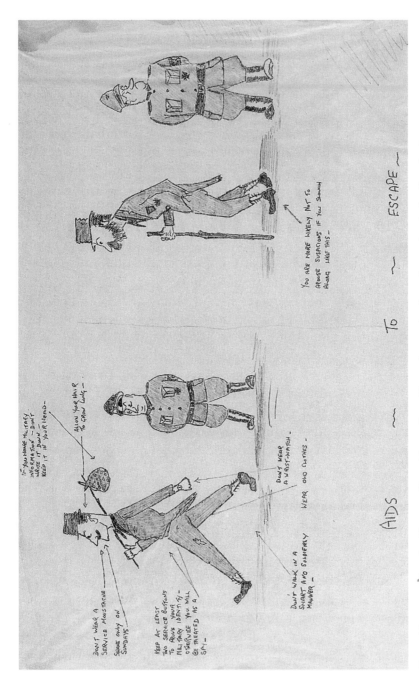

Created by a squadron intelligence officer, this excellent illustration encapsulates the evaders 'code of conduct'. (TNA:PRO AIR 40/1846)

arms and weapons. (In a purely survival situation, such as the jungle, where a machete or kukri could be essential, common sense had to prevail.)

An approach to civilians had to be cautious, in their own interests, since they would not render assistance if observed by others who might betray them. It was recommended that evaders approach isolated farms away from roads and built-up areas. The buildings should be observed from some vantage point for a few hours to monitor the traffic in and out, and to ensure that the buildings were free of the enemy. It was also worth checking to see if telephone lines were connected to the property. The actual approach had to be delayed until very early in the morning or at dusk, when the evader should wait until the person was alone and could not be seen by others. For those landing near built-up areas, they were advised to approach a priest or go to a café used by the poorer people. Once in the building, and convinced of the inhabitant's good intention, the evader had to declare his true identity, give full and accurate particulars and, without hesitation, reply to any questions put to him that might establish his identity. Aircrew were forcibly reminded that the punishment for assisting an evader was death, whereas the evader suffered no worse a fate than transfer to a prisoner-of-war camp.

Once an evader had found someone who would feed and hide him, it was essential to be patient, do as he was told, and await guidance. It was a golden rule that an evader should make no attempt to enquire about underground organizations or escape lines – a ruse sometimes used by enemy infiltrators and stool pigeons – but to wait until the organization made contact with him. If, within three or four days, the host did not appear either willing or able to assist further, the evader was recommended to move on and seek shelter elsewhere until he made contact with people who could arrange the rest of his journey.

Once in the hands of an organization, an evader had to place himself, unreservedly, under their orders, and answer all questions relating to his identity willingly and 'without hesitation'. If ordered to remain hidden until such time as an organization was able to pass him on, he had to carry out the order implicitly, moving only when he received information that the organization could no longer help him. If someone accompanied him on a journey, it was essential to obey the helper and follow instructions without question. Once his organized journey had begun, security was absolutely essential. An evader must never mention to the various helpers, to whom he might be handed, the names of his previous helpers or the methods used by them. On no account was he to write down the names and addresses of his helpers; if arrested when in the hands of an organization, he was to refuse to give names and addresses of his helpers, and he had to refuse to identify any of his helpers who might have been arrested at the same time.

For those evaders who were unable to make contact with an organization, it was essential that they stay calm, make a plan, but remain flexible enough to change it if opportunities or dangers arose. As one instruction in the *MI 9 Bulletin* commented, 'An evader must not be a slave to his plan or his map. To avoid the enemy is the real task, and they are not marked on his map.' Solo evaders were advised to keep stocked up with food and water as much as possible, and to pay particular attention to the state of their feet. They were advised not to rush and to take a 'day off' occasionally to rest. Evaders travelling by day or night should start looking for a place to sleep well before dusk or dawn – an outlying shelter was recommended. They were also reminded that moonlight and woods gave the same advantages to the enemy and the evader, but the hours of twilight were an excellent time to cover a piece of awkward or dangerous ground, as there was sufficient light to be able to move quickly without being seen clearly. A particularly dangerous area for an unaccompanied evader was the crossing of borders. He was advised to try and get information from local people, who were certain to know any details on guarding and patrolling, and to follow their advice. Finally, all aircrew were reminded of the value of acting and the use of bluff. An enemy soldier was just as likely to have little or no knowledge of the local language, and a startled sentry would probably be as surprised and frightened as the evader.

The problems facing aircrew who came down in enemy territory were far greater, and very few succeeded in making a successful evasion. Clearly they could not expect any help from the local population, so all the general guidelines had to be followed. During the period immediately after landing, most of the initial measures applied – leave the crash area immediately, destroy and hide any evidence of arrival, wait for the search activity to die down, and make a disguise. Almost all travel had to be carried out at night, and the aim had to be to reach an occupied or neutral country as soon as possible.

The guidelines outlined in the previous paragraphs were general and applied almost anywhere that aircrew might find themselves as evaders. In the parts that follow, some specific measures peculiar to the region will be highlighted, but the basic principles remained equally valid.

Chapter Four

Escape Aids

ONE OF THE ORIGINAL MEMBERS of Crockatt's team when MI 9 was established was a former First World War pilot, Christopher Clayton Hutton. Foot and Langley described him as 'the most wayward and original of them all, the joker in the pack'. In keeping with most imaginative inventors, he had many unique and unorthodox methods for achieving his aims, many of which got him into trouble with other departments and with his superiors. After one spate of trouble, Crockatt had to write to a provost-marshal: 'This officer is eccentric. He cannot be expected to comply with ordinary service discipline, but he is far too valuable for his services to be lost to this Department.'

Hutton had always had an interest in magicians and escapologists, and he was offered the post of technical officer with the specific task of developing and adapting aids for escape and evasion. His section became known as IS 9 (Z). He collected from second-hand book-shops all the escape books that he could find, and had them summarized. He also had the chance to discuss escape with one of the two MI 9 liaison officers, Pilot Officer A. J. 'Johnny' Evans, one of the few escapers from the First World War and the author of the book *The Escaping Club*. He offered Clayton some sound advice, indicating that a map, a compass, and food in a concentrated form were the most valuable aids for an escaper. As a result, Clayton immediately set about producing a series of maps. His first efforts to print a map on silk were a failure, but once pectin, a natural gelatine, was added to the printer's ink, a perfect imprint was achieved. Every aircrew was issued with an 18-inch square silk escape map, which was hidden somewhere in his

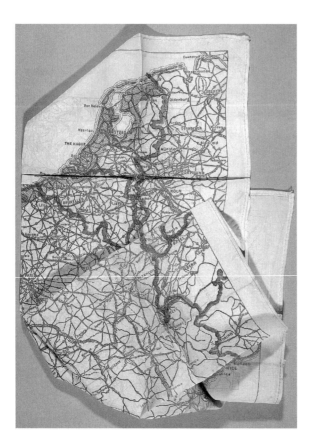

Many thousands of silk escape maps were produced. (Wing Commander D. Martin)

clothing or survival equipment. As the war progressed, silk escape maps were produced for all theatres of war, and new materials were found. Well over a million silk maps had been produced by the end of the war.

Hutton next turned his attention to the manufacture of magnetic compasses that could be hidden in various pieces of clothing. He invented many types, one of the most common being hidden in the collar stud, worn by most men in those days, when all the evader had to do was scrape off a thin layer of paint to expose the compass pointer. Others were hidden in trouser fly buttons, pipe stems and lead pencils. One Fleet Air Arm observer carried a compass in his collar stud, one in his fly button, one in his cap badge, and another behind one of his medal ribbons. He claimed that they were more accurate than the one he used for navigation in his Swordfish! As many as 2,452,862 compasses of various designs were manufactured and distributed.

Concealment of maps and compasses was important, and MI 9

offered advice to the RAF's operational commands. A letter signed by Johnnie Evans (shown on p. 28) explained how a tailor, Messrs Glandfield & Sons, had been contracted to sew the items into the linings of uniforms for no charge.

Many of Hutton's aids, such as saws, knives and mini-cameras, were designed for smuggling into POW camps. Some of them could, of course, be used by the evader, but the majority do not concern us in this narrative. One aid designed specifically with the evader in mind was a new flying boot. The warm and much-coveted fleece-lined flying-boot might be ideal for aircrew flying at high level, but it had serious drawbacks once an airman found himself on the ground behind enemy lines. It was very conspicuous, and it was no good for long-distance walking. Hutton invented the escape boot, which looked like an ordinary fleece-lined boot with a strip of webbing around the ankle. A small knife was hidden in the top of the right boot, and this was used to cut through the webbing to separate the fleece leggings to form a smart-looking black walking-shoe. The heels were hollow, allowing maps, compasses and money to be concealed. The fleece lining could be converted into a waistcoat!

Perhaps the most valuable aid to emanate from Hutton's fertile mind was the escape aid box designed to carry the third of Evans's valuable commodities for the evader – concentrated food. It was made from a pair of acetate plastic boxes, one fitting closely inside the other, and filled with malted milk tablets, Horlicks tablets, chocolate, a few Benzedrine tablets for energy, some halazone tablets for water purifying, matches, a rubber pint-sized water bottle, a magnetized razor blade, a needle and thread and a fishing line. These aid boxes provided the evader with sufficient nourishment for 48 hours, allowing him to lie up without the need to find food. The design of the box was modified as experience was gained, including making it slightly curved to fit human contours, enabling it to be carried in the battledress trouser map pocket or in the lower pocket of a dress tunic. It was also made waterproof. Over half a million aid boxes were issued during the war. Most aircrew also wore life-jackets, which were fitted with whistles, colour dye markers, a knife, and a battery and lamp. Large aircraft carried dinghies, and aids could be salvaged from them if the aircraft crash-landed.

Before flying on operations, aircrew went through a routine of dressing in their flying clothing, collecting survival equipment, and for those flying long-range sorties, in-flight rations. A crucial part of this pre-flight routine was the collection of escape and evasion equipment.

M.I.9/S.10(e)   MOST SECRET.

From : M.I.9.
      c/o P.A. to D.M.I.,
      Room 321,
      WAR OFFICE, S.W.1.

To   : Senior Intelligence Officer.

       We have had maps printed on special fabric capable of being sewn
into tunics, trousers or shirts, and also have a compass needle of low
strength sufficiently small to be concealed in tunics.

       It follows naturally that the better the workmanship employed in
securing these articles, the less will be the chance of their discovery
and incidentally the easier they will be to extract when needed.

       In the interests of security, it is undesirable that indiscrim-
inate use should be made of civilian tailors for this work.

       It may be that in some stations there is a skilled and reliable
man or woman who can undertake to do this work in a proper manner.
But in cases of doubt or where no local facilities exist, we have
arranged for reliable manufacturers to execute this work under our advice
in an approved manner.

       If therefore, any pilot or member of an operational crew wishes
to have maps and compasses concealed in his uniform, the tunic should be
sent to :
                  Messrs. Glandfield & Sons,
                    Brick Lane,
                    LONDON, E.1.

together with the particulars on a label attached to the garment, giving
the rank name and address of the owner and marked on the reverse side
with the word "MONKEY".   The tunic will be returned to sender with the
maps, etc. sewn in within 24 hours.

       Each tunic will be labelled with a number by Messrs. Glandfield &
Sons and one label, showing where the articles are hidden, will be sent
to the Senior Intelligence Officer of the Station in question.   The labels
will bear numbers to correspond to the numbers on the tunics.

       There will be no charge made to individuals or Stations for this
service, other than outward postage.

       Specimens of maps and compass to be concealed are enclosed, which
please retain as specimens and not for issue.

       It must be very clearly pointed out that on no account must the
fact of concealment of maps and compass needles be disclosed or discussed
beyond the operational pilots and crews themselves, not even to their
relations.

                                     Evans

10.11.40.   Flight Lieutenant, R.A.F.V.R.
Distribution to:-   for Lieut.-Colonel, G.S.

    BOMBER COMMAND - Groups Nos. 1, 2, 3, 4, 5, 6 and 7.

    FIGHTER COMMAND - Groups Nos. 10, 11, 12 and 13.

    COASTAL COMMAND - Groups Nos. 15, 16, 17 and 18.

                Group No. 22 (Army-Co-operation).

Johnnie Evans's letter outlining arrangements for concealing maps in uniforms.
(TNA: PRO AIR 14/354)

As mentioned earlier, many aircrew had maps and compasses already hidden in their flying clothing and uniforms. Before each sortie they were issued with a coloured purse containing the equivalent of £12 in notes of the currency of the countries in which they might have to travel to evade capture, the appropriate silk map, a compass and a hacksaw. An instruction in the *MI 9 Bulletin* indicates that not all currency was used for the purpose intended. It read: 'The signing of foreign banknotes as souvenirs must stop, as it renders the notes useless as currency. The holders will not be able to keep them anyway.' Aircrew were also issued with the standard aid box. For those aircrew operating over Germany, where no help could be expected from the population, a supplementary aid box was carried that contained sufficient nourishment for seven days. Those flying in the Far East carried specially designed aid boxes for tropical climates.

Blood chits were produced for those flying in the Far East and over Eastern European countries, particularly Russia. They served a dual purpose. First, they helped to overcome the language difficulty, so that aircrew could explain themselves to the natives. Secondly, they acted as a pledge to those who helped evaders, promising a reward redeemable when the enemy was ejected from the country. They were printed in many languages (as many as twelve could appear on those for operations over Burma), and they were issued together with the aid boxes and purses. Blood chits were not issued for Europe because of the ease with which they could be forged, but phrase-books in many European and Asiatic languages were compiled and produced.

The carrying of identity cards by the local population was made mandatory by German and Italian occupying forces. The design and type of identity card changed at irregular intervals, and different regulations existed between the occupied countries. This placed evaders at a great disadvantage, and the lack of an identity card often resulted in capture. All identity cards carried a photograph of the individual, and MI 9 instructed units that all aircrew were to carry photographs on all operations over enemy and enemy-occupied territory. From the results of careful observation on the part of reliable helpers, and interrogation of successful evaders, a clear and accurate picture was established on the types of photograph that were required. Precise instructions for the photographer were given, and these included the type of paper to use, the size of the image, the type of background, and the aspect of the subject. Aircrew were told to wear

Aircrew carried photographs to be used on false papers in the event of their being shot down. Units received instructions on the appropriate type of photographs. *(TNA: PRO WO 208/3268)*

a nondescript jacket, shirt and collar with a distinctive tie. They were strongly advised to be photographed without a moustache – on the Continent it was the exception rather than the rule for young men to grow moustaches. They were also reminded that individual members of the same crew should not all wear the same jacket and tie! Aircrew were told to carry at least two photographs and ensure that they were kept securely so that they could not be lost during a forced descent, or left in clothing or equipment likely to be discarded after landing.

Before concluding this account on escape aids, it is appropriate to mention another valuable contribution made by Hutton and his section. During 1943 and 1944, IS 9 (Z) clothed and equipped many IS 9 (D) agents and helpers. A special clothing store in Regent Street, London was created where agents could be fitted out with appropriate clothing. The preparation of containers for dropping supplies was also a major part of IS 9 (Z)'s work. From September 1944 the section was used for the purpose of obtaining special boating equipment for IS 9 (WEA)'s evasion activities in Holland. During the autumn of 1944 (and after VE Day in Holland), IS 9 (Z) dispatched thousands of parcels of food and clothing to helpers.

After the war, all three services, and the Americans, acknowledged that the work performed by Clayton Hutton and his IS 9 (Z) Section was of the greatest value, and an important contribution to the war effort. Without doubt, many people owed their lives and liberty to the equipment devised and issued by the section.

PART TWO

North-West Europe

Chapter Five

Introduction

B Y JUNE 1940, following the fall of Norway and Denmark, the Low Countries and France, German forces occupied the whole of north-west Europe except the United Kingdom. The withdrawal from France of the BEF left some 2,000 British forces free in France. It has been estimated that about half of them managed to return, the great majority having travelled south through France and over the demarcation line set up between the German-occupied north and the Vichy-controlled unoccupied zone in the south. Once south of the demarcation line they were still liable for arrest, but the Vichy police did not hand them over to the Germans. Instead, they were lodged in a series of forts in the Marseille region. The experiences of these early evaders heading south helped pave the way for the numerous escape lines that soon developed and proved so successful. For the next four years, with the exception of a few raids by Special Forces, there were virtually no ground actions in Western Europe, and thus the evaders came almost entirely from the air forces.

The Allied bomber offensive gathered momentum steadily from 1940, until raids by many hundreds of heavy bombers became an almost daily event. Each of these four-engine bombers carried crews of seven or eight men, and loss rates were high as the *Luftwaffe's* air defence system became increasingly effective. In the main, the routes taken by the aircraft to attack targets in Germany took them over the Low Countries and France, with the RAF operating predominantly at night and the USAAF by day. In the meantime, light bombers and long-range fighters, operating over shorter ranges, attacked targets in the same countries by day. As a result of losses, the number of Allied aircrew on the run increased on a daily basis.

For the many aircrew shot down over Germany and the occupied countries, almost all headed for Holland and Belgium *en route* to France, as this offered the only feasible route for returning to England. Owing to the heavily defended coastlines, there was virtually no opportunity to return by sea, but France had common borders with two neutral countries – Spain and Switzerland. The odds of success were heavily against an evader, but he had the advantage of being able to cope with the climate and environment, and could mingle with the local population, once he was properly attired, without attracting too much attention. Most importantly, the vast majority of the population of all three countries were anti-German, and many were prepared to assist him.

By 1941, the method of evasion was well defined. Having landed safely, aircrew headed for the occupied countries, where the majority were picked up by an organization and fed into a system of safe houses, whose owners hid and fed them before sending them to a collecting point in The Hague, Amsterdam, Liege, Brussels, Paris, Marseille or Toulouse. They were supplied with false papers and clothes before being taken by couriers on trains heading for the frontier zones, where they met guides who led them over the mountains to Spain. Later in the war, a few were recovered by naval operations from Brittany organized by IS 9 (D) in conjunction with the Royal Navy.

For evaders operating alone, their reception in the two neutral countries varied significantly. Entry into Switzerland presented no major geographical obstacles, and the Swiss border police were most unlikely to return an evader once he had arrived on Swiss territory. After brief interrogations at a police station they were handed over to the British Legation in Berne. Crossing into Spain presented an altogether different proposition. The natural barrier of the Pyrenees provided a formidable obstacle, which was virtually impassable without a guide. The border was declared a 'Forbidden Zone' through which civilians were not allowed to travel, and it was heavily patrolled by the Germans. If an evader succeeded in crossing the mountains, the Spanish border police were likely to return him to the Germans, so it was important to treat the border area in Spain as if it was enemy territory, and to continue evading until well clear. If the crossing had been with the aid of a guide, it was important to send him ahead to make contact with the British Consul, and await his return. Taking money or false papers into Spain was a crime that often resulted in a prison sentence, and as one intelligence officer used to brief the aircrew, 'Prisons in Spain are not nice places.' Many evaders were to discover that for themselves.

The Germans soon became aware that aircrew were evading capture and must be receiving organized help. Fortunately, troops could not be on the spot whenever aircrew crash-landed or arrived by parachute. Adding to the Germans' problems was the ever-growing army of those willing to assist aircrew, despite the much-advertised consequences displayed on the many posters in every town outlining the penalties for 'Aiding the Enemy'. However, the Gestapo made strenuous efforts to infiltrate the escape lines, and they achieved

The Germans were ruthless against those who assisted evaders. Terence Cuneo captures an all-too-familiar and awful scene. (TNA: PRO INF 3/1791)

considerable successes with the help of a few traitors who served them. The treatment of those caught sheltering evaders was brutal. Those considered to be unimportant to their enquiries into the wider organization were executed, sometimes with their families. If the real organizers and main characters were captured, all were submitted to severe torture and incarceration in a concentration camp, where many died. There was always the risk to an escape line through treachery, and Airey Neave estimated that 150 or more helpers died as a result of being betrayed.

Before turning to a review of the activities of the escape lines, and relating the experiences of aircrew who successfully evaded in the Low Countries and France, it is worth returning to the immediate post-Dunkirk era to consider how the lines became established. We have seen how Crockatt and his staff struggled to establish MI 9, and to foster interest in escape and evasion. The return of men who escaped from Dunkirk aroused some interest, but there was still a considerable degree of apathy among senior officers of all services – in particular, and very surprisingly, the RAF. The return of Wing Commander Basil Embry DSO (later Air Chief Marshal Sir Basil Embry) in August 1940, after being shot down during the Battle of France in May, suddenly alerted some elements of the RAF that it was possible for shot-down aircrew to return safely to fight another day. Embry was shot down on 28 May as he led a formation of 107 Squadron Blenheim light bombers against a target near St Omer. He was captured twice, but managed to escape on each occasion before making his own way home via Spain. Embry was a very charismatic and energetic officer with a very forceful personality. He had a distinguished record of service spanning many years in the RAF, and had been selected for promotion to group captain on the day he was shot down; he was well known and respected, so people listened to what he had to say. Foot and Langley commented in *MI 9: Escape and Evasion 1939–1945*: 'His example and his energy did much to fix evasion firmly in the heads of both MI 9's staff and of the Air Ministry's, as one of the modes of war to which they would thereafter need to pay full heed.'

Just before Embry's return, MI 6 had made their offer to establish an escape line from Marseille to Barcelona. The task was delegated to Donald Darling, a young man who had been in Spain during the Spanish Civil War. He spoke the language fluently, and he had an excellent knowledge of the Franco-Spanish border area between

Andorra and the Mediterranean coast. Darling travelled to Barcelona, assumed the codename 'Sunday', and immediately set to work to recruit guides to accompany evaders over the Pyrenees. One of the first to assist him was the very wealthy Nubar Gulbenkian, who was able to travel freely in Vichy France on an Iranian passport. Darling was able to put him in touch with one of his contacts, Michel Pareyre, a garage owner in Perpignan, and Gulbenkian successfully negotiated a deal with him. The arrangement required Pareyre to provide his garage for the reception of evaders before he passed them on to smugglers and guides who would take them into Spain. For each successful journey to Spain, the guides were to be paid £40 for each officer and £20 for other ranks. Darling established routes from wayside railway stations to the British Consulate in Barcelona, where, after some early difficulties, he was able to establish a reception system before evaders were passed to the British Embassy in Madrid, where he experienced even greater difficulties with the Ambassador, and finally on to Gibraltar.

Darling's activities soon came to the attention of the Spanish authorities, and in May 1941 he was forced to operate from Lisbon, where he remained until January 1942, when he moved permanently to Gibraltar to become MI 9's chief. From this time onwards, Darling interrogated every evader before arranging his passage back to England. By seeing each one, he was quickly able to identify trends, new opportunities, and the need for changes or reinforcement of procedures. It also allowed him to monitor the work and assess the validity of the helpers, and he was one of the first to recognize the treachery of an evader from Dunkirk, who had assumed an identity of Captain Harold 'Paul' Cole, a name that did not appear in the British Army List, and a man we shall meet later.

Once Darling had established the route from Perpignan through to Spain, he needed to create the link to Marseille, a city that was particularly suitable as a major reception area for clandestine activities. He made contact with Captain Ian Garrow who had escaped from Dunkirk to Marseille, and the first major escape line, later to become the famous 'Pat' Line, came into existence.

From these early beginnings, escape lines through Holland, Belgium and France developed quickly as more and more aircrew found themselves in occupied territory. There never seemed to be a shortage of willing helpers prepared to take the gravest risks to assist evaders, and their courage reached heights that few of us can either attain or fully appreciate. The chapters that follow will describe the many different organizations involved, illustrated by a wide selection of the routes and methods that evaders used.

Chapter Six

France and Belgium

WITH ITS COMMON BORDERS with two neutral countries, France was the key to the vast majority of successful evasions in north-west Europe. Those successfully reaching Switzerland, which included some who had arrived from Italy and a few from Germany, eventually had to travel through France before they could return safely to England. It was in France that the two most successful and best-known Second World War escape lines were established, and the names of Pat O'Leary and Andrée de Jongh, who established the Pat Line and the Belgian Comet Line respectively, will justifiably go down in history. There were, however, many other smaller lines that achieved considerable success. Also, many aircrew successfully evaded capture without ever making contact with an established line, but owed their success to the support and courage of individuals. The narratives that follow in this chapter offer a wide selection to highlight the variety of methods employed by evaders, and their helpers, to evade successfully.

THE PAT LINE

The origins of what later became known as the 'Pat' Line began in the summer of 1940 following the defeat of the BEF in France. Among the many British soldiers heading for the south of France to evade capture was a powerfully built Scot, Captain Ian Garrow of the Seaforth Highlanders. He was a survivor of the famous rearguard action fought by the 51st Highland Division at St Valery following the

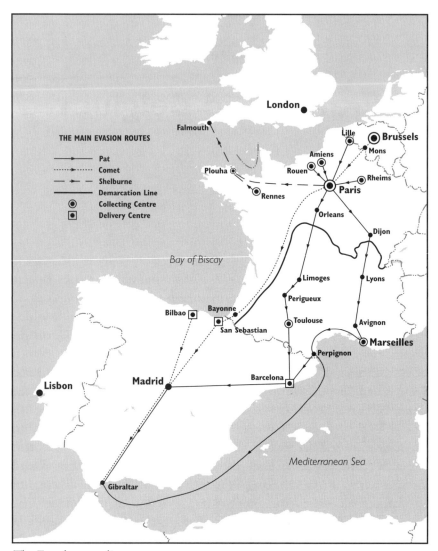

The French escape lines.

evacuation from Dunkirk. He successfully avoided capture before
reaching Marseille, where he arrived knowing nobody, without
money, and finding the city full of servicemen who had also made
their way south. He immediately recognized that something had to be
done to accommodate and feed them before making efforts to get
them home. His first priority was to establish a series of safe houses to
accommodate the evaders, and he made contact with members of the
British and Greek communities living in Marseille.

Heading south at the same time as Garrow was the Reverend
Donald Caskie, who had been forced to leave his Scottish

Presbyterian church in Paris. Once he arrived in Marseille, he too decided to remain and assist the stragglers of the BEF, and he was able to obtain permission to reopen the old Seaman's Mission building at 46 Rue de Forbin, which soon provided Garrow with a safe house for his developing organization. He had also been introduced to a remarkable couple, Dr Georges Rodocanachi, who was born in Liverpool of Greek parentage, and his wife Fanny, and their beautiful apartment became the main safe house in Marseille. Their Greek nephew, Georges Zariffi, became one of the most trusted couriers escorting evaders to Marseille and onwards to the Pyrenees. Garrow also became friendly with Louis and Renée Nouveau, who provided another safe house overlooking the Vieux Port. Around these unique people, Garrow established Marseille as his major reception point for evaders. Nouveau was able to put Garrow in touch with a Spanish guide, 'Vidal', an anarchist who had a number of excellent guides working under him, who coordinated the crucial crossings of the Pyrenees, the last major hurdle for the evaders. Garrow also made the important link with 'Sunday' in Lisbon to provide funds, and to establish the Spanish side of the escape line.

Ian Garrow recognized the need to create links with the north of France. Collecting centres in Lille, Rouen and Amiens were established to feed into a main centre in Paris, from where evaders were passed across the demarcation line *en route* to Marseille. He built up his network of couriers, one of the most successful in the early days being an Englishman claiming to be a Captain Harold Cole of the British Secret Service. It later transpired that he was a sergeant who had absconded with the sergeants' mess funds before Dunkirk. He used the alias 'Paul', and escorted a number of parties of evading airmen to Marseille, but his free spending and garrulous behaviour soon started to attract suspicion.

By the middle of 1941, Garrow had laid the foundations of the escape line when 'Lieutenant Commander Patrick O'Leary' appeared on the scene. He was Albert-Marie Guerisse, a médecin-capitaine in the Belgian Army who had escaped from Dunkirk to England, where he joined the Special Operations Executive (SOE), who gave him his alias as a French-Canadian and a commission in the Royal Navy. For his first assignment he was made second-in-command of a 'Q' ship, HMS *Fidelity,* tasked to carry out clandestine work on the south coast of France. O'Leary was sent ashore, where he was soon captured and interned at St Hippolyte du Fort near Nimes, the Vichy-controlled camp for British prisoners. Through a network of agents, he soon learned of the work of Ian Garrow in Marseille, and taking advantage of the parole offered to officers, he set up a meeting with him when his escape was arranged, and he arrived at the Rodocanachis' in mid-June 1941. It was to be his headquarters for the remainder of his time in Marseille.

Soon after his escape, O'Leary was persuaded by Garrow to join him in his work in Marseille. MI 9 in London approved this, and O'Leary soon started work as a courier and coordinator. It was not long before he met Paul Cole, and he took an instant dislike to the man. Garrow had also had his suspicions for some time, and in September they discovered that Cole had not been transferring funds to the helpers running the northern end of the line, but had been using them to pay for his own high living with his numerous mistresses. As O'Leary returned from the north with the proof of Cole's deception, the Vichy French arrested Ian Garrow. O'Leary took command of the line, and immediately confronted Cole in the Rodocanachis' flat, where he confessed. He was locked in the toilet while those present decided his fate, but he managed to escape through the window. He returned to Lille, where the Germans arrested him. Within days, he started his treacherous work, which included using bogus airmen. However, to maintain his cover, he continued to bring parties of airmen across the demarcation line until the Vichy French arrested him. Under sentence of death, he managed to 'escape' to work for the *Abwehr,* the German counter-espionage organization. It has been estimated that his treachery resulted in the deaths, at the hands of the Gestapo, of at least 150 French patriots and Allied evaders. O'Leary warned as many helpers and couriers as possible, but he was too late to save many of them. Among those lost was the gentle little Curé Abbé Carpentier who sheltered airmen in Abbeville, and forged identity cards and passes. He was arrested and later beheaded by the Gestapo.

O'Leary set about repairing the line and recruiting new members. He travelled down his own line to Gibraltar to meet 'Sunday' and Jimmy Langley of IS 9 (D), who had travelled out from London for a series of briefings. They discussed the new arrangements for running the line in the aftermath of Cole's treachery, and plans were also agreed to establish a radio link with Marseille, where evaders were arriving in increasing numbers. It was also decided that arrangements must be made to establish a sea link to Gibraltar from a beach at

Canet-Plage, near Perpignan, using the armed trawler *Tarana*. Finally, plans for the assisted escape of numerous RAF officers imprisoned at St Hippolyte du Fort, including American-born Squadron Leader Whitney Straight, were discussed.

In July 1942, the first sea evacuation took place, with others soon following, when many evaders, including Whitney Straight, were evacuated among other important refugees. However, as the year progressed, the Gestapo net was closing in on the line. Donald Caskie had been arrested, and O'Leary learned that Ian Garrow was to be deported to Germany. All this coincided with the Germans crossing the demarcation line in November to occupy the whole of France, so the Nazi flag was soon flying over Marseille. The Nouveaux had been under surveillance for some time, thereby being placed in great danger, and they were forced to leave their house. Louis Nouveau moved to Paris to try and reorganize the rapidly disintegrating northern arm of the line, while his wife remained in Marseille before she was eventually evacuated to England. The Marseille base for the line was also collapsing through betrayals, so O'Leary moved the operation to Toulouse, where he used the flat of Françoise Dissart, his trusted chief organizer in the city. Within days, he devised an audacious plan to rescue Ian Garrow, which was brilliantly accomplished on 6 December 1942, and Garrow crossed the Pyrenees a few days later. On return to England he was awarded the DSO for his work establishing the escape line.

In early 1943, disaster and tragedy struck the Pat Line. Paul Cole had reappeared, and the Germans had completely penetrated the network. It was also no coincidence that a new courier, Roger le Neveu (alias Roger le Légionnaire), had recently joined the organization as a volunteer to take airmen from Paris to the south. He was in reality a Frenchman recruited to be a German agent, and there were soon many arrests, including Louis Nouveau, who was deported to Dachau concentration camp. On 2 March 1943, le Neveu travelled to Toulouse to make contact with O'Leary, ostensibly to explain how Nouveau had been arrested. They met in a café. Within minutes, two Gestapo agents arrived, and Pat O'Leary was betrayed and arrested.

Just four days before O'Leary's arrest, the brave Dr Georges Rodocanachi was arrested. He had refused to leave Marseille, where his wife was ill. He was eventually taken to Buchenwald concentration camp, where he died on 19 February 1944. His beloved wife, Fanny, recovered and moved to London after the war to live near her brother.

Although the Pat Line continued on a small scale, it never regained its former capabilities. The experiences of Squadron Leader E. P. P. Gibbs and Sergeant J. Beecroft illustrate the diverse experiences of those evaders who returned to safety with the aid of the Pat Line.

Spitfire Pilot's 'Home Run'

Squadron Leader Patrick Gibbs was a regular officer with eight years' service when he joined the Spitfire-equipped 616 Squadron as a Flight Commander in June 1941. He had been a pre-war fighter pilot, but had spent the first 18 months of the war as a flying instructor. With no operational experience, he was keen to see action, so he volunteered to return to fly fighters. During his time as an instructor he had become an expert aerobatic pilot, a skill that was to pay handsome dividends within a few weeks of joining the squadron.

Squadron Leader 'Pat' Gibbs of 616 Squadron photographed at Tangmere shortly before he was shot down. (AVM J. E. Johnson)

As predicted by his colleagues, Gibbs did not last long in combat. On 9 July he led a section of Spitfires as the squadron, under the leadership of Wing Commander Douglas Bader, took off at 1.10 p.m. to escort bombers attacking Mazingarbe in northern France. Twenty miles inland, Messerschmit Bf 109 fighters attacked the Spitfires, and numerous combats broke out, with Gibbs and his number two attacking two of the enemy fighters. In a head-on attack he dispatched one, and as he turned to attack the second, a cannon shell smashed into his engine, which soon stopped as the glycol coolant poured out. He started to glide down for a wheels-up landing when two enemy fighters started to close in on him. Realizing that he was an easy target, he jettisoned his canopy, rolled the aircraft on its back and continued to glide to the ground hoping to give the impression that he was dead. A few feet above the ground, he rolled the aircraft the right way up before executing a perfect crash landing in a stubble field. He set fire to his Spitfire, and raced for the hedgerows before the German pilots could turn back.

Gibbs had landed 12 miles east of the French coastal town of Le Touquet. Following the evader's cardinal rule of getting as far away from the crash site as quickly as possible, he immediately set off at a brisk walk, using the hedgerows as cover until he came across a farm worker and his wife who directed him to a farmhouse where he was given great hospitality. After resting overnight, he walked through the day and night to another farm, where he was treated 'magnificently', and was able to rest for five days, which allowed the injuries he sustained in the crash landing to heal.

A doctor smuggled him across the boundary of the Forbidden Zone near Amiens on the pretext that he was suffering from an acute appendicitis. The doctor's niece then escorted him on the train to Paris, where a medical student and his wife gave him shelter. Forged identity cards and civilian clothes were provided, and 14 days after being shot down, a young girl student arrived to escort him to her aunt's house in Perpignan.

They travelled on the night train via Bordeaux to Salies-de-Béarn, 30 miles east of Biarritz, where they crossed the demarcation line into unoccupied France. To avoid the more stringent identity card checks, they travelled on to Perpignan using the slow local trains. Once in Perpignan, he said goodbye to his brave companion, and after a night's sleep, was briefed by a Frenchman on how to cross the border into Spain. He took the local train to Banyuls, a small coastal village close to the Spanish border, and left the station unhindered. However, as he was leaving the town, a gendarme stopped him to inspect his identity card, and recognized it as a forgery. Despite declaring his true identity, and pleading to the gendarme's 'patriotism', he was taken into custody.

The next day he was taken to the Vichy jail at St Hippolyte du Fort near Nimes and interned. Here he met four other British officers and some 90 soldiers who had tried but failed to escape the advancing German armies a year earlier. The camp was run on very civilized terms, with the officers allowed out on parole to the local town on the understanding that they would not escape. In addition to affording some pleasant social opportunities, parole allowed them to study the local area, and make important local contacts, which included meeting Ian Garrow and his members of the Pat Line. Gibbs was also able to escort a number of fellow prisoners to Dr Rodocanachi's surgery for a repatriation medical board, and this gave him further opportunity to discuss a possible escape. He was also able to send a telegram to his wife reporting that he was 'safe and well in unoccupied France'. After six weeks, this was the first indication to the squadron that he had survived, and the RAF was able to remove him from the 'missing in action' list.

After three weeks, Gibbs withdrew his parole agreement on the basis that it was an unfair advantage over the soldiers! He had made a simple plan to escape. Just as darkness fell on the evening of 18 August, he and Squadron Leader Whitney Straight approached the main gate with a colleague, Lieutenant Parkinson, who arranged for the gate to be opened on the pretext that he was going out on parole. He then created a diversion, which allowed Gibbs to dash through the gate and down the street to a pre-positioned bicycle, and cycle away. Unfortunately, Whitney Straight was apprehended. Once well clear, Gibbs discarded the bicycle, and set off to walk through the night along the railway to Nimes. At dawn he had covered almost 15 miles when he rested in the nearby hills, during which time he shaved off his moustache with a dry razor. He remained hidden until darkness fell, when he put on a beret and set off for Nimes for a safe house arranged by Garrow, where he stayed overnight. The next day he was taken to Marseille by one of Garrow's couriers, and delivered to Donald Caskie's Seaman's Mission.

He remained at the mission for a few days, during which time he met up with a party of four other British evaders. Early next morning the Greek courier Georges Zariffi arrived to collect the party, and he took them by train to Perpignan, where they were taken individually to a garage near the safe house run by Madame Catala, who was one of the local coordinators, for the onward journey across the Pyrenees. After a meal, they were taken part of the way into the Pyrenees towards the Spanish frontier in a large car driven by one of Madame Catala's couriers. *En route* they picked up one of Vidal's mountain guides. The car drove on, but stopped short of the border, where the five evaders and the guide got out to continue on foot. They set off on an arduous walk of 40 miles over the mountains, climbing at one point to 10,000 feet. They walked for two days, crossing the border at 9 p.m. on 26 August, when they descended to an isolated farmhouse owned by relatives of the guide. After resting for the night, they were collected by another guide, and taken to the nearest railway station, where the guide had already purchased tickets for the local train to Barcelona. By using this slow train, they avoided the possibility of identity checks, arriving safely after a six-hour journey. They left the station and boarded a tram to the British Consulate, which the guide pointed out before he left them. They remained three days in Barcelona before being driven to Madrid in the Consulate car, arriving on 30 August. Here, the Embassy arranged for their repatriation, and two weeks later Gibbs arrived in Gibraltar.

After 24 hours in Gibraltar, during which time he was debriefed by 'Sunday', Patrick Gibbs boarded a Sunderland flying-boat, arriving at Plymouth the next day. He had been away just over three months. He had followed all the evader's rules. He had attended lectures, carried his own survival kit and extra money, left the scene of his crash immediately, and headed straight for the Unoccupied Zone. His escape from St Hippolyte du Fort was well prepared and simple, and again he moved from the area quickly. He was fortunate to meet many brave helpers, but his own approach was commendable.

Shortly after his return, he and another evader were invited to have lunch with the Prime Minister, who wished to hear of their experiences. During the discussion that followed, Winston Churchill asked Gibbs if he had obtained the name of the French gendarme who had arrested him near the Spanish border. On learning that he had not been identified, Churchill retorted in a jocular vein, 'Pity, we could have put him on the list to be dealt with when we have won the war.' A few weeks later, Patrick Gibbs was awarded a Mention in Despatches.

Home via Switzerland and Spain

Sergeant John Beecroft and his crew of five took off in their 101 Squadron Wellington bomber from Bourn near Cambridge at 10 p.m. on 20 May 1942 to bomb Mannheim. They were 30 minutes from the target when the port engine failed, forcing them to abandon the operation and turn for home. Despite jettisoning the bombs to reduce weight, the bomber continued to lose height, and Beecroft had to make a forced landing. The young pilot made a good crash landing in a field near Sedan, the scene of many battles during the First World War, and all the crew were uninjured. Sensitive equipment, maps and charts were all destroyed before the five men set off to walk in a southerly direction with the aid of the issue button-compass. They found a wood at dawn, where they rested for the day and made a plan of action. They decided that they would stick together, walk only at night, and head for Switzerland.

For the next four nights they headed south with nothing to eat except the Horlicks tablets in their escape aids box. Although they were making good progress, they decided to seek assistance. They called at an isolated farm near the village of Hans, some 30 miles west of Verdun, where they were given food and shelter for the night. The Mayor of Hans called the next day with civilian clothes, bread coupons and a detailed map of the Marne area. He also advised them on how best to cross the canal and River Marne, which were major obstacles and patrolled by the enemy. When they set off the following night, most of the village came to see them off, and to bring them more food. After a few days, they intercepted the canal near St Dizier, which they crossed at an isolated spot before carrying on their journey to the south-east.

On the morning of 1 June they reached the small town of Rimaucourt, where they encountered three German soldiers guarding a bridge, who asked for their identity papers. They claimed to be farm workers on their way to a farm in the next village, and were surprised when they were allowed to pass. They realized that they had survived only because the soldiers' knowledge of French was no better than theirs. For the next two weeks, they continued to head south-east through the heavily wooded and hilly region of Alsace. They were fed at isolated farms, where they were also given useful information about the whereabouts of the enemy and places to avoid. Fortunately, there were few towns or major roads in the region, and the woods provided perfect shelter.

Finally, on the evening of the 15 June, they arrived at the village of Fournet Blanche, two miles from the Swiss border, where they slept in a barn. The following afternoon, the farmer took them to the River Doubs, which was flowing through a deep gorge, and formed the frontier with Switzerland. They had to scramble down a very steep, wooded cliff to get to the river, where they discovered that it was impossible for the two non-swimmers to cross, despite numerous attempts and assistance from the other three. They left to head north to find a more suitable place, but were eventually captured, to become POWs for the rest of the war. Beecroft and his two companions stripped off their clothing, which they tied to a log, and then started to swim across the river, with Beecroft pushing the log. Halfway across, Sergeant Harry Hanwell, the wireless operator in the crew, took over the log, and they continued swimming. As Beecroft climbed out of the river, he could see that Hanwell had also reached the bank a short distance away, but the third man was struggling. Shortly afterwards, he disappeared below the surface and did not reappear.

Beecroft and Hanwell dressed before heading away from the river until they came to a small café, where they were given a drink. The proprietor telephoned the Swiss frontier guards, who arrived to take them to the police station at La Chaux-de-Fonds, where they spent the night. Sadly, a search for the missing sergeant failed to find him. Next day, the two survivors were taken to Berne, where they were interrogated by the Swiss military police and Swiss Air Force police before being handed over to the British Military Adviser at the British Legation.

After eight days of rest and healthy eating, and a complete change of clothes, the two sergeants were taken to Geneva, where the British Consul, Victor Farrell, had established an organization for the onward journey of evaders. Lieutenant Anthony Deane-Drummond, a commando who had escaped from an Italian POW camp, had joined them. Farrell briefed them on the details of the next phase of their journey, and gave specific instructions for their reception in Marseille. After a few days in the Salvation Army Hotel, a car collected them just before dawn, and drove them to the frontier, where a guide escorted them across the French border before pointing out their next rendezvous. A series of guides took them to Annemasse, where they met 'Georges', who had already purchased railway tickets for them. The four men boarded the train for Marseille, arriving at 6 a.m. on

8 July, having spent the night in opposite corners of the compartment while dozing and not uttering a word. They left the station by a side entrance and were taken to a café in a poor area, where another courier, 'Jean', met them. He took them to a flat where a young girl was waiting for them. By a devious route, she escorted them to a block of flats in the port area, where the gendarme on duty outside looked away at the appropriate moment, and they entered the flat of Louis Nouveau and his wife. The use of so many couriers was a security measure. No one courier knew the whole system or more than one or two others in the network.

During the early hours of the morning of 12 July, Renée Nouveau took the three evaders to the railway station, where they were handed over to their next guide, 'Patrick' (O'Leary), who took them by train to Bezier, where they caught a local train to a station near the coast. The small party set off on a two-hour walk towards the beach, where they hid in a wood, to be joined during the late afternoon and early evening by more evaders, including Squadron Leader Whitney Straight, who had finally managed to escape from St Hippolyte du Fort. Just after midnight, they set off in small parties in single file to go down to the beach, where the guides spread out at 100-yard intervals, waiting for light signals from the sea.

Approaching the darkened coastline off Canet Plage was the converted trawler *Tarana* under the command of Lieutenant E. B. Clark RNR. The *Tarana* was a 347-ton motor trawler, which had been requisitioned to join the Polish Naval Mission based in Gibraltar,

The converted fishing trawler Tarana. *(R. Stephens)*

whose task was to rescue the many Poles who had made their way to southern France. The trawler had been modified to be an armed 'Q' ship, with guns hidden below decks and under fishing nets. After sailing from Gibraltar, the ship was repainted during the night to give it the appearance of a Portuguese fishing trawler, and it sailed for the south of France.

Having arrived a mile off shore just after midnight, a boat was lowered and manned by Sub Lieutenant Whiting and Able Seaman Ron Stephens who had volunteered for the role. With two agents on board, they started to row ashore. It was a dark, moonless night, making it difficult for them to be observed by any shore patrols. At 2 a.m. the evaders and their escorts saw the blue light signals from the *Tarana* indicating that the rowing boat was on its way. Hooded torches were used to guide the sailors to the beach, but to the evaders ashore the arrival of the rowing boat seemed to take an eternity. After 40 minutes, they heard the soft noise made by muffled rowlocks, and shortly afterwards the rowing boat beached. The evaders and returning agents made their hurried goodbyes to their brave guides before being ferried to the *Tarana*, where bread and cheese and steaming mugs of cocoa were thrust into their hands. With the party aboard, the trawler headed out to sea, with the passengers remaining below during daylight hours. After riding out a two-day storm, it picked up a party of 50 Poles from another ship before setting sail for Gibraltar. The night before arriving back at Gibraltar, the crew of the trawler restored its overall grey paint scheme, allowing the white ensign to be hoisted. After almost a week at sea in cramped and uncomfortable conditions, the evaders landed and were able to feel that, at last, they were safe.

After debriefing with 'Sunday', Beecroft and Hanwell had a few days' relaxation before they joined the SS *Llanstephan Castle* for the six-day voyage to the Clyde, where they arrived on 30 July – 10 weeks after they had been posted as 'missing'.

The return of the two young sergeants had all the ingredients of a successful evasion. They had trekked at night for almost four weeks, covering almost 300 miles on foot with assistance from local people only. They had avoided built-up areas to reach a neutral country, where they were able to rest before embarking on another dangerous journey through occupied France, but this time, under the control of a major escape line whose agents and couriers were taking great risks. Finally, the Royal Navy returned them to safety after picking them up during an audacious and daring sea rescue before taking them to Gibraltar. On 18 September it was announced that both men had been awarded the DFM. For security reasons, the citation could not make specific reference to their successful evasion, but concluded: 'On one occasion, their example of fortitude in most harassing circumstances was in keeping with the highest traditions of the service.'

Pat O'Leary's arrest on 2 March 1943 effectively spelled the end of the Pat Line. However, the redoubtable 60-year-old, chain-smoking Françoise Dissart survived. Remarkably, until the Liberation, she continued to shelter evading airmen in her flat opposite the Gestapo headquarters in Toulouse before sending them across the Pyrenees. She often travelled to the Swiss border to collect evaders before escorting them to Spain via Toulouse. She was never arrested, and

Ron Stephens (right) after receiving his Croix de Guerre. (R. Stephens)

survived the war. This amazing woman was awarded the George Medal for her incredible bravery. Louis Nouveau survived the horrors of Buchenwald, and he too was awarded the George Medal. His wife Renée was made a Member of the Order of the British Empire (MBE), as was Fanny Rodocanachi, who saw the honour as a tribute in memory of her brave husband. The Reverend Donald Caskie survived his imprisonment to return to his church in Paris, later being awarded the OBE for his services. Six crew members of the *Tarana,* including Ron Stephens, were awarded the Croix de Guerre by the French government for the numerous rescue sorties they undertook from the beaches in the south of France.

The Pat Line was the first of the escape lines, attracting a remarkable group of people led, first by Ian Garrow, and then Pat O'Leary. Over 600 Allied airmen and soldiers returned to safety, but over 100 brave helpers paid the ultimate price. The traitors met the fate that they deserved. Paul Cole continued his treachery, but in

The legendary 'Pat O'Leary' photographed with his wife and a colleague at the time of his investiture with the George Cross. (R. Stanton)

1945, French police cornered him in a flat, and he was shot dead during a gun battle. Roger le Neveu moved to Brittany, where he infiltrated the Shelburne Line. He was later captured by the Maquis, who 'liquidated him'.

The final word must be left for the inspirational Pat O'Leary. He was severely tortured by the Gestapo in an attempt to extract information about his contacts and activities, but he resisted. He was incarcerated in numerous concentration camps before being liberated from Dachau on 29 April 1945. He reverted to his Belgian name, but King George VI invested him with the George Cross as Lieutenant Commander Pat O'Leary. He returned to the Belgian Army and retired as a major general, having won gallantry awards during the Korean War. He was later awarded an honorary knighthood by the British government, and the King of Belgium granted him the rare honour of making him a count. He died in 1989, and will be remembered as one of the truly remarkable and most gallant men to emerge from the Second World War.

THE COMET LINE

'I realize that patriotism is not enough. I must have no bitterness towards anyone.' These were the last words of the British nurse Edith Cavell before she was shot by a German firing squad on 12 October 1915 at the Tir National in Brussels. Her crime had been to help Allied soldiers to escape to safety into Holland. Twenty-five years later, her words were to inspire another generation of Belgians who found they were living under the occupation of Hitler's Germany.

With her country occupied, 24-year-old trained nurse Andrée de Jongh (known as 'Dédée') decided she must return to her parents' home at Schaerbeek in Brussels to tend the wounded, and arrange for them to be kept at a series of safe houses before helping them to escape. Many Belgians came forward to help, with her father, Frédéric, headmaster of the boys' school at Place Gaucheret, taking a leading role. Once France had been occupied, she established a route through Paris to St Jean de Luz near Biarritz in the foothills of the Pyrenees. Safe houses were established along the route, and mountain guides were organized and routes chosen to take the 'parcels' across the mountains to San Sebastian in Spain. Her father coordinated the transfer of evaders on the Brussels–Paris route, and her aunt, Elvire de

Andrée de Jongh ('Dédée'), the inspirational Belgian leader of the Comet Line. (R. Stanton)

Greef ('Tante Go'), organized the operations in St Jean de Luz. Tante Go involved all her family, including her husband, Fernand, who worked as an interpreter for the Germans, which gave him access to blank identity cards and passes for the Forbidden Zone along the Atlantic coast. Most of the couriers escorting the evaders were young men and women, all under the age of 25. Dédée herself escorted the evaders from Paris to the Pyrenees before accompanying them over the mountains to San Sebastian with a fearless Basque, Florentino Giocoechea, whom she recruited as her chief guide.

In August 1941 she delivered three evaders to the British Consul in Bilbao, and sought a meeting with the Consul to explain the capabilities of her organization. She explained that she needed funds, but insisted that her line must remain under Belgian control, and the Consul undertook to alert London. On her next crossing a month later, Michael Cresswell ('Monday') from the British Embassy in Madrid travelled to Bilbao to meet her. He was captivated by her vitality, courage and initiative. As a result, the 'Comet' Line was firmly established, and 'Monday' met Dédée in Bilbao after every journey, this becoming the routine way of passing messages and funds.

The gallant Basque guide 'Florentino'. (R. Stanton)

The Gestapo were aware that there was an escape line, and made strenuous efforts to uncover it, including infiltrating bogus aircrew into the system. Frédéric de Jongh was forced to move to Paris in April 1942, when Baron Jean Greindl ('Nemo') assumed control in Brussels, working from the Swedish Red Cross canteen. Frédéric continued to organize the Paris operation, where he recruited new couriers, including young sisters Andrée and Michele Dumon ('Nadine' and 'Michou'). Nineteen-year-old Nadine took more than 20 evaders to Paris from the Belgian collecting points before her arrest in the summer and imprisonment in Ravensbruck. Her 20-year-old sister Michou became one of the line's most successful operators after the arrest of Dédée before having to evade herself, arriving in England in May 1944. Assisting in the dangerous crossing of the Pyrenees was Albert Johnson, an Englishman who had remained behind in France after the German occupation, and a young Belgian, Baron Jean-François Nothomb ('Franco').

Tragedy struck in Brussels on 19 November 1942 with the arrest of many of the key helpers following infiltration of the line by Gestapo agents posing as shot-down Allied aircrew. Dédée was so concerned for the safety of her father that she finally persuaded him in January 1943 to leave for England, and she took him among a party of evaders to St Jean de Luz. On 15 January, the weather for the crossing of the mountains was considered to be too bad for Frédéric de Jongh to travel, so Dédée set off on her 19th journey without him, and headed for the home in Urrugne of Francia Usandizaga, who ran the last safe house before the Pyrenees crossing. Just before the guide Florentino arrived at the rendezvous, the Gestapo raided the house, capturing Dédée, Francia and three evaders. On capture, Dédée tried to persuade the Gestapo that she was the leader of Comet in order to take the pressure off the others. The Gestapo would not believe that such a young and slight girl could be running such a complex organization. In due course, she and Francia were sent to Ravensbruck concentration camp, from where Francia did not return.

With the line broken, Frédéric de Jongh and Nothomb returned to reorganize the Paris link, leaving Tante Go and Albert Johnson to establish new links in the south-west. Fortunately, Florentino had avoided capture to continue with his vital role as chief mountain guide. Unfortunately, a traitor, Jacques Desoubrie (alias Jean Masson), had infiltrated the northern section of the line. Jean Griendl was arrested in Brussels in early February, and Desoubrie betrayed Frédéric de Jongh on 7 June. It has been estimated that Desoubrie betrayed over 50 members of the Comet Line, and his treachery almost wiped it out. After the war, he was tried and executed by the French authorities. Under sentence of death, Jean Griendl was killed in an Allied bombing raid. On 28 March 1944, 60-year-old Frédéric de Jongh was taken from his prison cell with two friends to face a German firing squad. After the war, his school was renamed 'Ecole de Frédéric de Jongh' in his memory.

In the south, Albert Johnson was arrested, but Tante Go managed to obtain his release, and it was decided that he should return to England. He had escorted no fewer than 122 evaders over the Pyrenees. Jean-François Nothomb travelled to Spain to discuss the continuation of the Comet Line with 'Monday', returning to take over Dédée's role of escorting evaders from Paris to San Sebastian. Michou continued to act as a courier on the route to the south despite the grave risks she ran following her exposure to the Germans by a collaborator. Others were recruited, allowing more evaders to escape to Spain. However, Nothomb was arrested in January 1944, and sent to a concentration camp. He had escorted 215 evaders over the mountains, a number exceeded only by Dédée herself who had taken 218. In the months ahead of the Allied invasion in June 1944, it became too dangerous to take evaders south by train because of the intensive bombing campaign against the French railway system. However, a number travelled to the south, and Florentino took two RAF sergeants over on 4 June 1944. They were the last customers of the Comet Line.

During the three years of its existence, over 800 airmen returned to the United Kingdom through the efforts of the Comet Line. One of the early airmen to return was Flight Sergeant Larry Carr.

~

Twenty-two-year-old pilot Larry Carr took off in his four-engine Halifax bomber to attack Cologne on 27 April 1942. It was his 14th operation since joining 102 Squadron, and the second since the squadron had converted from the Whitley bomber to the Halifax. He was flying over Belgium just after midnight when the rear gunner sighted a German night-fighter, which immediately opened fire, setting the bomber on fire. Two of the crew were killed during the attack, and it became apparent very quickly that the aircraft was doomed, so Carr gave the order to bale out. With the aircraft falling rapidly, he had difficulty getting to the escape hatch, and had only just managed to open his parachute when he hit the ground, with the aircraft crashing very close by. Clearly, he had escaped at a perilously low altitude.

Carr had landed in the Belgian province of Namur near the town of Hamois. He immediately buried his parachute and life-jacket and started to head south. A man who was accompanied by a gendarme soon confronted him, and they asked if he was English and 'did he want to return to England?'. On his replying, 'Yes', they said that they could arrange it for him, and immediately took him to the civilian's home, where he was hidden in the basement. His helpers were Maurice Wilmet and Gendarme Massinon, the latter leaving to make arrangements to move him from the immediate area of the crash. On his return, the two men took Carr to a farm some five miles away, where he exchanged his uniform for civilian clothes, and was able to rest. Two days later he left with Wilmet to catch the local train to Ciney, where he was to transfer to the express for Brussels. The gendarme joined them *en route*, and a 20-year-old woman, Fernande Pirlot ('Pochette'), met them at Ciney before taking them on to Brussels.

Once in Brussels, Carr stayed at a number of safe houses, meeting his navigator and second pilot during his stay with the Lizin family. Pochette acted as the courier and arranged for him to have photographs taken for an identity card. It was not considered safe for all three to remain together, so another young courier, Peggy van Lier, collected Carr and took him to the house of Carl Servais and his wife in a residential suburb. He stayed for a number of days, during which time he heard that the organization had been infiltrated, and many arrests had been made, including his two crew members.

Fernande Pirlot ('Pochette') of the Comet Line and one of Larry Carr's guides. (L. Carr)

After a week, Peggy van Lier returned to escort Carr into the centre of Brussels, where she introduced him to Dédée, who was to take him to Spain. He was given false papers and a railway ticket before they boarded the express for Paris. At the French frontier all the passengers had to disembark to pass through police and customs checks before the journey continued to the Gare du Nord in Paris, where Frédéric de Jongh met them. He escorted Carr across Paris to the Gare d'Austerlitz, where he received new forged papers allowing him to travel within the German-occupied area of France. Dédée and Carr boarded the night train for the Spanish border, arriving at Bordeaux at 6 a.m. before continuing their journey south. They were due to leave the train at Bayonne, but just before disembarking they saw Tante Go on the station, and she was able to warn them that increased security checks were in place on the station, and they must remain on the train and disembark at St Jean de Luz.

A Basque met them when they left the train at St Jean de Luz, but told Carr to leave by a goods entrance since strict control was in force at the ticket barrier. After meeting up outside the station, they left for an apartment where Carr was given new clothes for the journey over the mountains, and told to get some sleep. Late in the afternoon, Dédée and Carr left for the farm at Urrugne, where Francia Usandizaga had prepared a meal for them. They were told that the regular guide, Florentino, was unable to take them over the mountains that night, and a younger guide would escort them.

At midnight on 22 May, the guide arrived and the three of them set off along mountain tracks into the Pyrenees dressed as Basques. The guide set a fast pace as they climbed the hills behind the farm to a ridge, which they followed before descending into the valley of the River Bidassoa, which formed the frontier. With great caution, and in total silence, they had to ford the fast-flowing river, cross the road and railway running alongside the river on the Spanish side, and avoid patrols. Frontier patrols shot on sight, and Spanish patrols finding anyone crossing from France would hand them straight back to the German authorities. Having crossed the frontier safely, it was necessary to keep out of sight until Carr could be handed over to the British Vice-Consul in San Sebastian. After crossing the border, they climbed up from the valley to the mountains, where they kept to the high paths until it was daylight, when they rested at a farm. It would have been too dangerous to have been seen walking in the mountains in the early morning.

The photograph of Larry Carr taken in Brussels and used on his false papers. (L. Carr)

Later in the day the friendly Basque farmer wakened them. He provided them with a meal before they set off again once it was dark. They walked through the mountains all night, resting as dawn broke. The guide showed them the way down to a village at the end of the tramline to San Sebastian, and then left them. Dédée and Carr walked into the village, joined the queue of workers and boarded a tram, which they left near the centre of the town, where Dédée telephoned a contact, who arrived to take them by car to the British Vice-Consul.

Carr said goodbye to the amazing Dédée de Jongh, the slight young woman who appeared to know no fear. Once more she must return over the mountains. All those who met her found it difficult to believe that such an innocent-looking girl could make such arduous physical journeys, in addition to the great presence of mind and courage that she displayed at every stage of the journey from Paris to Spain. One of those she helped wrote: 'She was the force, the power and the inspiration that brought us from Belgium to Spain'.

Larry Carr was soon taken to the British Consul in Bilbao, and then to the Embassy in Madrid. He arrived in Gibraltar on 1 June to learn that Bomber Command had just launched the first 'Thousand

Bomber Raid'. Donald Darling, who was particularly interested in the difficulties occurring in Brussels, debriefed him in detail. Carr sailed from Gibraltar on 18 June on the aircraft-carrier HMS *Argus*, arriving at Gourock five days later. He was escorted to London, where he was taken to meet Jimmy Langley, Head of IS 9 (D), who was anxious to get the latest information of the threatened Comet Line, and to get a detailed report of his experiences.

After some leave, Larry Carr returned to flying duties, but his detailed knowledge of the helpers and the escape lines prevented him from returning to operational flying, and he flew with the Airborne Experimental Unit, and later with a communications squadron, ending the war in Norway. Following his evasion, he was awarded a Mention in Despatches.

Shortly after Carr's return, many Brussels members of the Comet Line were arrested, and some, including Gendarme Massinon, did not survive the war. Maurice Wilmet evaded the Gestapo by hiding in the cellar of his own house for over two years before the Liberation. His wife kept him hidden and supplied with food, and successfully led the Gestapo and all his friends to think that he had fled to avoid capture. He never fully recovered his health and died in 1960. Carl Servais avoided capture until

The widow and children of the executed Gendarme Massinon. (L. Carr)

just before the liberation of Brussels, when the Gestapo arrested him and many others. They were all put on a train, but railway workers took advantage of the confusion, and managed to divert it around the capital until the British captured it. Peggy van Lier escaped to England, where she was awarded the MBE – later she became Mrs Jimmy Langley.

There were many helpers in the Comet Line, and they paid a high price for their courage. Twenty-three were shot, including Dédée's father, and 130 did not return from German concentration camps. Pochette survived her ordeal in Ravensbruck, as did Baron Jean-François Nothomb, who returned to become a priest – the British awarded him the DSO. The courage of the women of the line was recognized by the award of the George Medal, the highest decoration that can be awarded to a foreign civilian for bravery, to Tante Go and Michou. The George Medal, together with the King's Medal for Courage, was also awarded to Florentino. Airey Neave said, 'Without him, Dédée and the Comet escape line which followed her could never have rescued so many airmen.' He died in 1980.

The final word on the Comet Line must be reserved for its creator, the remarkable Andrée de Jongh ('Dédée') who took over 200 airmen

'Dédée' de Jongh with the 'bomber' clock presented to her by the RAF at the time of her visit to London to receive the George Medal. (Imperial War Museum, London, CH 16803)

to safety across the Pyrenees on 218 journeys. After her arrest, she spent two years in Ravensbruck concentration camp, returning seriously ill. She recovered to return to nursing, becoming a sister in a leper colony in the Belgian Congo. In later years the King of Belgium made Andrée de Jongh a countess. Among her many awards was the George Medal, which she received from King George VI in 1946. She was a remarkable woman among remarkable people.

THE MARIE-CLAIRE LINE

The history of the French escape lines tends to be dominated by the largest two organizations, the Pat and Comet lines, but there were many other, smaller, operations, which also achieved some notable successes, and among them must be included the 'Marie-Claire' Line.

There were many remarkable characters involved in the dangerous work of assisting evading airmen, including the colourful, strong-willed, English-born Comtesse de Milleville who lived in Paris at the outbreak of the war. During the First World War she had served, in her maiden name of Mary Lindell, with the French Red Cross as a nurse, and had been decorated with the Croix de Guerre and the Russian Order of St Anne for her courage. She had married the Comte de Milleville, and settled in Paris, where she remained with her three children after the break-up of her marriage. With her striking good looks and her indomitable spirit, she was well known in the Paris social world.

Immediately after the fall of France in June 1940, she donned her bemedalled Red Cross uniform, which had her British medals mounted first, thus making her nationality abundantly clear. She immediately became involved in assisting evaders to cross the demarcation line into Vichy France. At a Paris cocktail party she managed to persuade Count von Bismarck and General von Stulpnagel, the German commander in Paris, that she needed a permit to cross into Vichy France to collect a sick child, and for her humanitarian work. She added that she would need to take a 'mechanic' with her. For good measure, she asked for some petrol coupons, and the Count arranged for her to receive an abundant supply. Her 'mechanic' was a non-French-speaking officer of the Welsh Guards who had been wounded at Dunkirk, but had avoided capture. On their route to Limoges she gave a lift to a *Luftwaffe* pilot, who entertained her in the officers' mess at his air base! She passed the Guards officer on to members of the Pat Line, who arranged his journey back to England, where he briefed the MI 9 staff on the 'remarkable' woman who had saved him from the Germans.

Mary Lindell, alias 'Marie-Claire', continued to drive evaders over the demarcation line before the Gestapo arrested and interrogated her in January 1941. She was sentenced to nine months in solitary confinement in the infamous Fresnes prison. Once her sentence had been completed, and before the Gestapo could consider further action against her, she headed for Ruffec, situated on the demarcation line north of Bordeaux, where her children had been taken. From there, dressed in her Red Cross uniform, she travelled south and crossed the Spanish frontier as a 'stranded governess' on 27 July 1942, before presenting herself to the British Consul in Barcelona. A signal to Room 900 announcing her arrival in Spain caused some consternation, and a few days later, she met Airey Neave to explain her activities, and to indicate that she wished to return to France to carry on her work assisting evaders. This presented MI 9 with a dilemma, since anyone who had already been in the hands of the Gestapo was a potential risk to the organization, in addition to the obvious danger to the agent. Eventually, Neave and Langley overcame their reservations, and she was the first female they trained specifically for setting up escape routes. She returned to France by Lysander aircraft on 21 October to set up an organization based on the Hotel de France in Ruffec. Unfortunately, she did not have a radio operator, and this proved to be a significant hindrance to her activities.

Mary Lindell soon established the Marie-Claire Line, and evaders were passed successfully to Spain. Shortly before Christmas, a car thought to have been driven by a collaborator ran her down, and she was seriously injured. She was admitted to hospital, but discharged herself in the new year despite being very ill. A few days earlier, Major 'Blondie' Haslar and Marine Bill Sparks had arrived in Ruffec. In due course, they became better known as 'The Cockleshell Heroes'. They were the only survivors of Operation 'Frankton', when some of their fellow commandos were drowned, and six were shot by the Germans following Hitler's infamous 'Commando Order'.

Mary's son Maurice transferred the marines to Lyon, where they met 'Marie-Claire', who promptly ordered Haslar to shave off his large, blond moustache. She then made an audacious journey to Switzerland to report to the British Legation, where she was able to send a message to Room 900 that the marines were safe. It was also apparent that she was very ill, but she insisted on returning to Lyon to organize the next stage of their journey. After many setbacks, because of the lack of a radio and Marie-Claire's illness, the two marines were finally escorted across the Pyrenees.

In May 1943, Maurice de Milleville was arrested and severely beaten in an attempt to obtain information about the Marie-Claire Line. He resisted and was eventually released. Shortly afterwards, his brother Oky was also arrested and tortured, then deported to a concentration camp, never to be heard of again.

The Marie-Claire Line operated by collecting evaders from many parts of France before moving them to safe houses in the Ruffec area. Once six or seven had been gathered, 'Marie-Claire' took them to the Pyrenees, where she handed them over to Spanish mountain guides. In the second week of November, she escorted her final group of escapers and evaders, which included Kenyan-born Flying Officer Mike Cooper.

~

Twenty-one-year-old Mike Cooper of Nakuru, Kenya, joined 616 (South Yorkshire) Squadron, equipped with Spitfire VI fighters, in May 1942. In July he was shot down and rescued from his dinghy in the English Channel. Three months later, he was shot down again and once more found himself sitting in a dinghy – this time in a German minefield. In a daring rescue just two miles off the coast of France, a Walrus amphibian landed among the mines and flew him to safety.

On 16 August 1943, he baled out of a Spitfire for the third time. He had taken off at lunchtime from Ibsley in the New Forest on a fighter sweep in support of bombers attacking an airfield near Le Havre. South of the target at 23,000 feet, his engine failed. During lectures on escape and evasion, it had been stressed that the coastal area was a heavily defended, restricted area, and aircrew should make every effort to avoid landing in the area, where capture was almost inevitable. Cooper turned his stricken Spitfire away to head south. At 9,000 feet, he took to his parachute for the third time, but on this occasion, there was no hope of rescue. He landed in an apple tree in the Calvados region near the town of Lisieux. After struggling to free himself from his parachute, he headed for a nearby wood, meeting a youth on the way who took him to meet two men. They took him to a shack,

Mike Cooper 'at readiness' with his 616 Squadron Spitfire. (Mrs Kitty Cooper)

where they provided him with some overalls, just before a German motorcycle patrol arrived looking for him. He hid in a hayfield, and when they departed he was encouraged to work in the field with other men gathering the hay. The ruse worked, as other soldiers passed the field without stopping. His helpers provided him with food, and he stayed in the shack overnight. German activity continued the next day, and so, once it was dark, he headed south and carried on walking for three nights. He stopped at isolated farmhouses where he was given food and shelter, but the farmers were frightened, and urged him to leave after an evening meal.

By the fourth day he was well clear of the immediate search area, and he knocked at the door of an isolated farmhouse, where he was fed, allowed to shave and wash, and had his clothes washed. Fernand Brad and his wife Silonge hid him in a hayloft until they could arrange a more permanent place to stay. That night, Robert Siroux, a neighbouring farmer, called for him and took him to his very basic and isolated farmhouse, where he and his wife Gabriel offered him shelter. Initially, Cooper had misgivings, but soon realized that this very poor couple had an abundance of kindness, as they treated him like a son. In case there was a search for him, he made a hiding place in the nearby barn full of hay. A prosperous farmer, Henri Beaudet, visited him and took some details to pass to the Resistance organization that would confirm Cooper's identity with London. He remained with the Siroux couple for two months before bidding them an emotional farewell. Beaudet had arranged for him to be picked up by a member of the local Resistance group, and taken by a horse and buggy to a house within five miles of the coast, and there he met Len Martin and Harry Smith, crew members of an RCAF Halifax which had been shot down a few days earlier.

Cooper and his colleagues were in the house of the local Resistance leader, M. Bodot, who told them that he was in contact with London and would soon get them rescued by a submarine. After a few days, it became apparent that the Germans had infiltrated the local Resistance group, and the three airmen were moved to a disused farm owned by the Coudrez family, who sheltered them for a few days before they were transferred to another house in a nearby coastal town. Cooper was most uncomfortable throughout this period since all his training had warned him to avoid the defended area near the coast. He certainly saw plenty of evidence of the Germans, but his forged pass was accepted each time he had to produce it.

Within a week, the three airmen were collected by a member of one of the underground movements, and taken to Paris by train, where they met their guide, M. Touly, who first took identity photographs of each of them for new passes, before he split them up to go to separate safe houses. Cooper was taken to the home of the

At the end of the war, Mike Cooper and his wife visited the Coudrez family. (Mrs Kitty Cooper)

Barthelme family in La Varrene-sur-Seine, on the outskirts of Paris, where he remained in the comfortable house with his brave helpers and their daughters. After 10 days, he was taken back to the Paris home of the Touly family, where he was reunited with Smith and Martin. Within a few days, a young girl, who was their guide for the journey south, joined them as they sat drinking in a café. She bought tickets at the main railway station, and instructed the three airmen to follow her at a safe distance, and not to talk on the journey. They boarded the train without difficulty, and six hours later they disembarked at Ruffec and walked to the Hotel de France. As they entered, a loud female voice greeted them in perfect English. It was 'Marie-Claire'.

After a detailed briefing on what she expected of them, the three were split up again, and Cooper was taken to a private house where he met an Australian bomber pilot, Allen McSweyn, an inveterate escaper who had finally managed to escape from Stalag VIIIB at Lamsdorf in September 1943. Seven days later, Captain Buck Palm DSO, a South African Air Force Hurricane pilot who had been shot down in the Western Desert, joined them. He had escaped from Italy, but was recaptured by the Germans near the Swiss border. *En route* to a German POW camp, he managed to escape again and reach France, where he made contact with helpers who escorted him to Ruffec. A Greek officer accompanied him.

With a party of six evaders, Marie-Claire and her helpers took the group by lorry and train to Toulouse and on to Foix, a small town near the Pyrenees. On the train, they received a warning that the Germans were looking for escapers and had set up a control point before Toulouse. Marie-Claire ushered all the evaders off the train at the next station, and the following day they returned to Ruffec, where the Greek decided to leave the party.

Maurice de Milleville left for the Pyrenees region to make arrangements for a second attempt. After 10 days all was ready, and the party left by train for Toulouse escorted by Marie-Claire and two of her assistants. They then took a slow train to Pau, where a French guide was waiting, and he rushed them to a bus that was just about to depart for the foothills of the mountains. Cooper and his colleagues were bitterly disappointed not to have time to bid Marie-Claire an appropriate farewell. The party left the bus at a remote spot to walk a few miles to a house where they were fed and met their French and Spanish mountain guides. To their surprise and concern, the evaders had little time to rest before they set off into the mountains in a steady and cold drizzle. They travelled all night and just managed to cross a dangerous road in a steep valley before dawn. Setting off up the next mountain, Harry Smith collapsed with acute chest pains, and had great difficulty carrying on. Cooper was also desperately tired and unable to help, but McSweyn and Palm dragged Smith up and over the mountain and into the next valley, where they had a brief rest and food at a remote house.

The guides insisted on continuing, despite the worsening weather. The climb became harder, and the drizzle turned to snow, which soon became a blizzard. Progress was desperately slow as they tackled yet another mountain. Nearing the summit, they noticed that the French guide had disappeared, so McSweyn retraced their steps to find that he had collapsed and died in the snow. A few hours later, and with Cooper in a state of near-collapse, they found a mountain hut, which they broke into. It was 24 hours since they had left the French house. They found some dry hay and were able to start a fire, which soon developed into a fierce blaze. It undoubtedly saved their lives, as all of them were suffering from the first stages of frostbite, and were too exhausted to carry on. After a sleep, they headed down the mountain, and stumbled into a small village, where a Spanish Garde Civile saw them and took them into custody. Their great ordeal was over and they were safe, although it was some days before a member of the British Embassy arrived to see them.

Mike Cooper with Mme Barthelme and Mme Touly, from two of the families that sheltered him. (Mrs Kitty Cooper)

They had to endure a frustrating period of interrogations before they were collected by bus to be taken to Madrid. Five days later, they arrived in Gibraltar, where Donald Darling interviewed all of them to obtain details of their evasion. On 20 December, they boarded a Dakota for Whitchurch airfield near Bristol, arriving in the early hours of the next day, 128 days after Cooper had parachuted into France. Shortly afterwards, it was announced that Allen McSweyn had been awarded the MC for his escapes and for his leadership during the treacherous crossing of the Pyrenees.

After recovering from his ordeal, Mike Cooper returned to 616 Squadron to be one of the first RAF pilots to convert to jet fighters when the squadron was re-equipped with the Meteor in July 1944. He remained with the squadron, finishing the war at Lübeck. He left the RAF in June 1946, and soon made arrangements to return to France with his wife to see his helpers. The Siroux, Coudrez, Touhy and Barthelme families survived the war, and he was able to introduce his wife Kitty to them. He remained in contact with his brave helpers, making a number of visits in the years ahead.

Two weeks after Cooper and his fellow evaders left Ruffec, the Gestapo arrested Marie-Claire at Pau railway station – they had been closing in on her for a number of months. On the journey to Paris she attempted to escape, but was shot and seriously wounded in the face and skull. A *Luftwaffe* surgeon saved her life, but despite being very ill with a high fever, the Gestapo deported her to Ravensbruck concentration camp. Her training as a nurse, which was utilized by the camp doctor, undoubtedly saved her, and she survived to return to Paris. Mary Lindell, the Comtesse de Milleville, was highly decorated by the French government, but inexplicably the British awarded this remarkable and wonderfully brave Englishwoman a mere Mention in Despatches. She died in 1986, aged 92.

RETURN BY MOONLIGHT

The role of the Special Duties squadrons of the Royal Air Force was to support the Special Operations Executive (SOE), which supplied the Resistance organizations in occupied countries. These clandestine forces were an important part of maintaining an offensive against the enemy; indeed, in some areas it was perhaps the only way to conduct an aggressive campaign. However, to be effective, supplies and arms were absolutely crucial, and the very great majority of these could be delivered only by air drops. Another essential element of this undercover war was the need for well-trained agents to be available to coordinate operations with the many Resistance groups and Underground movements. They too were usually delivered – and recovered – by air, giving rise to the need for two types of aircraft.

Bomber-type aircraft, such as the Whitley and the Halifax, were used for the delivery of large loads of arms and supplies. They were also used extensively to drop agents by parachute to reception committees on the ground. However, these large aircraft were unsuitable for 'pick-up' operations, when aircraft needed to land to collect important people or articles. For this type of operation, an aircraft with a short take-off and landing-run capability was essential. The single-engine Lysander aircraft was ideal for this type of operation, but it could only carry a maximum of three passengers, and a very limited weight of supplies. Occasionally, the twin-engine Hudson aircraft was used, but much bigger fields were required. Nos 138 and 161 Squadrons were formed in the United Kingdom for these types of operation, both achieving fame as 'The Moonlight Squadrons'.

Initially, most of the operations were to the near Continent, but as the war progressed the longer-range Halifax was able to fly to more distant areas. The number of drops increased, and 30 each month was being achieved by 1942. This increased rapidly over the next two years, rising to a record 267 sorties by the two squadrons by July 1944. By this time, other squadrons had been formed for Special Duties operations.

The main role of 161 Squadron's Lysander Flight was to deliver agents and collect those returning or other important people – they included two future Presidents and a Prime Minister of France. The squadron was not tasked to collect evading airmen. However, very occasionally, if a spare seat was available, a lucky evader had a quick return home. One such person was Sergeant John Tweed.

～

John Tweed had just celebrated his 21st birthday when he took off at 10.30 p.m. on 12 May 1943 to drop supplies to the French Resistance.

John Tweed pictured just after receiving his pilot's wings. He was trained in the USA and also wears the USAAF wings presented at his graduation. (Mrs Jessie Tweed)

He had only recently joined 138 (Special Duties) Squadron, and so was acting as the second pilot of Halifax BB 313, with Squadron Leader Robinson DFC as the captain. They had successfully dropped supplies to a Resistance group near the Swiss border, and were near the town of Troyes on their return, when their aircraft was hit by anti-aircraft fire. A fierce fire started, and the captain ordered the crew to bale out. The aircraft was very low, and before the crew could make their exit, the captain crash-landed in open country. The crew had not taken up their crash positions, so most were injured. Tweed sprained his ankles, badly damaged his hand, and suffered a deep cut on his leg.

After helping to free the injured from the wreckage, he hobbled off to find cover for the night, eventually finding a field of corn, where he slept for a few hours. An ambulance drove by during the morning, but there was no evidence of a search so he remained hidden until it was dark. He realized that he would have great difficulty travelling in his injured condition, so he took a Benzedrine tablet from his survival kit before staggering off in the direction of a village. As he entered the village of Pommereau, he saw a light in a house, which he approached. He crept along the wall to the window and was heartened to hear a radio broadcast saying, 'Ici Londres', followed by the Morse letter V and a drum roll. This convinced him that it was safe to knock on the door, which created a scuffle to switch off the radio. A woman holding a small boy came to the door, immediately recognized the RAF pilot's wings on his tunic, and she ushered him into a room where there were a number of men, including her husband. He had arrived at the house of the Charton family.

After he had been cleaned up and fed, he was taken to a semi-derelict farm building, where two of the young workers lived, and where he soon fell asleep. During the next week, Madame Charton modified his uniform to look like a farm worker's, and she brought food to him twice each day. After a week, a man visited from the village to ask a number of detailed questions. The following day, Dr Goupis, the village doctor, visited to attend to his various injuries, and said that 'arrangements' were being made. However, another 10 days elapsed before the next developments. John Tweed was not aware that he had unwittingly stumbled into the local Resistance network, and Louis Joubin ('Gustave'), the head of the Intelligence Section of the Goelette Resistance Group, had arranged for the doctor to visit him; he was now checking the details he had provided to ensure that he was not a 'plant' of the Gestapo.

Three weeks after arriving on the Chartons' farm, he bade them farewell as Dr Goutin arrived on his small motorcycle to take him to his next rendezvous. He met another doctor who drove him 40 miles to a house in Troyes, where 'Yvonne' sheltered him, and where he had his photograph taken for an identity card. Later that evening, an Englishman, who asked some penetrating questions, visited him and took him to another house for the night, where he also met a second Englishman. Tweed would see them both again. The following afternoon, Pierre Malsant (the Leader of the Goelette Resistance Group) arrived in his small car to take him to a safe house in the country – the Germans allowed him to have the car because his garage did good work for them and he was considered 'a model citizen'! He also gave Tweed his new identity – Phillipe Bonnard, a commercial traveller who was born in Vitry le François in 1918.

Tweed's new location was the café in the small village of Dierry St Julien, eight miles west of Troyes, owned by Maurice Bourgeois and his wife. He remained in a room above the café for the next three weeks, coming downstairs for exercise in the evenings. He was very well fed and Madame Bourgeois found small jobs for him to pass the time. A young Frenchman who was trying to get to England visited him, and they agreed to try and head for Biarritz before crossing the

John Tweed rests at the Chartons' farm with young Claude. (Mrs Jessie Tweed)

Pyrenees. The youth was sent on a trial run, but he was captured and severely beaten by the German police. With this avenue closed, Pierre Malsant decided to send Tweed to Paris, and first introduced him to his guide, Sam Chevalier, who escorted him on the train and provided shelter for two days before arranging for him to stay with Henri Boucher and his wife in their house in the Montraste district of Paris. He remained in the house for the next eight weeks.

In the second week of September, the Englishman from Troyes visited to tell him to prepare to move, returning an hour later to collect him. He took him to a fashionable café and handed him over to Pierre Piot, a man who used his office as a member of the Swiss Red Cross to cover up his assistance to Allied evaders. He lived in a very smart flat in the Rue Montmartre close to the Bourse, where he stayed for the next seven days until the Englishman returned in great haste at 8 a.m. on 17 September with the news that they were to leave at midday on a train for a place near Angers – for security reasons he was not told the exact location. At a small country station they disembarked, and were met by a prosperous young farmer who told them that the 'reception' was that evening. When the Englishman declared that he would be travelling with Tweed, and that he was Captain Ben Cowburn, leader of the SOE 'Tinker' group supporting the Resistance movement in the Troyes area, all became clear to Tweed. From the moment he had arrived in Pommereau on the night of his crash landing, he had been in the hands of the Resistance. The two men were taken to a farm, where they met four other 'passengers' before having a splendid supper.

Towards midnight, the party set off on bicycles to a very large meadow in the bend of the River Sarthe a few miles north of Angers. This was a landing ground run by the controversial agent Henri Déricourt. An hour after the party had arrived at the field, the faint sound of an aircraft could be heard, and the recognition signal 'R' was flashed by torch. The aircraft responded, and the reception committee immediately set up the basic flare path with their torches. A few moments later, a black Lysander, piloted by Wing Commander Bob Hodges DSO, DFC, the Commanding Officer of 161 Squadron and one of the earliest RAF evaders through France, landed and taxied back to the start of the flare path. With the engine running, three passengers were disembarked, messages and a parcel were exchanged, and three members of the ground party climbed into the cramped rear cockpit of the Lysander. It was airborne again within six minutes, just as a second Lysander, flown by Flying Officer Jimmy Bathgate, started its approach to land. The same procedure was followed, and Tweed, Cowburn and one of Déricourt's assistants climbed aboard. They were airborne two minutes later, heading for RAF Tangmere near Chichester. The whole operation on the ground had been completed in less than 15 minutes.

The flight back was uneventful, and John Tweed was back on

John Tweed returned to England in the back of a Lysander of 161 Squadron.
(TNA: PRO CN 5/33)

English soil four months and five days after he had taken off to deliver arms to the Resistance. It was fitting that members of the Resistance should have sheltered him, and that he had returned with one of the Special Duties squadrons. After recovering from his injuries, he returned to flying, and once France had been liberated, he joined a Lancaster bomber squadron. He completed a number of bombing operations over Germany before the war ended, when he left the RAF.

After the war, John Tweed returned to France to visit and thank his helpers. He later wrote this about them:

> Thanking them before I left was quite impossible, these gallant people just did not seem to realize the hazard attached to giving assistance to RAF personnel. It was always the same, a deprecating wave of the hand, 'It is nothing', or else they were sorry that they could not do more for you.

Captain Ben Cowburn returned to France to continue with his SOE sabotage operations, his greatest success being the blowing up of the railway round-house at Troyes, causing massive disruption to rail traffic. He was twice awarded the MC for his courageous work with the French Resistance. Louis Joubin survived the war, but his leader, Pierre Mulsant, was captured giving assistance to British evaders camped in the Forest of Fontainebleau in July 1944. He was interrogated by the Gestapo, and sent to Buchenwald concentration camp, where he was shot on 15 September 1944.

THE SHELBURNE LINE

The short sea route across the English Channel presented an obvious way back to the United Kingdom for aircrew shot down in northern France, but the Germans had created a heavily defended coastal zone, making attempts to cross the Channel fraught with danger. The RAF's raids on Brest, other French Atlantic ports and Cherbourg left many shot-down aircrew hidden in different parts of Brittany. Earlier attempts to set up a sea route had not been successful, but during his attempts to expand the northern arm of the Pat Line, Louis Nouveau had made contact with a determined leader of the local Resistance organization based in the village of Plouha on the Brittany coast – François Le Cornec. Members of his group had sheltered evading airmen before arranging their journeys to the south, and over the Pyrenees into Spain.

Following the success of the evacuations by trawler from the south of France, Room 900 began plans for a similar operation based around Plouha, utilizing Royal Navy ships. Selected to lead the organization was a colourful agent of Russian origin, Vladimir Bouryschkine, known throughout his career with MI 9 as Val Williams. He had played an important role as a member of Pat O'Leary's Marseille team before leaving for Gibraltar on the *Tarana*, arriving in England in September 1942.

After a number of setbacks, he returned to France by parachute on 28 February to establish Operation 'Oaktree'. With him was a French–Canadian wireless operator, Sergeant Ray Labrosse. Following the disasters that had beset the Pat and Comet lines, their task was to establish a network of new safe houses in Paris, and create an escape line through Guingamp to link up with Le Cornac at Plouha, where Royal Navy motor gunboats (MGBs) would land agents and evacuate evading airmen. The operation got off to a bad start when Labrosse's radio was damaged during his parachute landing on the edge of the Forêt de Rambouillet, so the crucial radio link with London was never established. Nevertheless, the two men made some progress and started to establish the Paris network under François Campinchi. Safe houses were also identified in Brittany. There were remnants of Louis Nouveau's northern links still intact in the Paris area, but the traitor, Roger Le Neveu (Roger Le Légionaire), had infiltrated them. This man's treachery had been discovered during the month of Williams's arrival, but appropriate measures to counter his activities were not taken, and he continued his deadly work for his German controllers. As a result, Val Williams was captured on 4 June. Without a radio, Ray Labrosse could not continue, so he got away through Spain with the help of Georges Broussine and his Burgundy Line. Most of the Oaktree organization was wiped out.

Although Oaktree was finished, it was not a complete failure, as over 100 airmen who had been gathered in Brittany were taken to Spain down the Burgundy Line. Fortunately, Campinchi's Paris organization remained intact, and Roger Le Légionaire had not managed to infiltrate the Brittany cell. Labrosse was certain that it was still possible to develop the Brittany sea-evacuation line, so he volunteered to return as a wireless operator. London decided that another attempt should be made. Sergeant Major Lucien Dumais, a tough French-Canadian, was chosen to be the new organizer.

Dumais distinguished himself during the ill-fated Dieppe raid (when he was awarded the Military Medal), managing to escape with the help of the Pat Line. He remained in Marseille assisting Pat O'Leary before he was evacuated on the *Tarana* in October 1942. He agreed to return to France to establish the Shelburne escape organization, with Ray Labrosse as his wireless operator and number two. They arrived in France by Lysander during the night of 18 November 1943.

Dumais was able to re-establish contact with Campinchi in Paris and Le Cornec in Plouha almost immediately. A suitable beach a mile from Plouha at Anse Cochat had been identified, and it soon became known as Plage 'Bonaparte'. The most difficult part of the operation was the transfer of the evading airmen from Paris to Brittany. They travelled by train on the Paris–Brest express, alighting at Saint Brieuc or Guingamp, where they either transferred to a slow train to Plouha or were picked up and taken there, arriving under the cover of darkness. Since too many 'parcels', as the evaders were described, delivered too soon would attract attention in the small village, it was decided that the evaders would not be brought to Brittany until three days before the planned evacuation. François Kerambrun drove a small lorry for the German garrison – he was also a member of the local Resistance group. He was allowed to use the lorry for private business during his off-duty hours, so it was he who collected the evaders and took them to the network of safe houses. Sometimes he had as many as 20 evaders in his lorry, but he was able to bluff his way through the checkpoints. He once said, 'The consequences of being caught with 20 is no different than if I had two with me, so I would prefer to make one journey, not ten.' Such bravery was the hallmark of the French patriots. Once the timing of the evacuation had been confirmed by London, the airmen were taken from these places to a house belonging to Jean Gicquel, another key member of the Resistance. This house, which was to become legendary throughout Brittany, was located a mile from 'Bonaparte' Beach.

By late January 1944, Dumais was ready to send his first 'parcels'. Tasked to collect them were the MGBs of the 15th MGB Flotilla based at Dartmouth. These heavily armed boats carried a crew of 36, and were powered by three silenced 1,000 h.p. Paxman–Ricardo diesel engines allowing the MGB to cruise at 30 knots. The first operation was arranged for the night of 29 January 1944. On receiving the BBC message, 'Bonjour tout le monde â la Maison d'Alphonse', the airmen moved to Gicquel's house, known for ever afterwards as 'The House of Alphonse'. The airmen were then guided along the difficult path through a minefield and down a steep cliff to the beach, where specially designed surfboats with muffled oars arrived, after verifying a pre-arranged signal, to transfer them to the MGB waiting a mile out to sea. One of the guides was 18-year-old Marie-Thérèse Le Calvez, whose mother, Leonie, provided one of the safe houses. She was a remarkable and fearless young woman who became one of the key members of the local Resistance. This first Operation 'Bonaparte' recovered 19 airmen, and was a complete success. Other equally successful operations followed in the next few months. Returning with other evaders on MGB 503 on the night of 23 March was a young Canadian fighter pilot, Flying Officer Ken Woodhouse.

Twenty-year-old Ken Woodhouse from Prince Albert in Saskatchewan, Canada, took off from Biggin Hill in his Spitfire IX of 401 (RCAF) Squadron at 1.30 p.m. on 16 March 1944. His squadron was acting as escort to a force of light bombers attacking targets over northern France. Shortly after crossing the French coast, the engine of his Spitfire failed, and he was forced to bale out, landing in open country near Beauvais. Fourteen-year-old Marc Rendu, who was working in a field, watched his descent, and he immediately ran to fetch his father, Maurice, who arrived moments after Woodhouse landed. Within two minutes, the downed pilot had been bundled into the back of Maurice Rendu's small truck, and covered with sacking – moments later a German patrol arrived on the scene. Woodhouse was driven away and taken to the home of Maurice's father, Wilfred Rendu, where he met two American airmen who had been shot down a few days earlier.

After two days, when the initial search for Woodhouse had died down, the chief gendarme of Bresles, who was a leading member of the Resistance, and Wilfred Rendu, drove the three evaders to Beauvais, picking up *en route* six other shot-down airmen hiding in the area. A guide then took them by train to Paris, where Woodhouse was sheltered in a house overlooking the Luxembourg Gardens. The following day he was taken to 62 Rue Tiquetonne, the apartment of Genevieve Schneegans and Olympe Vasseur, who looked after him and an American, Keith Suter from Kansas.

After two days, he was collected by another guide and taken to the Lycée St Louis in the heart of Paris, where he met Maurice and Marguerite Cavalier, and two fellow Canadians. The Cavaliers had an apartment in the building where Maurice had set up a room to forge identity cards, restricted-zone passes and travel passes. He had obtained the names of young men from Brittany who had died, and whose identities he used for the evaders. He also acquired specimen signatures of local mayors and German authorities in various regions, together with rubber stamps, seals of various provinces, and all the inks and papers needed for forged documents. He chose the name of Louis Alphonse Pierre Kervizic for Woodhouse, and added his physical description, photograph and thumbprint to the card before forging the signature of the mayor of the town where the dead Louis Kervizic had lived. Finally, he added the appropriate seal of office. He then prepared passes authorizing entry into the 15-mile zone along the northern coast of France before giving Woodhouse a train ticket for St Brieuc in Brittany.

*Ken Woodhouse in his
401 (RCAF) Squadron
Spitfire. (K. Woodhouse)*

Within minutes of leaving the Cavaliers' apartment, Woodhouse had to show his pass when two Paris gendarmes stopped him and his guide. It passed their scrutiny and he was taken to the railway station, where he was passed to a young female guide called 'Mimi'. To his great surprise, he recognized one or two other men in the party that she had gathered, including Keith Suter and the two Canadians. The train was crowded and took all night to reach St Brieuc, where the nine evaders changed to a local train and spread themselves throughout the uncomfortable carriages. Some German soldiers were travelling on the train, causing numerous alarms, not least when one asked for a light for his cigarette. The guide indicated to Woodhouse and an American evader that they should alight at Guingamp, where another guide took them to the house of Mme Françine Laurent, a nurse. After she had fed them, they were able to wash before being offered a bed.

Mme Laurent was another of the many remarkable women of the French Resistance. Behind the stovepipe leading into a chimney, she kept a tin box that held the names and addresses of the airmen she had

The false papers provided by the Cavaliers for Ken Woodhouse. (K. Woodhouse)

helped. Woodhouse and the American added theirs to the list, which contained 32 names by the end of the war. She and her husband also stored arms, ammunition, explosives and a radio set for the local Resistance. They had narrowly avoided capture by the Gestapo by fleeing the area after the arrest of a colleague, but had returned to carry on their heroic work. She did this in the full knowledge that the Germans had just executed their friend and some of his family, including the wife, a daughter, and three boys aged between 14 and 18.

Twenty-four hours after Woodhouse arrived at the Laurents' house, he was collected by François Kerambrun, who appeared with his truck, already loaded with six other evaders dressed as farm workers. At selected spots, one or two were handed over to other guides. Eventually, Woodhouse and three others were dropped off, when they were met by Marie-Thérèse Le Calvez, who took them along hedgerows to a farm building where they were sheltered and given food.

Late the following evening after a final meal, she returned with a man to escort them to the final rendezvous. At one point the party of eight had to scatter when a German patrol passed nearby. Eventually, they reached the 'House of Alphonse', the final assembly point, where they discovered almost 30 other evaders, together with François Le Cornec, his chief guide Pierre Huet, the 'beach master' and signaller Job Mainguy, and other guides. Here the evaders were warned in no uncertain terms of the extreme danger of the situation, and how they were to be guided through the minefield and down the steep cliff to the beach. In total silence, Huet and Marie-Thérese led them to the beach, where they were hidden among the rocks as Mainguy signalled with a hooded torch. Shortly afterwards, Woodhouse saw two small boats, each manned by two Royal Navy sailors, pull on to the beach. The evaders were quickly ushered aboard, offered mute farewells to the brave French helpers, and the boats pulled out to sea, leaving a few evaders ashore. After some minutes of rowing, the boats pulled alongside a motor gunboat, MGB 503. They were quickly hauled on board before the rowing-boats returned for the rest of the party. Eventually, the MGB slowly steamed away under the command of Lieutenant R. M. Marshall DSC, RNVR, making as little noise as possible. Once clear of the coast, it was full speed for the River Dart, which was reached just after dawn. Operation 'Bonaparte V' had been successfully completed. The evaders were told to keep out of sight, and they were transported to London in great secrecy, where they were debriefed by the staff of MI 9.

Ken Woodhouse returned from Brittany on MGB 503. (R. Stanton)

Ken Woodhouse (centre) returned to Paris in 2001 to unveil a plaque in memory of the Cavaliers. On his left is Olympe Vasseur who sheltered him in her Paris flat. Marc Rendu (left) was 14 years old when he and his father rescued Woodhouse from under the noses of the Germans. (K. Woodhouse)

Keith Woodhouse had returned to England just seven days after he landed in France, and he was soon on his way home to Canada. His evasion was the result of the brilliant organization of Dumais and Labrosse, and the incredible bravery of the French people who made the Shelburne Line so successful. Sadly, there was a price to pay. The Cavaliers were betrayed to the Gestapo and Maurice was arrested. His wife was warned of her husband's arrest, giving her the opportunity to avoid capture, but she insisted that 'my place is with my husband'. They were both deported to German concentration camps. Maurice died in Dachau, and the fate of his brave wife, who was sent to Ravensbruck, remains unknown.

There were two more trips to 'Bonaparte' Beach before D-Day. Shelburne was responsible for the rescue by sea of 128 airmen and seven agents. Through their system of guides, they also arranged the safe passage of 98 men to Spain, and a group of 74 were sheltered in the Forêt de Fréteval until the Allied armies liberated them in August.

By the liberation of France, Shelburne had rescued 365 airmen. Incredibly, this was achieved without the loss of a single evader. Unfortunately, the 'House of Alphonse' did not survive. The Germans discovered its use and set fire to it. The ruins stand today as a memorial to the bravery of the French members of the Shelburne Line.

Lucien Dumais and Raymond Labrosse were both awarded the MC for their work establishing and organizing the Shelburne Line. Ken Woodhouse has remained in contact with his French helpers, making regular visits to see them and to remind them of the gratitude of all the evaders.

WITH THE MAQUIS

On the night of 3/4 May 1944, RAF Bomber Command mounted an attack with 362 bombers against a German military camp and tank ammunition storage depot near the French village of Mailly-le-Camp near Troyes. The raid was part of the preparations for the D-Day landings, and was considered by most bomber crews as a relatively straightforward sortie compared to the intensity of those against targets deep in Germany. On this particular occasion, they were to be proved wrong, as radio failures in the master bomber's aircraft caused great confusion, allowing German night-fighters to wreak havoc among the orbiting bombers. No fewer than 42 were shot down, an unacceptably high loss rate of 11.6 per cent, with over 250 aircrew losing their lives. Patriotic French families and members of the underground movement sheltered some of the 50 who parachuted to safety, among them Flying Officer Maurice Garlick of 12 Squadron.

Garlick, a 31-year-old Londoner, was the navigator in Flying Officer Peter Maxwell's crew, one of the most experienced on the squadron. They took off at 10 p.m. from Wickenby near Lincoln to join the stream of bombers heading for the French coast. They arrived at the target to find total confusion, with over 300 heavily laden bombers circling and waiting for orders to bomb. Eventually, the deputy master bomber realized the tragedy that was unfolding as the German night-fighters started to take their toll, and he ordered the bombers to attack. Maxwell's aircraft had just dropped its bombs when the aircraft jolted violently as the mid-upper gunner called that the port wing and engines were on fire. An unseen night-fighter had hit the aircraft from underneath. The pilot and the flight engineer,

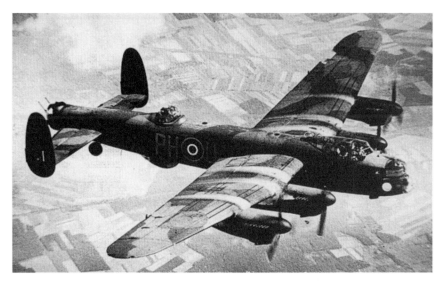

A Lancaster of 12 Squadron. (P. H. T. Green collection)

Sergeant John Crighton, tried to put out the fire and feather the engine, but to no avail. Maxwell gave the order to bale out.

Garlick made a clean exit from the aircraft, and floated through the darkness until he hit something that caused a great flash and bang, rendering him unconscious. When he recovered, he was lying in a wheat field somewhere in the area of Romilly. He was in great pain, with both his legs useless, there was a strong smell of burnt flesh and he noticed that his trouser legs were also burnt. He could see a high-tension cable lying on the ground close by, and it was clear that this was what had arrested his fall. He was fortunate to be alive. He was in a state of shock, and once he regained his senses he pulled the parachute over himself to keep warm.

He lay in the field for about 30 minutes, working out a plan of action, after which he opened his escape kit, ate a Horlicks tablet, and used his compass to find out which direction was south-east towards Switzerland. He cut open his trouser legs, removed his flying boots and started to bandage his legs with strips torn off his parachute. His right leg was paralysed and was burnt from below the ankle to the calf. His left leg was also very badly burnt from the foot to above the knee. After attending to his legs he fell asleep for a few hours.

He awoke at dawn and realized that he must get away from the immediate area, as it was inevitable that someone would soon arrive to inspect the damaged high-tension cable. He collected his belongings together, and crawled to the edge of the field, where he buried his parachute and helmet. He continued crawling across another field until he reached a railway line, which he crossed with great difficulty. He then had to crawl up an embankment, where he was able to survey the immediate countryside. He noticed a wood about two miles away in a south-easterly direction, and he made this his objective. After a rest he continued his crawl, with frequent rests in depressions and bushes. He heard and saw several farm workers, but was conscious of the advice given during lectures on escape and evasion to approach only individual farmers. In a small copse he cut down some saplings to make a pair of crutches, and using some parachute cord to make a sling for his right foot, he hobbled and crawled to his objective. Living on Horlicks tablets, chocolate, and rainwater that he was able to catch in the lid of his emergency pack, he took two days to cover the two miles to the wood. By the time he reached the wood the blood circulation had started to return to his legs, causing him great pain.

The woods were not as extensive as he thought, so after a night's rest he continued with the aim of finding an isolated farmhouse. At one stage he was resting by a cart track, smoking the last of his pipe tobacco, when a dozen German soldiers appeared. He avoided being seen by diving into a ditch, but it was a stark reminder of the risks of travelling in daylight. After eating some potatoes and wild rhubarb, he hobbled and crawled along for the remainder of the day and night. During the afternoon he was able to see the spires of Troyes Cathedral, which allowed him to fix his position.

On 7 May he continued to crawl and hobble until about 11 a.m., when he saw an isolated farmhouse. He hid in a hawthorn bush opposite the house, watching the movements of its occupants. An elderly farmer came out, and after observing him for two hours, Garlick approached him on his crutches and told him who he was. At nightfall, the farmer invited him into the house where he was given a meal of eggs, bread and cheese washed down by cider. The farmer's daughter bathed his legs, and he was able to shave. He was given a jacket, a pair of trousers and a penknife to replace the knife that he had lost. The family did not want him to stay the night as they said it was too dangerous, but they gave him more food and drink to take with him, refusing any kind of payment for all their help.

Garlick hobbled through the countryside for the next six days, travelling mainly at night and resting in woods and bushes by day. By 14 May, 11 days after he had been shot down and injured, he realized that he was becoming very weak and must seek help, since the burns on his legs were becoming infected. He came to an isolated and large farmhouse near Bucy, and decided to observe it until the evening, when he spotted a youth working in a field. He approached him and was soon taken to the farmhouse, where the maid of the house gave him some food and bathed his legs. Garlick had arrived at the farm belonging to Charles Decreon, the head of the local Resistance group, who soon arrived to meet him. Once Decreon was convinced of Garlick's identity, he agreed to help him. Since German agricultural inspectors called at the farm frequently, it was decided that he could not remain. A few hours later, an elderly lady and her daughter arrived and were introduced as 'good patriots and friends of the Allies'. They took him away by car to their house in Ossey Les Trois Maisons in the Aube area.

Garlick was immediately put to bed on arrival. The following morning he was treated by an unknown doctor, who visited every day for the six days that Garlick remained with the ladies. The daughter had to remain in the house for the whole period, feigning illness to justify the doctor's visits. The doctor refused all offers of payment, as did the two ladies who nursed him faithfully throughout his stay. With the news of the arrest of the leader of the Troyes Resistance group, who was a close friend of the two ladies, it was decided to move Garlick, as searches by the Gestapo were inevitable. He was moved to the house of two spinsters who lived at the other end of the village, a place where the doctor could continue to treat him. A number of other evaders were brought to the house, one of them a fluent French speaker, who had acted as liaison with the Maquis organization. He convinced himself of Garlick's identity before telling him that, once the Allied troops landed in France, it was intended to gather all the RAF evaders in the area, and take them to a wood near Lisière-des-Bois to form a sabotage group under the command of Flight Lieutenant G. Foley, working with the Maquis.

News reached the village that the Gestapo were about to conduct a search, so Garlick was moved back to Charles Decreon's farm, where he met Foley. They stayed for the night before being moved on 26 May, dressed in a new suit, a beret, and a pair of slippers, to a house in Estissac. He had arrived at the home of the local Maquis leader Joseph Lebrun, the father of five small children and the local postman. He said that he knew everyone in the village and the local area, including the gendarmerie, and that he had arranged with the police to be alerted if the Gestapo arrived in the village. He had also been a medical orderly during the First World War and he was concerned about the state of Garlick's legs. He called a Maquis doctor who examined his legs and prescribed a new treatment of saline solution and antiseptic powder. Lebrun changed the dressings every day, and under this treatment his legs started to heal. His morale received a further boost on 29 May when his bomb aimer, Sergeant Paddy O'Hara, was brought to the house to keep him company.

Garlick remained with the Lebruns until a few days after D-Day, when he learnt that the Germans had attacked the local Maquis in a wood and two RAF evaders had been among those killed, including one of his air gunners, Sergeant J. Davidson. The flight engineer of the crew, John Crighton, had got away and was taken to join Garlick. The three evaders remained together until they were liberated. With the American forces advancing slowly, there was little the three men could do, and an idea to make for Switzerland had to be abandoned when a travel ban was imposed.

In the second week of August they were warned that the Gestapo were going to search the village. They immediately left for the nearby woods, returning after dark. The same thing happened the following day, but this time they were told that the Maquis leader's house was to be searched, so the evaders were joined by Lebrun, who took them to a friend's farm in the next village. During the middle of August, it was decided to form a number of small groups of the Maquis instead of re-forming the large organization. By this time, Garlick was well enough to join a small group headed by Lebrun, and they moved to the Forêt d'Othe, where they camped out with the intention of causing as much trouble to the Germans as possible until they were liberated by the American forces, who had by then reached Le Mans. The group was equipped with arms dropped by the Allies, and the local people provided food.

When the group heard that the Americans had reached Auxerre, Lebrun took his car, which they loaded with Sten guns, and by a circuitous route the four men drove to an American outpost a few miles outside the town. They met the colonel, and in a long conversation with him Lebrun and Garlick gave him a detailed brief on the organization of the local Maquis groups. He asked the three evaders to remain with Lebrun's organization rather than return immediately to England, and also invited them to gather all the local Maquis leaders together for a conference. The next day, the colonel and two of his officers made their way to Lebrun's house, where they met all the local leaders, with Garlick acting as interpreter. Three days later, the village of Estissac was liberated.

The Liberation was tinged with sadness as the Germans had shot five young men a few days earlier 'for terrorist activities'. The three RAF men were asked to attend the funeral in an official capacity to represent the Royal Air Force, so they went to the Americans and asked if they could borrow uniforms, which the Americans readily agreed to. After this sad event, the villagers were able to celebrate their freedom.

On 2 September, Garlick and his two colleagues spent their last night with the Lebruns. They had shared their home for three months, and also the dangers. There were tears when it came to the time to depart. There were no suitable words of thanks for people who put their own and their children's lives at such risk. After three days in Paris, Garlick and his two fellow aircrew were flown to Hendon. None returned to operational flying.

Garlick's pilot made his own way home via Spain and returned a month before his colleagues. Joseph Lebrun, the brave rural postman, and his family moved to Paris after the war. A few weeks after the liberation, his wife gave birth to a son – they called him Maurice after a certain RAF navigator. Charles Decreon continued to live in Bucy, proud of the citations from Supreme Headquarters signed by General Eisenhower, and from the Royal Air Force signed by Air Chief Marshal Sir Arthur Tedder.

There are many remarkable people in this account, but the last word must remain for Maurice Garlick. Badly injured, unable to walk, and suffering agonies, he epitomized the courage of men who were determined not to fall into the hands of the enemy. His conduct and indomitable spirit were justly recognized when he was awarded the OBE.

Chapter Seven

Holland

Holland straddled the main bomber route to Germany, and as the strategic bombing campaign intensified, many aircrew found themselves landing among the Dutch people. The country is heavily populated, and the flat open terrain is so cut by many waterways, some presenting formidable obstacles, that travel in Holland presented aircrew on the run with many more problems than in other countries in north-west Europe. There were countless bridges, and all the important ones over the major rivers were guarded, making progress towards Belgium and France very difficult. It was considered to be particularly difficult to travel at night for any long distances without help. A coastal defence zone about 15 miles in depth was established and much of the population was relocated. Evaders who came down near the coast had to use great ingenuity to get clear of the area, and the majority were unsuccessful.

The vast majority of the Dutch population were prepared to give an evader assistance, but the main difficulty in Holland was making the first contact with an organization. The Germans were very much in control of the country, and made regular use of the members of the Dutch Nazi Party. The population was, understandably, very nervous of being seen helping evaders, who were advised to approach isolated farms – it was also known that lower-grade railway workers and barge crews were good contacts. Aircrew were warned never to ask a helper, 'Are you Dutch?' since the person would think this meant, 'Are you German [Duitsch]?' This misunderstanding caused some unpleasant incidents and could be avoided by using the word 'Netherlander' or 'Hollander'. One evader reported that he found the

*The radio operators of the Resistance movements and MI 9 took grave risks
punishable by death. Artist, Terence Cuneo. (TNA: PRO INF 3/1787)*

Dutch farmers and workers did not understand 'RAF' but did
understand 'British Tommie' and 'Churchill' accompanied by the 'V'
sign.

The difficulty of establishing and supporting an escape line in
Holland was exacerbated by the infiltration of the Dutch Resistance
movement by the German secret police (*Abwehr*) in April 1942, an
event that did not come to light for almost two years. As a result, the
Abwehr were able to intercept all radio communications from London,
and Langley and Neave in Room 900 were unable to provide support
to local organizations, most of which were unknown to them.

The most successful line in Holland was the 'Dutch–Paris' line run
entirely without support by John Weidner. He had studied at
Collonges, close to the border between France and Switzerland, so he
knew the area well, and took his evaders to this area before they

crossed into neutral Switzerland. Many of his evaders were Jews, but once he discovered that military evaders could be interned in Switzerland, he started to send them through Paris *en route* to Spain. One of the many successes of the line was Flight Lieutenant Bram van der Stok, one of only three men to successfully escape from what has since become known as 'The Great Escape', the infamous escape from Stalag Luft III when the Gestapo executed 50 of the recaptured aircrew. Van der Stok was sheltered in Holland before he passed down the Dutch–Paris line *en route* to Spain and Gibraltar. In addition to almost 200 aircrew, the line saved 1,000 Jews, but at the cost of some 150 members who were arrested, 40 of them never to return, including Weidner's sister Gabrielle.

Once the Comet Line had started to operate again after its setbacks, Neave was keen to establish a link from Holland to Brussels to link up with Comet. Suspicions that all was not well in the Dutch Underground movement increased during 1943, so Neave arranged to drop a Dutch agent, Dick Kragt, blind – that is, without a reception committee on the ground. Kragt (alias 'Frans Hals') had a Dutch father and was a trained radio operator, and he was parachuted into Holland in June 1943. Unfortunately, he was dropped in the wrong place, and he lost his radio, the crucial link with Room 900. However, Kragt was a tenacious individual who eventually established contact with Comet, and he was able to pass over 100 aircrew across the border to Brussels, where Comet arranged their onward journey. However, Kragt's greatest achievements stemmed from his availability at the time of the failure of Operation 'Market Garden' at Arnhem in September 1944. By this time he had received a radio operator and was in regular contact with Neave, who was immediately able to redirect his efforts to help the many evaders from the failed airborne operation. Dick Kragt's work during this period was of the greatest value, and many men owed their freedom to his gallantry.

Once the Allied armies neared the Dutch borders in September 1944, circumstances for aircrew evaders changed, and many chose to lie up or work on the land waiting for liberation. Following the defeat at Arnhem, there were many soldiers in hiding, and IS 9 (WEA), with Kragt coordinating the Dutch support, mounted a series of daring operations to rescue them. Airey Neave has described Operations 'Pegasus I and II' in detail in his book *Saturday at MI 9*.

Allied air activity over Holland increased significantly from September 1944. The heavy bombers continued to overfly the country *en route* to targets in Germany, and the RAF started to fly many airborne resupply sorties by transport aircraft. Thousands of ground-attack sorties in support of the advancing armies were also flown. The inevitable consequence of this greatly increased air activity was that many more aircrew were shot down to find themselves in an evasion situation. During the fighting in Holland, aircrew flying the dangerous low-level attack sorties in support of the Army were strongly advised to wear a khaki battledress. Mistakes were made by both the Dutch and the Allied troops when evaders in blue uniform were seen in the fighting area, since their appearance from a distance was very similar to the Germans in their field-grey uniforms. As the intensity of the ground fighting increased in late 1944, there were cases of the Germans opening fire on aircrew as they descended in their parachutes. Pilots were reminded of the merits of crash-landing or carrying a delayed-action parachute drop to overcome the danger.

The narratives that follow involve aircrew shot down over Holland, but their experiences and eventual escapes to freedom were very different.

SOLO FROM HOLLAND TO SPAIN

Ontario-born and Toronto-educated Flight Lieutenant Julian Sale RCAF was captain of a Halifax bomber of 35 Squadron detailed to attack Duisburg on the night of 12/13 May 1943. He took off from Graveley near Cambridge just before 10 p.m. The aircraft had crossed the Zuyder Zee, and had almost reached the turning point before heading south towards the target, when a German night-fighter attacked it. The aircraft was badly damaged and Sale gave the order for his crew to bale out. Just as he was moving to the escape hatch, the aircraft exploded and he was thrown clear. He landed in the top of a pine tree near the small Dutch town of Haaksbergen and clambered down the tree, but was unable to recover his parachute. He decided to leave his life-jacket at the foot of the tree. He had lost one of his flying-boots during his descent, so put both socks on the one foot before heading away.

On landing, he knew he was near the Dutch-German border, so his first aim was to head west, since he was not sure if he had landed in Germany. As dawn broke, he hid in a thicket between two farms hoping to determine if he was in Holland, but no safe opportunity

Flight Lieutenant Julian Sale RCAF (third left in back row) with his air and ground crew. (RAFES)

occurred for him to find out. Once dark, he again set off in a westerly direction along small tracks and minor roads, covering 20 miles before he took cover in another thicket. He had filled his water bottle with milk from a churn, and he ate Horlicks tablets from his aids box. At dusk on 14 May he convinced himself that he must be in Holland, so decided to approach a farmer for food and some footwear. The farmer was friendly, but nervous, and was able to understand who he was. He gave Sale some food and a pair of clogs, pointed out the direction for Arnhem, but asked him to move on because of his fear of the Germans.

Sale walked all night along secondary roads, passing through numerous villages, when he took off the clogs for fear of making too much noise. His feet were badly blistered, so he rested through the day before setting off again once it was dark. His feet were in poor shape so he had to abandon the clogs, and by the end of that night he had walked almost 40 miles during the previous three nights, but felt that he could go no further without some shoes and food. Towards dawn on 16 May, he reconnoitred a farmhouse on the outskirts of the village of Linde. He knocked on the back door, and declared himself by sign language before entering. He was well received and found he was surrounded by a most helpful, but very frightened, Dutch family.

They gave him a complete outfit of clothes, and a pair of socks and shoes. The son of the family brought a friend who explained that the Germans had discovered that local people had been assisting shot-down aircrew, and there had been some arrests. He urged Sale to give himself up, but he refused. The family gave him a bed in the attic and fed him throughout the following day. Sale found the family 'intensely patriotic, Dutch Royalist and pro-British'. That evening, they gave him a large-scale road map and sent him on his way.

With good clothes, he decided to walk by day, and use bigger roads, in order to make more distance. On one occasion, he helped a German officer to push his car, which had broken down. He decided to bypass Arnhem to the north, and headed for Oosterbeek, where he hoped to find a crossing point over the Neder Rijn. At dusk, he had reached the Arnhem–Nijmegan railway bridge, which he thought was unguarded. He had just got on to the bridge when he was hailed by a soldier who then fired at him as he raced off the bridge and down the riverbank. Once it was dark, he looked for an unchained boat, but had no luck. He stripped off his clothes and bundled them in his overcoat, secured them to a plank of wood, and propelled the plank across the 100-yard-wide river. By morning, he had reached the River Waal at Druten, where there was a ferry crossing. A friendly Dutch boy, who spoke a little English, told him that there were no controls on the ferry, so he exchanged a British half-crown for a few cents, which allowed him to pay the ferryman.

After crossing on the ferry, he headed for the next obstacle, the River Maas, which he reached later that day. Some workmen helped him across on a private industrial railway. Once again he approached an isolated house, where a schoolteacher who spoke some English gave him food and some new socks. As he walked through a small village the next day, a Dutch policeman stopped him and asked to see his papers. Sale was explaining his situation when the policeman suggested in broken French that he was 'a Frenchman going home from Germany'. Sale assented eagerly, they shook hands and the policeman wished him good luck.

In St Oedenrode, he knocked at the door of a house that he thought was a priest's house. Instead, he found three elderly ladies who invited him in to have some food, and to meet three residents from the town. After two nights' rest, his new helpers gave him a new pair of boots, three days' food, a road map and a bicycle. They also briefed him on a safe location to cross the Belgian border. At 3 p.m.

on 22 May, he reached the border, where he asked a Dutch family if there were soldiers guarding the crossing, and he was told that it was safe. He headed towards Antwerp, but was soon stopped by two policemen and identified himself. They were friendly, but advised him not to keep the bicycle since it had no Belgian licence plaque, and the blue Dutch plaque was too obvious. Sale kept the bicycle and improvised a Belgian plaque from an old cigarette carton.

He headed south through Belgium, and by the late evening he had passed through Louvain and Charleroi, and was close to the French border, having cycled over 100 miles in the day. The following day, a friendly Belgian farmer personally took him through the town of Grandneu on the frontier, thus avoiding the customs post. Sale had arrived in France 11 days after being shot down, and during that time he had walked and cycled almost 200 miles – some of the journey without shoes.

Sale had some knowledge of French, and his general plan was to head for Spain, keeping to the east of Paris. He hoped to make contact with 'an organization', but apart from being given some bread coupons, he had to press on alone. He cycled through the day, approaching lonely farms each evening, almost always gaining access to a barn. Few farmers accepted any payment for his food, and he was regularly provided with enough food for his journeys. For two days, he had only one pedal on his bicycle, and punctures became a regular feature as he progressed south through Laon, Chateau-Thierry, Sens, and on to Bourges, where he arrived at the demarcation line. As he had no repair outfit, he pushed his bicycle until he arrived at a small town where he was able to get repairs. Throughout his journey, he used coloured card and tin to improvize a local licence plaque, and he was very alert for police patrols whenever he entered a small town.

The demarcation line between the Occupied and Unoccupied Zones of France was regularly patrolled, and presented a major obstacle to the evader. Sale approached a landowner a few miles south of Bourges who helped him cross at an unguarded bridge. Safely over, he continued south, aiming to cycle up to 100 miles each day, which he achieved to reach Castres on 1 June. A day later, he reached the small town of Revel, where he stayed on local farms for almost three weeks. Since leaving the Belgian border eight days earlier, he had covered just over 500 miles.

Shortly after arriving in Revel, he met a young Frenchman who had tried to escape to Switzerland, but had been forced to return to

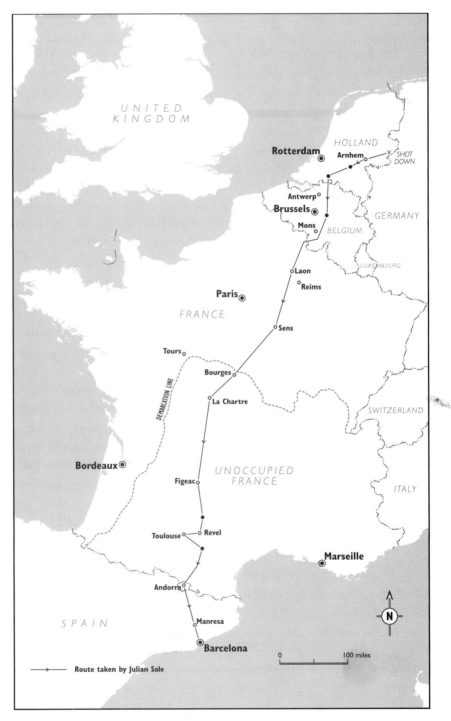

The route taken by Julian Sale RCAF.

Revel because of the tight security near the Swiss border. They agreed to join forces to make an attempt to cross the Pyrenees. On 21 June, Sale abandoned his Dutch bicycle that had served him so well. He and his companion left for Toulouse, where they caught a fast train to Carcassonne before transferring to a local train that took them to Quillan. After a 15-mile bus ride to Belcaire in the foothills of the Pyrenees, they stayed at a small hotel where they were able to contact a mountain guide who had gathered a party of six others who wished to cross the mountains. The party set off early on the morning of 24 June, but the guide became lost, which resulted in an overnight stop in the open. They started climbing early the next morning, and reached a point two miles from the frontier with Andorra by mid-afternoon when the guide refused to go any further. Sale and his French companion continued alone, crossing a 7,000-foot mountain and snow drifts to reach the frontier, which they crossed late on 25 June. They stayed overnight in a shepherd's hut before walking into the small Andorran town of Canillo the next morning.

In Canillo, they met a man who put them in touch with a Spanish smuggler who agreed to take them to Barcelona. A short car journey took them to the closely guarded Spanish frontier, and that night they crossed the mountains on foot into Spain with the smuggler and some of his associates. Over the next 10 days, they descended from the mountains, reaching the town of Manresa after a 90-mile walk – Sale claimed that this was the most arduous phase of his journey. The guide left them to go ahead to Barcelona to make contact with the British Consul, who arrived on 7 July to take the two men to the Consulate, where they remained until their onward journey to Gibraltar could be arranged.

Julian Sale left Gibraltar on 5 August, arriving in Liverpool five days later, and three months after he had baled out of his stricken bomber. With the exception of three short train and bus journeys, he had walked and cycled over 800 miles without once being supported by any of the escape lines. Local Dutch, Belgian and French people had been his helpers along the route – one of the longest solo evasions during the war. By any standards, his effort and determination to remain free places him as one of the great Air Force evaders. The authorities obviously agreed when it was announced in October that he had been awarded the DSO for his epic journey, an extremely rare award for such an action. The citation concluded: 'His unconquerable spirit of determination, great gallantry and fortitude have set an example beyond praise'.

The indomitable Canadian returned to 35 Squadron in the Pathfinder role, and to continue flying at the height of the strategic bomber campaign over Germany. Promoted to squadron leader, he was awarded a bar to his DSO for an outstandingly courageous action when he crash-landed his burning Halifax to save the life of one of his crew whose parachute had been destroyed in the fire. A few months later he was awarded a DFC for his gallantry as a Pathfinder leader. On 19 February 1944 he took off to target mark Leipzig. A German night-fighter attacked his Halifax, setting it on fire and seriously wounding Sale. Somehow, this tenacious Canadian managed to parachute from his burning bomber, but tragically he died of his wounds on 20 March 1944 in captivity.

DUTCH PILOT EVADES IN HOLLAND

Twenty-year-old Dutch-born Pilot Officer Jan Bernard Marinus Haye, known throughout his RAF career as 'Dutchy', was the pilot of a 57 Squadron Lancaster III bomber that took off on the night of 13 May 1943 from Scampton, near Lincoln, to bomb the Skoda works at Pilsen. It was his 23rd bombing operation. At about midnight on the outward journey, a Messerschmitt Bf 110 night-fighter attacked his Lancaster near the Dutch-German border. The bomber was set on fire, and Haye immediately turned west in an attempt to get over Dutch territory, but he started to lose control of the Lancaster and ordered the crew to bale out. Once he was sure that all the crew had left the aircraft, he jumped from the front escape hatch. The aircraft had been shot down by one of the *Luftwaffe's* most successful night-fighter pilots, *Hauptman* Herbert Lutje of *III/NJG 1*. He shot down no fewer than six RAF bombers on the night of 13/14 May, and by the end of the war he had been credited with the destruction of 53 aircraft.

Haye landed in a cornfield about 15 miles north-west of Enschede. He was uninjured and immediately buried his parachute, life-jacket and battledress top. He was wearing a civilian shirt with an open neck, and he pulled his trousers over his flying boots. He opened his aids box and purse, putting the contents in his trouser pockets before setting off for a nearby farm. He heard voices from inside, but the occupants were speaking with a strong dialect, which he did not recognize, so he decided not to knock at the door in case he had landed on the German side of the border. He headed west before

Pilot Officer 'Dutchy' Haye pictured with his mother shortly after receiving his commission in the RAF. (Mrs Joanne McHugo)

calling at another farm, where he was told to go away. However, he soon saw a sign, 'Verboden toegang' (entrance forbidden), and this confirmed that he was in Holland. He continued walking along sand tracks and through fields before calling at another farm, where he was again refused entry. Soon afterwards, he discovered that there was a strict curfew in Holland from 8 p.m. to 4 a.m., which explained why the Dutch farmers would not come outside.

After resting in a barn overnight, Haye approached a woman working in the fields. He spoke to her in Dutch, but she was very frightened when he declared who he was, and he was forced to move on. Without doubt, the Dutch families living in isolated farms very close to the German border were particularly fearful of reprisals should they be found helping an evading airman. It must also have been very disconcerting to be approached by someone speaking fluent Dutch who claimed to be in the RAF. Using 'plants' with a perfect command of the native language was a common ruse used by the Germans in all the occupied countries. The reluctance of these Dutch farmers near the border to help Haye is entirely understandable under these frightening circumstances.

Haye continued west, skirting past the town of Almelo before calling at another farm. This time, once the farmer realized that Haye was a RAF pilot, he took him to a barn where he gave him some bread and milk, but he was unable to meet Haye's request for a new pair of trousers. Haye was aware that they were conspicuous and he must take care. He had noticed a number of men dressed in civilian clothes riding a peculiar upright bicycle with saddlebags on the back, and he recalled that policemen in Holland usually rode on such bicycles. Therefore, whenever one approached him, he squatted down, so that his trousers were obscured, and pretended to be eating.

Once he was clear of the Almelo area, Haye headed south and soon came to a canal called the Twikkelsche Vaart, where there was a ferry with a number of people using it. Seizing an opportunity when there was no-one else about, he approached the ferryman. He spoke to him in Dutch, telling him that he was a pilot, and had only 20 gulden in notes. The ferryman agreed to take him over without payment. On the other side they met a man with a cart, who knew the ferryman, and he took Haye on his cart to a farm, where he gave him some food and an old pair of gumboots with the tops cut off. As he left the farm, a boy followed him on a bicycle for some distance before approaching him to ask where his aircraft had crashed! After a brief conversation he took Haye to a farm where the occupants welcomed him very warmly and gave him his first substantial meal since his arrival in Holland. They also gave him a suit of clothing, changed his banknotes into small money and gave him a bicycle. They refused any kind of payment. Finally, they gave him advice and directions on how to reach Amsterdam.

After leaving his helpers he almost made a fatal mistake. As he left a small town, he stopped to ask a man for directions, but by mistake he spoke in English. The man looked bewildered, so Haye spoke to him again in German, and finally in Dutch, explaining that he was a German visitor to Holland. As soon as he could, he hurried away, glad to have avoided causing suspicion. Just before curfew time he stopped near Klarenbeek, and went to a farm where he told the farmer who he was. He was given food and a blanket, and shown to a barn where he was able to spend the night. The farmer also told him that the back of his bicycle should be painted white to adhere to the local regulations. During the night, as Haye slept, the farmer painted the necessary white markings on the rear of his bicycle.

Early next morning he filled his water bottle and hung it over the handlebars before leaving for Apeldoorn, where he saw many German soldiers, and on to Amersfoort further west. As he rode along he examined his water bottle, and to his great concern he noticed that it was stamped 'made in England'. He immediately threw it away. He had previously lived in the town of Hilversum, and as he approached the town he was tempted to find some old friends to seek their assistance, but he thought it would be wiser to avoid it in case he was recognized by less friendly acquaintances. Instead, he cycled to the nearby town of Laren, where a boy told him of a family in the next town who might be prepared to help him. On his arrival, they gave him some food and advised him that once he reached Amsterdam he should go to the Warmoesstraat (the notorious red-light street), where the prostitutes might be willing to shield him. He continued on his journey, and as the curfew hour approached, he called at a café, where he declared himself. He was taken to a farm where he was given food and shown to a barn for the night. His hosts were very scared, but he soon discovered that they had only just been released from a concentration camp. Nevertheless, before he left the next morning, this brave couple gave him a meal and enough bread coupons to last two weeks.

As he got close to Amsterdam, Haye realized that his bicycle had rubber tyres, which was unusual in wartime Holland, so he threw it away and carried on to Amsterdam on foot. He was given directions to the Warmoesstraat, where he went into a small bar with a German name above the door. He struck up a conversation in Dutch with the barmaid, and eventually told her that he was in the RAF and needed help. She told him in a low voice that she didn't care who he was, but her father and sister, who were sitting at a nearby table, were pro-German and he had better leave the place immediately. He went to another bar for a drink, and while there he saw a police car call at the bar that he had just left. He realized that the prostitutes of Amsterdam were not likely to be able to help him, so decided to head for The Hague, where he hoped to contact Dutch fishermen who might be able to get him to England.

After resting in a cinema, he tried to get a meal at a cafeteria, but found that practically all the food available required coupons, which he did not possess. He headed for the railway station and bought a ticket to The Hague. Unknowingly, he boarded the wrong train since he had bought a worker's ticket that was only valid on certain trains. He had to get off the train at Zandvoort, where he was taken to the station-master's office to face a few difficult moments explaining his error. Fortunately, he was not asked for an identity card, and he left with the correct ticket and a refund, for which he signed with his real name and a false address. He then caught a train for The Hague, arriving in the late afternoon.

Waiting at the station he saw a woman whom he had known well before the war, and her husband, whom he also knew well, soon joined her. He approached them, and not unexpectedly, they were extremely surprised to see him. He told them that he was serving in the RAF and they immediately took him to their home, where he remained for the next two weeks. During this time numerous people in the Dutch Underground, who also provided him with identity papers, visited him. One of the visitors was 26-year-old Anton Schrader. Just before the outbreak of war, he had returned from Indonesia to study at university, but his plans were disrupted and he had to accept a senior position in the Ministry of Food. He was responsible for the distribution of food, which gave him access to the use of boats on the Dutch canals and waterways, an ideal job providing cover for all his underground activities, mainly organizing the escape of Dutch civilians across the North Sea – over 100 during the course of the war. He was about to organize another crossing to England, and he offered to include Haye in the next group to make the dangerous voyage to freedom.

'Dutchy' Haye pictured with Anton Schrader (left) shortly before leaving for England. (Mrs Joanne McHugo)

During the next eight weeks, Haye stayed for most of the time at Schrader's house in The Hague, and it was during this time that he met a beautiful young woman, Elly de Jong, who worked for Schrader in the Ministry of Food and assisted him with his underground activities in addition to gathering intelligence for sabotage operations. It was a meeting that would have a profound influence on the lives of 'Dutchy' Haye and Elly. By 26 July, Schrader had completed the arrangements for the next North Sea crossing. Haye, together with eight Dutchmen and Alfred Hagen, another RAF evader, was picked up by an open truck carrying some oil barrels to be taken through Rotterdam to the small town of Noord Beijerland, near Dordrecht. On arrival the party boarded a barge loaded with potatoes belonging to Kees Koole who had joined Schrader in his work assisting evaders. Concealed in the hold was a 20-foot wooden launch. The captain was Dolph Mantel, who immediately set off for the wide channel known as the Holland's Deep where the Meuse River entered the sea, timing his departure in order to reach the coast under the cover of darkness. The launch was hoisted overboard by using a derrick before the eight men were transferred successfully.

The launch was equipped with a recently overhauled Ford V-8 engine and a small outboard motor. There was also a small sail and four oars available. Four hundred litres of fuel, a supply of lubricants, a small quantity of water and four double loaves of bread were on board. The boat immediately got under way, initially travelling at quarter speed only in order to slip quietly past the inevitable coastal patrol boats, before speeding up to make the maximum distance from the coast before daylight. The following day the main engine failed, and the outboard motor gave only intermittent help – and they could still see the outline of the Dutch coast! The sail was rigged and the men took it in turns to use the four oars as they continued their westward voyage on a very calm sea. The weather was blisteringly hot so they took it in turns to swim and cool off. On the third night the weather started to change, and they had to ration the limited supply of food and water. On the fourth morning HMS *Garth*, a Royal Navy destroyer on convoy escort duties, saw them when they were about 10 miles off the Thames Estuary, and the evaders were soon scrambling aboard. By lunchtime the men had been landed at Sheerness. Haye had arrived back in England 11 weeks after baling out of his Lancaster. On returning to his squadron, he learned that four of his crew had survived to become prisoners of war, but his two air gunners had been killed.

*Elly de Jong of the Dutch
Resistance who fell in love with
'Dutchy' Haye. They were
married after the war.
(Mrs Joanne McHugo)*

'Dutchy' Haye was one of very few aircrew who evaded successfully direct from Holland. The majority of those who succeeded in returning to the United Kingdom travelled through Belgium and France to Spain. With a complete knowledge of the Dutch language, he could afford to approach certain places and organizations in the knowledge that he would arouse less suspicion than a non-native. He also had the good fortune to meet an old friend who was sympathetic to the Allied cause. However, notwithstanding these advantages, his was a remarkable achievement concluding with a perilous voyage across the North Sea in a broken-down open boat.

'Dutchy' Haye eventually returned to operations flying Lancasters with 83 (Pathfinder) Squadron. He survived the war and was awarded the Dutch DFC for his patriotic services. However, this was not the end of his remarkable story. After VE Day, he was given permission to visit Holland to see Elly de Jong, the girl he had fallen in love with during his eight weeks in The Hague. He was horrified to learn that she and other members of her Resistance group had been betrayed and arrested. Elly had been sentenced to death and sent to Ravensbruck concentration camp. She was transferred to Mauthausen, from where she was liberated before the sentence could be carried

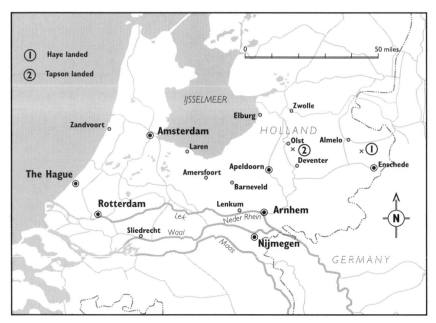

*Southern Holland showing the main towns where 'Dutchy' Haye and
Charles Tapson travelled and were sheltered.*

out. Soon after the war, she married her RAF pilot, 'Dutchy' Haye,
and they were happily married for over 50 years.

'Tonny' Schrader lived an amazing double life worthy of a book. He
was betrayed after the Germans picked up a group of evaders, and he
had to flee along his own route, arriving in England on 9 October
1943. He was employed by the American Office of Strategic Services
(OSS), and parachuted into Holland, where he established a radio link
with the Allies. He was captured by the Germans and forced to
transmit messages to England, but he took the precaution of including
a code word that indicated that he was transmitting under the
influence of the Gestapo. General Eisenhower awarded him one of
America's highest awards for gallantry, the Silver Star, for his services.

WITH THE DUTCH RESISTANCE

Flying Officer Charles Tapson from Melbourne, Australia, and his
London-born navigator Pilot Officer Frank Batterbury took off from
Lasham in Hampshire in their Mosquito VI of 107 Squadron at 9.30
p.m. on 5 October 1944. They had been tasked with a night-intruder
sortie over north-eastern Holland. Flying at 1,000 feet, they dropped

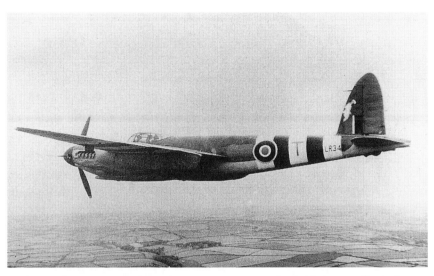

A damaged Mosquito IV limps home on one engine. (P. H. T. Green collection)

a flare before turning in to attack a railway junction near the town of Deventer, 30 miles north of Arnhem. As Tapson pressed the release to drop the 500 lb bomb, the aircraft was hit by intense light flak, which blew off the nose of the Mosquito, making the aircraft almost uncontrollable. Somehow, Tapson managed to crash-land the aircraft in a field between two woods. Batterbury scrambled through the top escape hatch before helping out his concussed pilot, who had also received bad cuts to his face. The sensitive navigation equipment was detonated, and the parachutes and life-jackets were thrown into the aircraft, which was soon burning fiercely.

The two men headed west after Batterbury had dressed his pilot's wounds, and they walked until just before dawn, when they headed for a wood to hide throughout the day, keeping a close watch on two nearby farms. As darkness fell, they approached one of them and were given food and water before being taken to the neighbouring farm, owned by the Kolkman family, who provided shelter for the night. The farm was near the village of Olst, a few miles north of Deventer, and the family had strong connections with the Dutch Resistance movement. However, their farm was only a half-mile from a German SS camp, and it was not considered safe for them to stay longer. That afternoon they were taken to a rendezvous in a nearby wood, where they were told to wait. Two men in uniform soon approached them, and they thought they had walked into a trap and were to be handed over. Their fears were short lived since the two men were Dutch policeman from Olst, and they were there to safeguard the arrival of the leader of the local Resistance, M. Detombs. On arrival, he rigorously checked their identity before telling them to remain in the wood until it was dark, when the two policemen would return for them.

They were taken to the nearby farm of M. Suntink and his wife, where they were given a hiding place in a secret room built high in a barn, and accessible only by a long ladder. The farmer's wife dressed Tapson's wounds and Detombs's brother-in-law brought shaving materials and books. This was their home for the next two weeks, during which time they were unable to leave the room for more than a few minutes each day. The farmer and his family did everything they could to make them comfortable, but the presence of a German

Charles Tapson was wounded during the crash landing and was treated by Dutch patriots. Terence Cuneo captures a similar scene. (TNA: PRO INF 3/1790)

work force constructing a major defence system nearby prevented them from any outside activity or exercise. They discovered that two glider pilots in hiding after the Arnhem operation were being sheltered nearby, and the Resistance intended to evacuate all four men from the area, which was due to be declared a prohibitive zone. The two glider pilots were brought to the farm early on 20 October to join the Mosquito crew. At lunchtime, the four men were hidden in a large horse-drawn hay cart, and in broad daylight the farmer brazenly, and with immense courage, drove the cart through German checkpoints to a farm close to the river.

At 6.30 p.m. Detombs appeared to escort them through a wood down to the river, where the two policemen they had met two weeks earlier were waiting for them. They climbed the dyke and waited for a green signal lamp to indicate that it was safe to cross. The two policemen then led them through the German defences to the side of the Ijssel River, where a small boat had been positioned. The four evaders were rowed across the 200-yard-wide river, where three more members of the Resistance met them. The courageous policemen took the boat back. The leader of the new group was the local Dutch Reformed Church priest, called Couvee, who split the party in two and took Tapson and Batterbury to a farm where they spent the next 10 days receiving daily visits from the priest.

At dusk on 1 November, Couvee arrived to take them to the church in Welsum, where two more members of the Resistance met them with bicycles ready to escort them to the manse in Veesen. There the local priest, Louis Buenk, welcomed them in perfect English. They were greeted by the strange sight in flickering candlelight of 10 men of the Veesen Group sitting around a table being given instruction on firearms. The manse was a hive of illicit activity; Buenk later showed them a trap-door under the carpet in the dining room, which led to a hideout containing a large arsenal of weapons and ammunition obtained from RAF airdrops. During their 16-day stay at the manse they assisted with a project to build a new shelter to hide the arms. The site chosen was under the church vestry, and eight other evaders, who were being sheltered in the area, were included in the work that started at 11 p.m. each night, finishing just before dawn. After five days, the new hideaway was complete.

On 17 November, the two glider pilots and an officer from the Royal Artillery arrived at the manse ready for the next stage of the attempt to return the men across the Allied lines. At 2 p.m. a horse-

drawn cart loaded with freshly dug turnips arrived at the back of the
manse. The turnips were unloaded and the five men, each equipped
with a Sten gun and a food parcel, lay on the floor of the cart before
the turnips were piled back on top of them. Just as they set off, the
men heard Louis Buenk shout a blessing to them. For the next three
hours they remained in their uncomfortable position while Henk
Zwaan drove the cart through a German artillery camp and on
towards Elburg. Throughout the journey, members of the Resistance,
who rode bicycles at a discreet distance ahead and behind the slow-
moving horse and cart, escorted them. Finally the horse could go no
further, and the five evaders were ferried on the bicycles to a barn rear
Elburg. At the end of the war, Tapson wrote: 'I pay a special tribute to
the Veesen Group under Louis Buenk'.

On arrival at the barn, the leader of the Elburg Resistance Group told
them that they were to join another 75 evaders, mostly Arnhem veterans,
in woods near Renkum, east of Arnhem, prior to a mass evacuation
across the Neder Rijn River to join up with Canadian forces. A
previous operation, Pegasus I, had been arranged successfully by Airey
Neave and his men from IS 9 (WEA), and this was to be Pegasus II.

At dusk on the evening of 18 November, Tapson and Batterbury,
together with 12 other evaders, were loaded on to a lorry, all carrying
picks and shovels to make them look like a labour gang. They travelled
south at speed on main roads with headlights on – a perfect target for
a Mosquito night-intruder, a fate that did not go unnoticed by Tapson
and Batterbury! On arrival at their destination, they disembarked from
the lorry as two guides hurried them along to the final rendezvous for
the river crossing. Further delays occurred, as they had to take evasive
action from unidentified strangers, and make a detour around a
German post. As they were making a further detour through a wood
they heard bursts of gunfire coming from the river area, and realized
that the main party had run into trouble. They later discovered that a
German sentry had confronted the column of evaders, and shooting
broke out. The large party had to scatter and seek shelter in the area,
but it was estimated that 16 evaders, two Dutch guides and a number
of commandos had been killed, with others captured.

For three wet and miserable days the men had to shelter in the
wood while Dick Kragt, who had been the coordinator on the Dutch
side for both Pegasus operations, made new arrangements for them.
He decided to split the group up into small parties. Tapson was taken
to the farm of Jacob Bois near Barneveld, where he remained in

Dick Kragt, who masterminded the rescue of many evaders in Holland. (RAFES)

hiding for the next three months. Batterbury was teamed up with a Flying Officer Adrian Davies, a Typhoon pilot of 263 Squadron, shot down two weeks earlier while dive-bombing the railway near Zwolle, a town a few miles north of Olst.

Batterbury and Davies were taken to the farm of G. van den Brandt a few miles to the east of Barneveld, and given accommodation on the top of a 20 ft haystack, protected by a 'pagoda'-shaped metal roof, where they remained throughout the day. There was very little light, and the two men's only exercise for the next four weeks was when they were able to take a very short walk from the haystack to the farm kitchen. During this period they suffered from acute stomach pains. Permission was eventually obtained from Kragt allowing them to take a short daily walk on a prescribed path within the farm. Reading was their only pastime, and this was only possible on sunny days or when there was snow on the ground. During their nine-week stay conditions were extremely severe, and the cold and lack of exercise began to tell on them. It was clear that a new shelter was needed for the two men, and on 21 January 1945 they were moved a few miles to

Jacob Bols's farm, where they met another RAF pilot who had been there for 10 weeks. Two days later they were moved to a more permanent refuge.

On 25 January, two guides arrived to escort them on bicycles to the farm of W. van der Kemp at Nijkerk near the Ijselmeer, where they were allowed to work as farm hands. He had seven children and was a very staunch worker for the Resistance, accepting great risks to himself and his young family. After two weeks on the farm they set off on a series of daily journeys, heading west towards the lower Waal River where Dick Kragt had joined up with Dick van Brugge and Klaas Heijboer of the 'Lek' team. They had set up a new operation with canoes following the abortive Pegasus II operation, and this had become the established escape route from northern Holland. A British Army officer had joined Batterbury and Davies, and the three stayed overnight in a series of safe houses. On the night of 11 February they stayed in a house at Schalwijk just north of the river before setting off in the early hours of the following morning with three guides. At 9 a.m. Boon van Waterstraat, a waterman, rowed them across the wide Lek river before taking them to his house. There they were met by Klaas Heijbor, who took them to Groot Ammers, a small village 30 miles to the west. They remained for two nights before Heijbor took them south towards the Waal River near Sliedrecht, where three more Army officers joined them. After an abortive attempt to cross the river to Canadian lines in the early hours of 16 February, they made another attempt the following night when Lang Jan, a local Resistance leader, led them over the river in canoes to a dam where Captain Coates of the IS 9 (WEA) organization was waiting for them with a larger boat. The evaders bade farewell to their gallant Dutch friends just after midnight and set off across the Nieuwe Merwerde, at the mouth of the lower Waal, reaching the Allied positions at 7.15 a.m.

After his three-month stay with the Bois family, and five days after his navigator reached freedom, Tapson finally left their house. Together with a Canadian soldier and guides, he set off on a bicycle to travel westwards to the escape route established across the Waal River. On 28 February they arrived with the Stapper family in Doorn, where they stayed until 6 March. On that day 15 Germans arrived to requisition the house for a hospital, and they proceeded to inspect the house. Tapson and his Canadian colleague hid in a cupboard in one of the rooms, which the Germans entered a few minutes later. Mrs Stapper told them that refugees from Arnhem used the room, which thankfully satisfied them. The Germans moved in later that day, followed by 50 soldiers who started to dig trenches in front of the house and to put a control post on the road. They left at the end of the day, leaving the German medical personnel in the house. As they sat down for their evening meal, Stapper went up to the room to release the two men from their cupboard before quietly leading them downstairs past the Germans. Tapson described Stapper as 'one of the coolest men I ever met'.

Over the next few days, the evaders and their guides moved from one safe house to another as they cycled towards the Lek, which they had to cross at Vreeswijk. The crossing point was a heavily guarded bridge, where the guide would lead them to a point just short before he turned away, leaving Tapson and his colleague to cycle over the bridge 100 yards apart. With hearts thumping, they crossed success-fully to meet two more guides who were waiting for them on the far bank ready to take them to a safe house. When another pair, escorted by a girl courier, followed an hour later, they were apprehended, although the girl managed to escape to give the alarm. Despite the onset of the curfew, the Dutch guides decided to move Tapson and his fellow evader to a safer farm. Here a courier, Map Dogterom, the local schoolmistress, met them and told them that arrangements were being made to get them to the Allied lines. From this point, their route followed the same as that used by Batterbury and Davies a few weeks earlier.

After crossing the Lek in a rubber dinghy, they were taken to Heijboer's farm in Groot Ammers for the night. On 13 March a guide took them to Sliedrecht, where they had to wait for 24 hours before the tide was suitable to make the hazardous crossing. At 9 p.m. on the following day, they set off to row across the wide river. Owing to a heavy mist they were lost in the river for over an hour, but Tapson's escape compass helped considerably. After almost five hours of rowing, they reached the Allied lines. Tapson had been on the run for almost six months.

Tapson and his navigator, Frank Batterbury, were reunited a few weeks later when they completed a refresher flying course on the Mosquito before returning to 107 Squadron at Epinoy, France, on 22 May 1945.

Following the failure of the Arnhem operation, many men were hiding with the help of the Dutch Underground. As the air war moved north through Belgium and Holland, many aircrew shot down over Holland found themselves among the Arnhem evaders. The reaction of the Dutch people was truly amazing. They took the most enormous risks, but they were determined to shelter the men who had fought to help them achieve their liberty. The words written after the war by Charles Tapson sum up the feelings of all those who owed their freedom to the Dutch people when he said, 'Our success was due entirely to the heroic efforts of the Dutch Resistance'.

Chapter Eight

Scandinavia

THE INVOLVEMENT OF MI 9 in Scandinavia was on a very small scale due to the limited amount of offensive operations carried out in the region. After the Allied withdrawal from Norway in the spring of 1940, apart from a few raids by commandos there was no ground action in Scandinavia other than those by the local Resistance forces. Compared to other theatres, air operations were limited and generated few aircrew evaders.

With its flat farming country, good communications and friendly people, Denmark provided plenty of opportunities for evasion lines. German troops were sparsely distributed in the Danish countryside, thus giving the evader a good opportunity to get well away from his landing area before the arrival of a German patrol. The morale of the Danes was very high and the great majority were extremely anti-German and pro-Allies. Most Danes could speak English, and this made contact with potential helpers much easier than in other occupied countries. Aircrew were advised to seek assistance from priests or doctors. As in other countries, small farms, of which there were very many, were recommended. Briefings also stressed the need to avoid the coastal defence zone on the west coast, and to head north-east in an attempt to get a boat to Sweden – the only feasible route to return to Britain.

The Danes were slow to establish lines to freedom, but their success getting a young Canadian, Donald Smith, across to neutral Sweden by boat in April 1943 prompted the establishment of an escape line from Frederikshavn, in north Jutland, to Sweden. Smith was the flight engineer of a Stirling bomber returning from an attack on Stettin when his aircraft was shot down. Various Danish farmers helped him until he met a member of the Resistance movement who eventually canoed him across the Kattegat to Sweden. He was the first of a number of aircrew evaders to use this route to safety. When the Germans ordered the arrest of all Danish Jews a few months later, over 7,000 were taken by boat by their fellow countrymen to Sweden. A RAF pilot who took the boat trip to Sweden was Flight Sergeant Rowland Williams.

FROM DENMARK ACROSS THE KATTEGAT

By intercepting German signals traffic, British intelligence staff discovered that the *Luftwaffe* intended to fly reinforcement aircraft, including Heinkel He 177 heavy bombers, to Aalborg airfield in northern Denmark. They were due to arrive at the Danish airfield at 11 a.m. on 17 May 1944. Eight long-range Mustangs of 122 Wing based at Funtington in Sussex were tasked to intercept them. The aircraft flew to Coltishall in north Norfolk to refuel for the long North Sea crossing, and to receive a final briefing before taking off at 9 a.m. Flying one of the 65 Squadron Mustangs was 20-year-old Welshman, Flight Sergeant Rowland Williams.

As the Mustangs arrived over the airfield at Aalborg, they encountered numerous training aircraft and bombers in the local area. Williams attacked two Junkers Ju 34 training aircraft and shot them down before pursuing a Junkers Ju 88 bomber that was escaping at low level to the north. He closed on the aircraft and opened fire, setting the starboard engine on fire. As he pulled up to make another attack, he felt his Mustang shudder when a piece of debris from the bomber hit his aircraft's engine, causing it to stop. He was too low to bale out, and as his engine gave signs of catching fire, he had to make a hurried forced landing in a large field 15 miles north of Aalborg.

During the landing, Williams suffered mild concussion and hurt his shoulder, but he was able to scramble clear. He saw people approaching, so he headed for a small copse to hide, where he decided to discard his uniform blouse. He removed the pilot's wings from his uniform, in case he needed them for identification purposes later, and then set off in a different direction to avoid being followed. He found an irrigation ditch surrounded by willows where he remained for a few hours. During this time, he noticed a large barn, but before he

Rowland Williams's Mustang attracts the attention of German soldiers in a field near Aalborg. This photograph was discovered in Germany in 1990. (R. Williams)

could head for it, a lorry-load of German troops arrived to search it. As soon as they departed, he headed for the barn, working on the assumption that, having already searched it once, the troops were unlikely to return. He reached the barn and hid in some hay, but soon afterwards a woman came to feed some chickens and her dog alerted her to Williams's presence. She ran off and a farmhand arrived shortly afterwards, and showed him a safer place to hide within the barn. He spent an uncomfortable night before the farmhand returned at dawn with a sandwich, but it was clear that he wanted Williams to move on.

During his pursuit of the German bomber, Williams had noticed a large forest to the north-east, and he decided to head for this area. He made rapid progress to cover the five miles, and was able to hide in the wood all day. He noticed a farm on the far side, which he observed all day before approaching it as dusk fell. The farmer's wife immediately admitted him. He had arrived at Storlogtved farm, owned by the Callisen family, where he was given a good meal, some civilian clothes, and a road map of Denmark. He stayed in their barn overnight before leaving early the next morning, when he was urged to go to a nearby refectory at Albaek, where he would receive help. However, he had decided to change his original plan, which was to head for the east coast where he hoped to find a boat for neutral Sweden, and to head south instead, and make for Copenhagen, where, he reasoned, there would be a better chance of crossing into Sweden.

To cross the wide Limfjord, he had to head for Aalborg, so he set off along a road. In due course he heard a large lorry approaching, which he soon discovered was German. Thinking that it would arouse suspicion if he jumped in the hedge, he carried on walking. As it passed him, he was astonished to see that his Mustang was on the back, having been dismantled. Emblazoned on the side was a name, 'Mike – First of the Few', which his fitter had painted on a few weeks earlier to celebrate the birth of Williams's son. Seeing this, and realizing that his clothes had not attracted any suspicion, gave him an overpowering desire to get back to England.

He continued south to cross the Limfjord that ran through Aalborg. Once he reached the 500-yard-long bridge on the northern side, he stopped to consider how he was going to get past the guards to cross the bridge. Just as he was contemplating the problem, a convoy of eight covered lorries of the German Army came along, each carrying parties of displaced persons used for forced labour. The convoy stopped at the control point, giving him just enough time to climb over the tailboard of the last lorry to sit with the labourers, one passing him an identity card to wave to the guard who made a perfunctory check. Once over the bridge, the lorries continued into the centre of Aalborg, where they stopped at traffic lights, allowing Williams to jump out and disappear among the crowds. He headed out of the town to continue his southerly journey. After spending the night in a wood, he realized that he would have to get some assistance since his feet were very badly blistered and turning septic. He watched a farmhouse for a number of hours before approaching it, and was relieved when the farmer invited him in. He was given some food before his host telephoned for a doctor.

Two men arrived, one an English-speaking doctor called Ropholtz, to treat Williams's feet. After bandaging them, the doctor told Williams that he would have to take him to his house in Kjletrup for further treatment. It transpired that the doctor was married to an English widow, whose son, Walter Lonsdale, was the other man with the doctor, and who was the leader of the local Resistance group. Williams remained with the family for two days before Lonsdale escorted him by train to Randers, a town some 50 miles to the south. Lonsdale went ahead to check that the safe house was clear, but he returned to say that the signal indicating that all was safe, a pot of flowers in the window, was missing. He made further enquiries and discovered that the whole Resistance group had been betrayed the day before, and most had been shot by the Gestapo.

Lonsdale and Williams left Randers immediately, taking a train to Aarhus, Denmark's second city, where they headed for the town hall. Williams was subjected to a detailed interrogation by a British secret agent before being handed to a courier who took him to the home of Lasse Egebyerg, the editor of the main Jutland daily newspaper. During the seven days that he stayed at the editor's house, the chief organizer and leader of the Resistance movement in Jutland, a man known as 'Tolstrup' visited Williams. He organized his onward journey to freedom, which started with a train journey back to Aalborg!

Niels Otzen, a photographer, who took photographs of Williams for an identity card, looked after him for two days before Police Inspector Kaj Mortimer arrived to move him to another safe house. He put Williams in the sidecar of his motorbike as his 'prisoner' to drive him over the Aalborg bridge, which had given him so much difficulty two weeks earlier, and on to the Albaek Refectory. There he was looked after by the Reverend Hindsholm, who had assisted many refugees in the past. He had, quite incredibly, returned to the safe place

The photograph of Williams taken in Aalborg for his identity card. It was taken in front of the well-known statue in the centre of the city to add authenticity.
(R. Williams)

recommended by the Callisen family two days after his unscheduled arrival in Denmark.

He stayed in a secret room for the next 24 hours before he was driven 20 miles to the small port of Saeby, where he met Jens Christian Jensen, the captain of the fishing trawler *Laura*, and seven other passengers. The boat sailed at 9 p.m. taking a route through water too shallow for German patrol boats. The plan was to make a rendezvous with a small Swedish boat for the passengers to be transferred, allowing the trawler to return to Denmark under the cover of darkness. For reasons unknown, the rendezvous failed, so Jensen took the very brave decision to head for the Swedish port of Gothenburg. In the early hours of the morning, a Swedish Marine Police launch intercepted the *Laura*, and took off the eight passengers. The crew announced that the Allies had landed in Normandy. It was 6 June 1944.

Williams was de-loused by a Swedish nurse before being taken to the British Consul. Within a day, he moved to the British Embassy in Stockholm, where he received a new set of clothes. Since he had arrived in Sweden unarmed, he was entitled to be repatriated rather than interned. After four weeks of pleasant living in Stockholm, he put on very heavy flying-clothing prior to climbing into the specially adapted seat in the bomb bay of a BOAC Mosquito. After climbing to 30,000 feet over neutral Sweden, the Mosquito headed for Scotland above the normal operating height of German fighters before

The fishing boat Laura *took Williams to Sweden. (R. Williams)*

descending to land at Leuchars in Fife. Williams arrived in London on 4 July to meet the MI 9 debriefing team and then enjoy some leave.

Rowland Williams returned to 65 Squadron, which was established in Normandy, and he flew many low-level ground-attack and long-range escort sorties. In October, it was announced that he had been awarded the DFM for 'his skill, courage and devotion to duty'. After the war, he became a leading member of the RAF Escaping Society, and he continues to make regular visits to see his brave Danish helpers.

~

For those who succeeded in reaching Sweden, a period of internment in the prison at Falun, 80 miles north of Stockholm, was the first stage of their journey through Sweden. Here they were subjected to a fairly benign interrogation and had an opportunity to visit the local neighbourhood on parole – a far cry from the privations experienced by their colleagues incarcerated in a Spanish jail. For those who qualified for repatriation, there was only one route home, and that was by courtesy of the British Overseas Airways Corporation's courier service that operated between Bromma airport near Stockholm and the Coastal Command airfield at Leuchars in Fife, Scotland. The air route had been opened in May 1940 following the British withdrawal from Norway, and it continued until the end of the war. The route was operated with Lockheed 14 aircraft for the first few years before 10 Mosquito Mark VI aircraft were introduced in 1943. The high-flying and fast Mosquito climbed to a safe height before crossing the North Sea and remained at high level until over Sweden and out of reach of the *Luftwaffe* fighters based in Denmark. On its return, the Mosquito climbed over Swedish airspace before turning west to make a high-speed dash for Leuchars.

The bomb bay of the Mosquito was modified to carry one passenger clad in thick Irvine flying-jacket and trousers and wearing an oxygen mask. It was less than comfortable, but for someone who had crossed the snow- and ice-clad mountains of Norway on his way to freedom, two hours of cold and discomfort was a small price to play. One of the RAF officers to return with the BOAC Courier Flight was Wing Commander Don Bennett, the Commanding Officer of 10 Squadron, who had been shot down attacking the German battleship *Tirpitz* in Trondheim Fjord on 27 April 1942. He

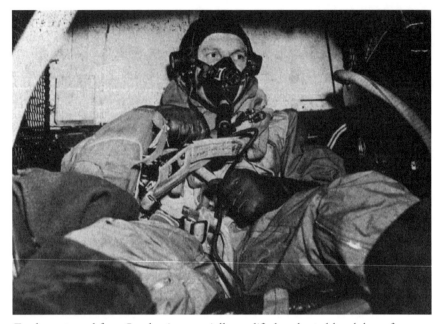

Evaders returned from Sweden in a specially modified, unheated bomb bay of a Mosquito. (Air Historical Branch)

went on to become the Air Officer Commanding No. 8 Group and the leader of the Pathfinder Force.

Between 1941 and VE-Day more than 1,200 trips were made, of which nearly 500 were made in 1944 alone. It is a service that has attracted little attention, but those evaders who returned by courtesy of the Flight will always remember it as their final route to freedom.

Norway presented an evader with a very different problem from Denmark. A huge country 1,000 miles long, with a third of the coastline inside the Arctic Circle, the mountainous terrain, long winter nights and the weather provided a formidable problem of survival for any evader. The average density of the population of Norway is the lowest in Europe, with few towns and not many villages, except on the main lines of communication. Most of the people outside the towns live in self-supporting agricultural settlements or in the coastal fishing villages. Many live on isolated farms. Such terrain did, of course, also provide major problems for the occupying German forces whenever a manhunt had to be mounted. With a very loyal population and a strong and very effective

Resistance movement (Mil. Org.), evaders stood a good chance of success once they had established contact with an organization.

There were three ways of escape from Norway. The *MI 9 Bulletin* described the first way as a 'fighting patrol to the Swedish border'. By this they meant that a bomber crew could make their own way to the border in good weather conditions in sparsely populated areas without the aid of the local population. A number of Halifax bomber crews, including Wing Commander Don Bennett, returned in this manner. The second method was to head for Sweden with local help, essential in the winter or if the weather was poor. Even at the height of summer, for those who had to make the crossing north of the Arctic Circle conditions could still be very difficult in the sparsely populated mountains. The four surviving members of a Liberator of Coastal Command successfully evaded due entirely to the help given by local Norwegians.

THROUGH ARCTIC NORWAY TO SWEDEN

Flying Officer Rae Walton and his crew were tasked to fly a reconnaissance sortie to north Norway to search for the German battleship *Tirpitz,* which had been reported moving north from Trondheim. They took off from Stornoway in their Liberator long-range patrol aircraft (AM 924) at 7 a.m. on 28 May 1942 to patrol the area from Trondheim to the North Cape, well inside the Arctic Circle. The crew had been together for almost a year, and were one of the most experienced on 120 Squadron.

They had been on patrol for almost 12 hours when they decided to search the area of the Vestfjord between the Lofoten Islands and the mainland near Bodø. The visibility was in excess of 100 miles but there was very little cloud cover, so Walton decided to leave the area on a south-westerly heading at 5,000 feet. They had just settled down for the return journey when Flight Sergeant Edwin Allgood, who was manning the rear gun turret, saw four Messerschmitt Bf 109 fighters closing in for an attack. The fighters, led by *Unteroffizier* Robert Merkl, had taken off from the nearby airfield at Bodø for a routine patrol in Vestfjord. They belonged to *10/JG.5,* a fighter unit that had just arrived in the north of Norway. Immediately Allgood saw the threat he gave instructions to dive left as the fighters opened fire, and Walton responded by turning and putting the heavy aircraft into a steep dive. As the Liberator descended through 2,000 feet, the fighters set up a coordinated attack, with each aircraft approaching from a different direction. During this attack, Allgood was hit and died in his turret. Flight Sergeant John Pickering was manning one of the waist guns, and he too was wounded, but he immediately pulled Allgood clear of the rear guns and took his place, since he realized that this was the most vulnerable area for another attack by the fighters. Flight Sergeant Bryan Smith, who was manning the starboard waist gun, was severely wounded during this attack as he opened fire.

Walton managed to keep control of his badly damaged aircraft, which had lost a large piece of its port fin and rudder, and he had levelled off at about 50 feet above the sea when the fighters closed in for a third attack. Pickering managed to hit one of them, and it immediately sheered off to take no further part in the action. The others closed in to hit the aircraft repeatedly with their cannon. As they broke away, both engines on the port side of the Liberator failed. Walton handed over control to his Australian second pilot, Pilot Officer Terry Corkran, in order to confer with the navigator about the shortest route for an emergency landing at one of the airfields in the Shetlands. As he left his seat, the starboard inner engine failed, and with virtually no rudder control Corkran could not prevent the aircraft from entering a shallow spiral dive. The port wing hit the sea and the big aircraft crashed without catching fire.

Walton came to the surface very near the aircraft, which had broken up on impact. He scrambled onto the port wing, where he was able to release the dinghy and inflate it. Despite the wounds to his left arm, Pickering was able to release the starboard dinghy and then pick up Corkran who had surfaced nearby. Walton picked up the navigator, Flight Sergeant J. Culnane, and the flight engineer, Sergeant Ernest Booker, before joining the other dinghy and tying the two together. They soon located Allgood and Smith floating in the sea, but sadly both were dead. The crew estimated that they had crashed 50 miles south-west of the Lofoten Islands.

In the excellent visibility they could see the tops of the distant mountains, and they set off to paddle ashore. During the night the sea became rough, but the crew took it in turns with the paddles. Culnane, who had reported that he had banged his head during the crash, was unable to paddle and made little effort to keep warm in the very cold conditions, and he lapsed into unconsciousness after 24 hours. During the second night he died. Walton's dinghy had partly collapsed and was swamped, making it virtually useless, so he and Booker transferred to the other before they cast off the waterlogged dinghy carrying Culnane's body. His body was later recovered and he was buried in the servicemen's graveyard at Narvik.

The four survivors continued to paddle eastwards throughout the second day. They ate the Horlicks tablets and were able to purify some water, but had difficulty digesting the hard biscuits. They found the rum 'very welcome and a Godsend which they would not like to have been without'. By late afternoon they were too exhausted to continue paddling, but the current was carrying them towards the land. After 48 hours in the dinghy, Einar and Inge Ingerbrigtsen, who had been out fishing for the day, found them. They had heard about the aerial combat and realized immediately that the four men must be the survivors, so they landed them at an isolated village on Moskenesøya the most southerly of the Lofoten Islands, where they were taken to the house of Johan Nordman. He gave them shelter and arranged for John Pickering to receive medical attention, including the removal of some shrapnel from his shoulder.

Plans to get to the mainland and then overland to Sweden were discussed, and the four survivors were introduced to two brothers, Sigurd and Leif Hamran, who were local fishermen. They had friends who lived on the mainland in the small town of Beiarn who they knew had helped other people to cross the border, and it was decided that the airmen would be taken there before starting their journey to Sweden. However, since there was still a great deal of snow in the border region, the brothers decided to delay the journey for a few weeks until the snow conditions were better. In the meantime, there had been a great deal of activity by German patrol boats searching for survivors in the sea areas around the island, and it became very important to hide the four men. The two brothers took them by trawler to an isolated cove, where they were established in a cave for the next three weeks. Local people supplied them with food and clothing throughout their stay on the remote island. Prominent among the helpers were members of the Johansen family from the larger village of Stamsund.

On 27 June the Hamran brothers had to collect some materials from a small town south of Bodø, and they decided to transfer the men to Beiarn valley, from where they would start their journey to Sweden. The four men were collected and taken to a specially prepared hiding place in the hold of the brothers' trawler, the *Hans,*

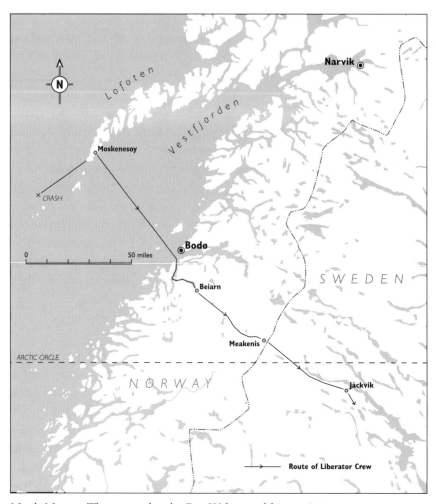

North Norway. The route taken by Rae Walton and his surviving crew.

before sailing early in the morning. During the six-hour crossing of the heavily patrolled Vestfjord, the trawler was investigated by low-flying aircraft and patrol boats on a number of occasions, but the trawler sailed on. It transpired later that the aircraft and patrol boats were trying to warn the fishermen that they were sailing very close to a minefield. The trawler arrived in the fjord at the head of the Beiarn valley late in the afternoon, and Sigurd Hamran rowed ashore to meet his sister and her husband. They put him in touch with Sigmund Bernsten, the local taxi driver, who was able to drive all round the area without attracting special attention. By coincidence, Hamran and Bernsten had known each other previously.

At 9 p.m. Hamran called at Bernsten's home to seek assistance.

Bernsten immediately agreed to help, but had insufficient petrol – a problem resolved when Hamran offered some from his trawler. They returned to the trawler, where the car was filled with petrol and the four airmen were transferred, together with the two fishermen. The taxi had to negotiate a number of difficult places, including a building housing German soldiers. Bernsten switched off the engine, and the taxi coasted past silently before resuming its journey along the valley. At 11 p.m. the taxi arrived on the edge of Beiarn at the farm of 60-year-old William Øvernes, who immediately agreed to help the four evaders to cross the border. Walton and his colleagues bade the two fishermen brothers a fond farewell as they returned to their trawler. They had looked after the airmen for almost four weeks, and had made the dangerous journey from Lofoten to Beiarn at very great personal risk. Walton and his crew also said goodbye to the taxi driver, Sigmund Bernsten, who had so willingly used his taxi, having been given virtually no advance notice of the task.

William Øvernes contacted an English-speaking friend, Trygve Blämoli, who took the men to a remote 'gamma' – a roughly built hut of wood, stone and turf used by reindeer herdsmen. Over the next few days, Øvernes collected food and clothing suitable for crossing the mountains – he also provided rucksacks for each of the men. Maps were drawn and the airmen were briefed. It was stressed that each part of the map had to be destroyed once the appropriate section of the route had been completed, and in this way, their route could not be traced if they were captured. A few days later, Trygve Blämoli led the party from the gamma and took them up the valley as far as he was able before pointing out the route for the evaders to follow in order to reach the Swedish border.

The airmen made slow progress, sometimes achieving just half a mile in one hour. Some still had only their flying-boots, which were totally unsuitable for the mountains, and they suffered badly with sore feet. They climbed during the cold of the night, although it was never dark at that time of the year, and sheltered in woodmen's huts and caves during the day. They decided to avoid the small villages and isolated houses in case they encountered any German patrols. The first sign that they were approaching the Swedish border was a reindeer fence, which they had difficulty climbing, and soon found a Laplander's earthen hut where they stopped to rest. They had not slept for three days, were very wet, weak and hungry, and they collapsed in a state of exhaustion. It was 1 July, five weeks after they had been shot down.

Terry Corkran, Ray Walton and Ernest Booker rest in Sweden after their ordeal. (T. Corkran)

Two children who had walked to the mountains for some fishing found them the following day. They ran back to the border post at Merkenis where they lived and alerted their father, Seth Vikberg, a member of the Swedish border police. He immediately set out for the hut and found the exhausted men. Walton commented in his report that all the men were too weak to climb the mountain that lay between them and Merkenis, the only habitation for almost 100 miles, and some of the party would almost certainly have died had they not been found. Vikberg immediately arranged for the men to be carried to his house in Merkenis, where they remained for a few days to recover, and 'were very hospitably entertained'.

The men were taken to the police post at Jackvik before travelling by boat and bus to Arjeplog, where they received treatment in the hospital and where the police interviewed them. Within a week they were taken by train to the Falun internment camp, where Swedish intelligence officers, who made no attempt to press them on military matters, interviewed them, seeking details of the help they had received from Norwegians. The evaders also received visits from members of the British Legation. During their stay at Falun they were able to gather information from some of the other inmates, many from different countries and services, and this provided some valuable intelligence when they were debriefed in London by MI 9 staff. After two months in the relatively civilized camp at Falun, they were taken to Stockholm, and on 1 September they were flown from Bromma airfield to Leuchars in an aircraft of the BOAC courier service.

For his leadership and courage during this harrowing experience, Ray Walton was awarded the MC. Three years later it was announced that he had been awarded the AFC for his skill and leadership flying Liberators of 232 Squadron based in the Far East. His second pilot, Terry Corkran, returned to Australia after the war and has enjoyed a long retirement in Brisbane.

WINTER ESCAPE FROM TELEMARK

By late 1944, the Special Duties squadrons of No. 38 Group were busy dropping supplies to the numerous underground movements in the occupied countries, including Norway. Eight Stirling Mark IV aircraft were tasked to take off from their base at Rivenhall in Essex on 2 November 1944 to drop supplies at various dropping zones in southern Norway. Flying his personal aircraft was Rivenhall's 30-year-old Station Commander, Group Captain Wilfred Edward Surplice DSO, DFC, DFC (Dutch), a veteran of many bomber and supply-dropping operations. Instead of the aircraft carrying the standard squadron code letters, the Group Captain had his initials 'WE–S' on the side of his Stirling LK 171. On the nose of the aircraft was emblazoned 'Shooting Stars' and the names of his crew who had all completed bomber tours, and were filling ground appointments in the Rivenhall Flying Wing Headquarters. Whenever the Group Captain decided to fly on operations, he took his 'scratch' crew with him. The navigator was Squadron Leader Kenneth Bolton DFC, who had been shot down over Belgium in April 1943, but had managed to link up with the Comet Line and successfully evade capture by travelling through France and over the Pyrenees to Spain. Joining the crew to observe the supply-dropping procedures was Lieutenant Michael Hicks, the SOE liaison officer at Rivenhall.

After take-off, the Stirling headed for the dropping zone in the Telemark region of southern Norway, where it was to drop supplies to

Group Captain W. Surplice and crew stand by their Stirling 'Shooting Stars'.
(Halvor Sperbund)

Detachment 16.1 of the Mil. Org. in Numedal. As the aircraft approached Norway the weather started to deteriorate, forcing Surplice to descend to 2,000 feet to try and stay visual with the ground. He circled the area looking for the lights of the reception committee, but the visibility deteriorated in thick snow showers, and with mountains surrounding the area Surplice was forced to climb into the clouds. The Stirling was still in cloud at 14,000 feet but was becoming increasingly difficult to control as ice built up on the wings and in the engine intakes. The stores were jettisoned as Surplice struggled to keep control of the ice-laden aircraft, which started to lose height. Surplice was fighting a losing battle, and as the big aircraft wallowed on the verge of a spin, he ordered the crew to bale out as he tried to hold the Stirling steady. Bolton was the last to jump – his parachute had fouled one of the throttles and opened in the aircraft. He bundled it into his arms and jumped from the front hatch. To his great relief, the parachute opened just before he landed on some scree alongside a lake. As he descended, he saw a large explosion as the Stirling smashed into a nearby mountain. The selfless Group Captain was later found dead at the controls, having given his life to allow his colleagues time to bale out.

As Bolton collected his thoughts he saw Pilot Officer Robert 'Red' Chapin, the rear gunner, and Warrant Officer Robert Dalton, the flight engineer, and they joined up. Shortly afterwards they came across Mike Hicks, but there was no sign of the other two members of the crew – they were captured two days later to spend the rest of the war as POWs at Stalag Luft I. Before the flight, Hicks had borrowed some flying-boots, which were too big for him, and they had been lost during his parachute descent. Before the party could move in the snow and ice conditions it was essential to provide him with some footwear. By cutting up sections of a life-jacket and a parachute, the four men made a makeshift pair of shoes, which were bound with parachute cord.

The four men wandered around in the snow for the next two days looking for shelter in the inhospitable terrain before finding a cabin in which they found a small quantity of dry wood, some dried fish, potatoes and coffee beans. They lit a fire to cook a meal and make coffee. They found a newspaper published in Rjukan giving them some indication of their location. They also found a pair of rubber galoshes, which provided Hicks with footwear more comfortable and appropriate for the winter conditions. Overnight a very bad snowstorm developed, forcing them to remain in the hut until 8 a.m. on 6 November, when they were able to set off in an easterly direction towards some large lakes. They made very slow progress because of the deep snowdrifts, and by 4 p.m. they were too exhausted to continue. They cut down some saplings with an axe they had taken from the hut, and made a rough tent using Bolton's parachute. They were able to make a fire and boil some coffee. After spending an uncomfortable and cold night in the shelter, they set off the following morning to walk round a lake, and soon found a more substantial chalet, which they broke into. They had not been there long when they saw a boat carrying two men crossing the lake heading for the hut. One of the men spoke English and told Bolton that their two colleagues had been captured in the local town. Before departing he gave them some food and briefed them on certain torch signals that would be used at 7 p.m. indicating if Germans were in the area or if it was clear.

A few hours later, the second man in the boat returned alone with more food and a note written in English by a member of the local Resistance group. The note stated that they were not to light a fire or leave the hut in daylight, and they were to wait at the hut until

Bolton, Dalton, Chapin and Hicks with one of their Norwegian helpers (centre) during their journey to the coast. (Halvor Sperbund)

someone contacted them. At 7 p.m. they received the torch signal 'OK' from the other side of the lake, giving them the all-clear to light a fire and cook a meal. A few hours later, the English-speaking man returned with Axel Prydz ('Ludwig'), a leading member of the local Mil. Org., a man with a wide network of contacts. The six men crossed the lake in the boat. Prydz wanted to take advantage of the darkness, and immediately took the evaders on a five-hour trek to a barn where they remained for the following 36 hours while arrangements were made for the rest of their journey.

The men were given instructions to leave the barn at midnight on 10 November and walk to the small town of Tinn to arrive at a bridge at 2 a.m. where they would be met. Just after the appointed time, three men appeared from the shadows to escort them to a remote hut in the hills, where they remained for the next six days. Here they met Jens Anton Paulsson, the leader of the Telemark Mil. Org., and one of the saboteurs of the Norsk Hydro 'heavy water' plant at Rujkan, and he and Prydz were keen to recover the containers the crew had been forced to jettison. They sat down with Bolton to attempt to determine where the arms and supplies might have landed. They also undertook to search for the aircraft and discover the fate of

Group Captain Surplice. Throughout the time Bolton and his colleagues spent in the hut, Prydz and Paulsson, together with members of their local group, supplied them with food. In the meantime, Prydz contacted the Mil. Org. group responsible for the escape sea routes to Sweden.

Early in the morning of 16 November, Einar Thronsen, who was responsible for the next stage of the escape, travelled to Rjukan, where Paulsson met him before they went to the hut to collect the four evaders. Thronsen had managed to 'borrow' the Norsk Hydro car used for local journeys, and Bakke Svendsen drove the party to Gransherad, where they were due to meet a contact. Thronsen and the four men had a nerve-racking time on arrival since the contact failed to appear on time, and Svendsen was in an understandable hurry to return the car. Only two of the RAF men had civilian clothes, so the party had to endure a tense wait by the local church. Eventually the contact arrived driving a wood-burning car. Shortly after the party started the next stage of the journey the car skidded off the road near a built-up area, but Thronsen dared not use the RAF men to push the car back on the road since there were so many people about. He gathered some local men to help, claiming that the men in the car were mental patients and he could not risk letting them out. Eventually they arrived at a safe house, where each had a hot bath and their first shave since arriving in Norway.

The journey south to the coast was continued the next morning, when the evaders travelled on two horse-drawn sledges. There had been a fresh fall of snow overnight so it was a very strenuous journey for the horses, the two drivers and Thronsen, who had to stamp down the snow ahead. The night was spent in the woods before a taxi was commandeered the following morning to drive them to a remote area where they stayed in a hut on an island in the middle of a lake. Thronsen travelled to Skien to meet up with Trygve Etland, the district commander of the local Mil. Org., to make plans for the next phase of the operation. By 23 November arrangements had been made and Thronsen took the evaders by road to the small town of Bamble, and Etland's members took over the responsibility for the RAF men. Taking the lead role in organizing safe houses and travel arrangements for the next few weeks was a young woman, Lillen Dahll Vogt.

Initially, the men were taken to a camp in the woods where they stayed in tents and huts for the next few days before setting off for the

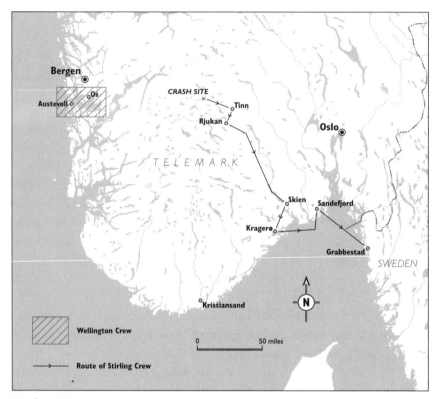

Southern Norway

coast with 'Olaf' and later 'Arnim', as escorts, walking some of the
way, and travelling by small boats on the lakes at other times. They
were sheltered at farms and in summer chalets in the hills as they
made their way south. On the afternoon of 30 November they arrived
at the coast and boarded a motorboat that took them to Fossingfjord,
where they stayed with a member of Etland's group for three days.
They were then transferred to Schweigaard Island, a remote island in
the Kragerø archipelago, where Mrs Liv Schodt provided shelter for
the next week.

   The Mil. Org. had been taking Norwegian refugees to Sweden from
Kragerø for some months, and arrangements were made to take the
four evaders on the next trip. The organizer of these hazardous trips
across the Skaggerak to Sweden, a crossing of almost 60 miles, was
Einar Frøysaa. At the beginning of December he had gathered a party
of 20 Norwegians ready for the next voyage. The trip was to be the
first made in the fishing boat *Augusta*, which he had just acquired. A
few difficulties had been encountered getting the trawler ready, and the

lack of knowledge about the engine, allied to a shortage of fuel, gave
Frøysaa a number of headaches. He sailed down the coast to Arendal to
provision the boat and service the engine before returning to Kragerø,
where the Norwegian refugees had arrived from Oslo.

On 10 December Bolton and his colleagues were taken by boat to
Kragerø ready for the voyage. Bad weather intervened for the next
five days, and they had to survive in some very basic shelter, with
limited food and no chance to exercise during daylight hours. Frøysaa
admired their 'stoic calm without any complaints despite the tough
conditions'. On 17 December, conditions improved, although the sea
was still rough once they left the shelter of the islands. Out on the
open sea, the weather conditions deteriorated rapidly. Frøysaa had to
go to the bow to keep a lookout for mines, but the rolling and
pitching of the trawler made it virtually impossible for him to stand.
The engine failed on numerous occasions during the next two days
before the rudder broke and a rope fouled the propeller, forcing
Frøysaa to accept a tow to the port of Sandefjord to seek repairs. The
evaders and the Norwegian refugees had suffered badly from
seasickness, but it was imperative to get them off the trawler quickly
to safe accommodation. In the two days since leaving Kragerø, the
trawler had travelled a mere 25 miles.

The group had to wait ashore for the repairs to be completed, and
for the weather to be suitable before the voyage could be resumed.
During the night of 21 December, the whole group was led to the
trawler, which sailed at 2 a.m. Conditions were still bad and the
passengers had to remain in the hold, which was battened down, and
where 'the stench was almost unbearable'. After six hours of sailing,
the Swedish coast was sighted, and at 11.45 a.m. the *Augusta* anchored
in the small Swedish fishing port of Gräbbestad and the passengers
were disembarked. Frøysaa clearly admired the four RAF evaders
when he wrote after the war:

> The Englishmen behaved exemplarily and they were always
> willing to help in difficult and dangerous situations. Despite the
> terrible conditions there was never a cross word from our
> English guests, despite the fact that they knew what to expect if
> we were captured by the Germans.

This is a truly remarkable statement from a man who chose to ignore
the dangers he faced – the sacrifice of his own life to save four strangers.

It epitomized the attitude of all the resolute Norwegians involved in this hazardous 40-day operation conducted in the depths of winter.

The four airmen were soon taken to Stockholm, where they had a few days to recover before flying from Bromma airfield to Leuchars on 2 January 1945.

After the war, the Norwegians buried Group Captain W. E. Surplice in the Oslo War Cemetery. In 1982, Kenneth Bolton and Robert Dalton returned to Norway at the invitation of aircraft historians who had been to the crash site with the intention of placing a memorial. The two men met for the first time since the war on the flight to Norway where they met a number of their helpers before the Royal Norwegian Air Force flew them by helicopter to see the remains of their crashed Stirling LK 171 on the 4,450 ft mountain of Skarfjell in the Telemark region. It was a poignant moment for the men when they saw the remaining wreckage and the memorial fashioned from one of the twisted propellers mounted on a concrete base. A bronze plaque had been placed on the base commemorating the aircraft's supply mission, and the sacrifice of Group Captain W. E. Surplice, 'who managed to keep the plane airborne until the crew baled out, but was killed in the crash'. The memorial made from parts of his personal aircraft ensures that a very gallant officer will always be

Robert Dalton and Ken Bolton returned to Oslo in 1982 to meet their helpers. Here they are pictured with Axel Prydz (centre). (Halvor Sperbund)

remembered – as are the brave Norwegians who helped his crew to evade capture.

Kenneth Bolton was twice an evader, one of the very few, and his words to a Norwegian helper, 'I felt and still feely deeply indebted to the Norwegians who helped us', are undoubtedly equally appropriate to those of the Comet Line who helped him to safety in the spring of 1943.

~

For those stranded near the coast in the south of Norway, the only realistic chance of avoiding capture was to remain in hiding, contact the local population and hope that an opportunity to return by sea might arise later. There was virtually no chance of individual aircrew procuring a boat suitable for crossing the North Sea. However, once in the hands of the Norwegian Resistance Movement, the Mil. Org, there was the possibility of returning on the 'Shetland Bus'. The story of the Norwegian fishermen who ran a boat shuttle service between the Shetlands and the coast of Norway is one of the epic stories of the Second World War. The full history can be found in David Howarth's book *The Shetland Bus*.

RETURN BY THE SHETLAND BUS

Flying Officer Gordon Biddle and his all-Canadian crew of 407 (RCAF) Squadron took off from Wick in north-east Scotland just after midnight on the night of 26 September 1944. They were tasked to fly their Wellington GR XIV aircraft of Coastal Command on an anti-submarine patrol off the coast of Norway. A few hours into the sortie, and flying at 1,000 feet above the sea, the starboard engine suddenly exploded and caught fire. After Biddle and his second pilot, George Death, successfully extinguished the fire and shut the engine down, the two pilots found that the aircraft could not climb. Biddle ordered the crew to jettison all loose equipment to lighten the aircraft. He also decided to jettison fuel until he had just sufficient to return to the airfield in Scotland. When Death tried to close the jettison valve it failed, and fuel continued to escape until the main tanks were empty. This left 450 gallons in the reserve tank – sufficient for 30 minutes' flying time only. Biddle had no other choice than to turn for the Norwegian mainland and hope to find a suitable area to make a crash-landing.

The crew continued to jettison equipment and sensitive material, such as codebooks, as the two pilots tried to gain some precious height. At 6 a.m. Biddle brought the aircraft over a fjord, where a small convoy opened fire on the crippled Wellington, to look for a suitable area in the rugged terrain to carry out a crash-landing. The failure of the other engine through fuel starvation left him with no choice, and slicing through some electricity cables Biddle got the Wellington down more or less in one piece, and the crew escaped virtually uninjured. It had been a superb piece of flying. The aircraft had landed within sight of the small school at Haugland, near Os on the west coast of Norway, 15 miles south of Bergen. The place was within an active military defence zone, but by good fortune, the German patrol manning the nearby watchtower had left the previous day. The Canadians destroyed their parachutes and harnesses before setting fire to the Wellington just as the local schoolmaster, Magnus Askvik, appeared on the scene together with other local people. He advised them to move from the area quickly, and they followed his advice to head towards the next fjord.

The Canadians took off their battledress tunics, and turned them inside out to hide their brevets and 'CANADA' shoulder flashes. After a two-hour walk, they stopped to discuss their situation. They realized that it was only a matter of time before the Germans located the crash site, and started a search for them. They also recognized that their only chance of escape was to contact the local population to seek assistance. Descending a small hill, they saw a cluster of four houses, and the navigator, Maurice Neil, decided to approach one of the houses. He met Ingeborg Bjornen, who had seen and heard the low-flying aircraft in trouble, and she immediately led the crew to a cave in the forest, where she told them to remain while she contacted her father. Twice during the day she brought them milk, returning again at 7 p.m. with food. She also had the welcome news that she had arranged for them to be moved.

Einar Evensen lived on a nearby island and was a leading member of the local Mil. Org., and he had been alerted to the crash and the plight of the crew. He immediately set out to find the location of the aircraft, but his search was fruitless. Returning to his home at lunchtime, he received a message from Ingeborg Bjornen's father telling him of the crew's whereabouts, and he immediately contacted three of his most trusted colleagues, who agreed to accompany him to collect the airmen. They decided that the safest place for the Canadians in the first instance was a boathouse on the small island of Strøno. Although it was directly across the fjord from a German fortification, it was unlikely that the Germans, knowing that their aircraft had crashed on the mainland, would look for the evaders on an island.

A neighbour of Ingeborg Bjornen arrived to take the Canadians through the woods to a small cove, and a rowing boat arrived at 8 p.m. to take them to a rendezvous with a second boat, which three of them boarded. The two boats then set off on a dangerous journey of a mile, which took them past a German guard boat and under a bridge where there was a permanent military patrol. Hugging the coastline, the Norwegians rowed silently, having taken the precaution of wrapping sacking round the rowlocks and oars. The light breeze rustling the leaves ashore made more noise than the sea against the boat. Fortunately, it was also a pitch-black night with a light drizzle falling. The final stage of the boat journey went across the arm of the fjord to the island, where they landed to be guided over moss and heather to a hut. Here they saw their rescuers for the first time, including Nils Røttingen, who had spent many years in America, and who was able to explain details of the Norwegians' plans for them.

Much had happened during the Canadians' first day in Norway. Realizing the danger to the airmen, the Norwegians had sprung into action immediately, and some daring and courageous actions had got the crew away from the immediate area of the crash. In the meantime, the Germans quickly moved into the area to start a widespread search. They also herded all the population into the school to be interrogated, but nothing was divulged. Evensen had also contacted his chief, Magnus Hauge, asking to see him the following day, when they would discuss the next stage. At their morning meeting they agreed to contact Jakob Hjelle who led the neighbouring Deknings group of the Mil. Org.

For the next five days, the Canadians remained on the island, leaving the boathouse before dawn to hide in the nearby wooded hills before returning after dark to spend the night under cover when food was brought to them. The Germans continued to carry out intensive searches, and the airmen were able to watch from their secure hideout the movements of the patrol boats in the fjord. During this time, the Norwegians were very busy making arrangements to get the airmen

back to safety. Hjelle had contacted Helén Mowinkel-Nilsen, the local
SOE-trained Norwegian agent, and the leaders of the local Mil. Org.
groups agreed that the intensity of the German searches dictated that
the evaders should be transferred to Hjelle's group, who would hide
them in the mountains on the mainland until arrangements could be
made for their rescue.

On 30 September, the airmen were told to shave off their
moustaches and beards, were given civilian clothes, and told to be
ready to move from Strøno the next morning. Evensen and Thorvald
Jacobsen arrived at 10 a.m. to take the Canadians to Lønningdal in
Evensen's motorboat, a distance of about 15 miles. With the evaders
hiding under a tarpaulin, half the journey had been completed when
a German patrol boat suddenly appeared, heading directly for the
obviously overloaded motorboat. Evensen held his nerve, and
continued to steer directly for the patrol boat, which finally sheared
off when 200 yards away. The motorboat carried on past the U-boat
base at Hatvik before landing its passengers at Lønningdal, where
Hjelle and Mowinkel-Nilsen were waiting to take over the task of
sheltering the evaders and organizing their onward journey. They
were given appropriate footwear for the next stage of their journey,
and taken to a hut in a very secluded and secure place in the
mountains, where they remained for the next seven days. Here they

*The hut 'Little Canada', used to hide the Canadians and built by Frederik Øvredal
(left) is still in use today. (Bjarne Øvredal)*

met Haldor Øvredal, who was on the run from the Gestapo, and Ivar Dyngeland, the former Sheriff of Os, who was also on the Germans' wanted list. These two men were their companions throughout their stay, providing food, companionship and, most importantly, security. The hut had two beds and a small loft, and the men were able to sleep on the bunks and benches in turn. The Norwegians had also supplied cooking utensils, food and sleeping bags.

Mowinkel-Nilsen's radio operator contacted SOE headquarters in London to alert them that the six Canadians were in the hands of the Norwegian Resistance. Initially, there was a misunderstanding when the radio operator transmitted that eight men were safe, and this caused London to doubt the origin of the message. However, when they received the correct information, they reacted quickly. Within a few days the BBC transmitted the message, 'Keep the meat cakes hot', meaning that the Canadians would be picked up in two days' time at a holm (islet) called Ospøy near the community of Austevoll south of Bergen, and a regular landing place for the famous 'Shetland Bus' of the Royal Norwegian Navy Special Unit operating from Scalloway in the Shetland Islands.

On the evening of 8 October, the airmen left the hut, which they had christened 'Little Canada', and were taken down the mountains to a house where they were given a typical Norwegian meal. During the night they walked through the forests to board a small boat to be

Lars Orrebaken (left) and Haldor Øvredal who played important roles in the rescue of the Wellington's Canadian crew. (Bjarne Øvredal)

taken to a remote beach near Lønningdal. Hjelle was waiting for them, having been in the area for the last few days making all the arrangements, including ensuring that all the danger spots were guarded by his men armed with automatic weapons. He had organized the return route, obtained boats and crews, detailed duties for each stage and fixed exact timings for the plan. It worked perfectly. At midday, Lars Orrebakken manoeuvred his boat *Snogg* to the quay at Lønningdal where Hjelle was waiting to direct him to the beach to pick up the Canadians and Haldor Øvredal, armed with a Sten-gun and five magazines, who would accompany them. As the *Snogg* headed out into the fjord, the two Norwegians counted up to 15 patrol boats, and noticed that a number were observing them through binoculars, so they waved and shouted greetings. When the *Snogg* passed Hatvik, Biddle was very eager to get up on deck to take the positions of the submarine berths in case he returned to attack them! Haldor Øvredal had to keep him under the decking.

They sailed on towards Austevoll, where they transferred the Canadians to the fishing boat of Sverre Østervoll, the chief contact in the area for the Shetland boats. He took them on a three-hour boat journey to a windswept islet with a disused hut where they spent two miserable days sharing bunks and awaiting the arrival of the Shetland Bus. Østervoll rowed to the island each evening to bring them food, and to shake his head to indicate that he had no news for them. Finally, on the third evening, his smiling face told the Canadians all they wanted to know, and they followed him down to his boat.

Early in October news had reached the Scalloway base of the Shetland Bus that six Canadian airmen were to be picked up. The legendary Norwegian sailor, Leif Larsen DSC, CGM, DSM and Bar, was tasked with the operation, and he and his crew left Scalloway on 11 October in their converted US Navy submarine chaser, the *Vigra*, with stores for the Mil. Org. Larsen headed for Austevoll, conducting the last part of the voyage under the cover of darkness, before arriving off the Norwegian coast at 8 p.m. Larsen swung the *Vigra* between the small islands before manoeuvring the boat alongside a steep cliff close to where the Canadians were sheltering. The rendezvous was near to a German naval base, and in an area of constant sea patrols by the enemy, so he did not drop anchor in case he had to make a quick getaway. In view of the dangers, the orders issued to Larsen advised him to withdraw immediately if the party were not at the rendezvous.

It was typical of Larsen that he waited for over four hours before he succeeded in making contact with the shore party, and it was a further two hours before Sverre Østervoll arrived in his small fishing boat with Gordon Biddle and his five colleagues on board. They were transferred to the *Vigra*, and were at last able to converse with the non-English-speaking Østervoll through an interpreter, allowing them to express their gratitude for the remarkable assistance that they had been given by so many Norwegians. After unloading an agent and supplies for the Resistance to Østervoll's fishing boat, Larsen threaded his way at slow speed through the islands until he reached the open sea, when he was able to increase speed for a fast return to Scalloway, where the Canadians arrived after a rough crossing during the early hours of 12 October.

Life stopped for a few minutes the following evening for the brave people of Os and Austevoll as they sat around the radio listening to the BBC. Then came the message that they were all waiting to hear: 'It is raining in the mountains.' The Canadians had arrived back safely.

Gordon Biddle and his Canadian colleagues would have been the first to recognize and admit that their success in avoiding capture was due to the gallant efforts of the local Norwegian people and members of the Mil. Org. From the moment that Ingeborg Bjornen sheltered the crew in a wood to the final episode when Leif Larsen and his Norwegian sailors brought the *Vigra* into Scalloway harbour 17 days later, the Canadians were entirely in the hands of their Norwegian helpers. What makes this story all the more remarkable is to appreciate that this rescue operation involved so many individuals and

The ex-US Navy submarine chaser Hitra, *the sister ship of* Vigra *of the Shetland Bus. (J. Irwin)*

organizations, with the attendant risk to security, and was conducted under the noses of the German forces in a highly defended military area. The Germans were aware of the crash and the survival of the crew almost immediately, so they were able to mount an extensive air, sea and land search for them within hours. That they failed, and the six Canadians successfully evaded, is testimony to the guile, resource-fulness, skill and courage of those many Norwegians involved.

As always, there was a price to be paid by the local population. Some of the families of the helpers were arrested, tortured and imprisoned, and Magnus Hauge suffered the same fate. However, after the war, many of the Norwegians were honoured, and Leif Larsen was awarded the DSO for carrying out many clandestine operations in the *Vigra,* when the citation made special mention of his rescue of the six Canadian airmen.

Maurice Neil and Harvey Firestone, two members of the Wellington's crew, returned to Os in 1966 to meet and thank their Norwegian helpers. They carried with them a letter from the Canadian government to the citizens of Os in which the Minister for Veteran Affairs concluded:

> The airmen have told me of the wonderful cooperation and help you gave them, at great personal risk, to avoid capture. On behalf of the Government and people of Canada, may I commend you for your gallant actions in those far off days and also offer the thanks of every veteran in Canada.

PART THREE

The Middle East and Mediterranean

Chapter Nine

Introduction

After the Italian Army's first incursions into Egypt in September 1940, the British Commander-in-Chief in the Middle East, General Sir Archibald Wavell, established a secret organization, given the name 'A' Force, under the command of Lieutenant Colonel (later Brigadier) Dudley Clarke, with his headquarters in Cairo. Its role was 'to organize by every available means the deception of the enemy high command'. It was also tasked to train fighting men in the art of escape and evasion and to provide them with any help they might need. This latter organization was known as 'N' Section. From September 1941 until the end of the war its leader was Lieutenant Colonel Tony Simonds.

Until Dudley Clarke's arrival in Cairo in the autumn of 1940, no MI 9 organization existed in the Middle East, and he may justifiably be regarded as the founder of MI 9 in the area. He had a considerable knowledge and experience of MI 9 work in Great Britain, and he took a keen interest in its establishment in the Mediterranean area, despite his main priority being the development of 'A' Force. As a result of signals exchanged between Clarke and Brigadier Crockatt in London, the start of the MI 9 organization in the Middle East, corresponding to MI 9(b) in the War Office, was approved. A Charter was issued in early January 1941 establishing MI 9 – 'N' Section – 'with the object of securing information from British POWs, and assisting them to escape'.

Although Clarke understood his instructions, the handicaps under which he started MI 9 in the Middle East were considerable. No organization for escape and evasion had existed in the area before the war, and there were no 'Underground' or 'Resistance' movements which could be utilized for the rescue of escapers and evaders. Quite apart from the lack of an active escape organization, there were many difficulties in organizing MI 9 work because of a shortage of staff, transport, wireless facilities, and, above all, the active support of the other secret departments already well established in Cairo. In due course, these handicaps were overcome, very largely through the persistence of Dudley Clarke.

The original charter was soon amended to recognize two distinct aspects to MI 9's work – escape work and preventive training. However, the ebb and flow of the campaigns in North Africa generated many escapers and evaders, and the small MI 9 staff had to concentrate on the operational aspects of their work, with the result that preventive training could not be carried out to any significant degree. Furthermore, the organization soon found itself heavily involved in new operational areas, in particular Greece and Crete, where the eventual retreat and withdrawal of Allied forces generated a huge influx of evaders.

For its first year of existence MI 9 grew up piecemeal, and was largely an ad hoc organization formed to meet the varying and pressing needs as they arose. However, as the tasks, responsibilities and commitments became more clearly defined, it was possible to evolve a working system of staff and operational control. In the European area, particularly in the earlier stages, MI 9(b)'s escape and evasion activities were well supported by the other two large secret organizations, MI 6 and SOE. In the first year of the Middle East war, this procedure was also followed because of the lack of operational staff in MI 9. The arrangement was not entirely satisfactory for a number of reasons: lack of security, the risk of compromising agents from the other organizations, and the vast areas to be covered were just a few.

With the arrival of Tony Simonds in the autumn of 1941, MI 9 was able to develop more independently. He had worked closely with SOE during a previous appointment, and his experience was a great help to MI 9 in several ways. He also started to recruit and employ agents and operational service personnel who became engaged in MI 9 work on a full-time basis. He established links with MI 6 and the Long Range Desert Group (LRDG). In his post-war report he paid tribute to the assistance and support of other clandestine and secret organizations, in particular the cooperation afforded by MI 6 for the provision of crucial wireless links during MI 9's activities in Greece and the Balkans.

As the MI 9 organization gradually evolved, so the division between active operational personnel and those engaged on preventive training became more strictly defined. By the middle of 1942, both aspects had developed significantly, and the essential coordination between the two departments had been established. The operational sections were responsible for contacting, organizing, and rescuing all service POWs, escapers and evaders in any occupied area in the Middle East theatre of operations. The preventive training organization was responsible for training all service personnel in escape and evasion techniques. The two disciplines were entirely complementary. The training organization needed to know the capabilities of the operational sections, their techniques, and knowledge of 'rat lines' and escape routes. By knowing that personnel had been instructed on escape and evasion techniques, the task of contacting and rescuing escapers and evaders was made easier for the operational personnel. Simonds recognized the essential need for close liaison between the two sections, and he instituted a system allowing personnel to switch from one to the other in order to understand the requirements of each.

Operations in the Middle East covered a vast area, with many different types of terrain and circumstances, with the result that the methods of operation varied according to the theatre concerned. However, in broad outline, the principle of operations was based on sending rescue teams based on 'Field Sections' to selected areas behind enemy lines to form an organizing and rallying point for rescue, escape and evasion operations in that area. The composition of the field section could vary, but was usually one officer, one senior NCO, a wireless set and a vehicle. The availability of wireless communications was vital. In addition to the task of contacting POW camps and other field sections that were organizing the evacuation of escapers and evaders, each field section also had the responsibility of providing escape intelligence information to assist the training staffs in the compilation of bulletins and briefing materials.

Methods of evacuation varied greatly. In areas such as the desert it was possible for military forces to operate deep inside enemy-occupied territory, where aircraft and the transport of organizations such as the LRDG could be used. Sea evacuations were common in the Aegean Sea area. Where partisan groups operated, aircraft were often used. Once the invasion of Italy had started, evaders found themselves in a situation very similar to those operating in Western Europe, and they relied heavily on local helpers.

Once the American forces entered the Middle East theatre, the escape and evasion organization expanded rapidly, with the same close cooperation between MI 9 and MIS – X soon established. The organization of MI 9 was also modified to take account of the wider range of operations in the Middle East area of operations. On 1 November 1943 'N' Section of 'A' Force was divided into east and west, with Simonds remaining in Cairo to run 'N' Section East, while Wing Commander E. Dennis controlled 'N' Section West from Algiers – this was often referred to as Advance Headquarters 'A' Force. In August 1944 Clarke's area of responsibility had become so large and cumbersome that changes had to be made. Responsibility for MI 9 work in the Mediterranean theatre passed from 'A' Force to the Operations Division at Allied Forces Headquarters at Caserta, near Naples, with the establishment of IS 9 (CMF) for the Central Mediterranean area, and to IS 9 (ME) in Cairo for the Eastern area, the latter with Simonds still in charge.

After an understandably slow start, MI 9 established a most effective organization in the Middle East and Mediterranean area. However, Colonel Tony Simonds OBE made the very pertinent comment in his long post-war report:

It is a matter of regret, firstly that no MI 9 organization existed before the war, and secondly, that one was not created and organized in the area before January 1941. Had either of these events taken place, the organization would have been in a better position to tackle the large tasks which later fell to MI 9 for operation in this area, and undoubtedly most escapers and evaders would have been rescued, and more people trained in escape duties.

He is right, of course, and it is the purpose of such post-war reports to draw such conclusions. However, it should not detract from the manner in which the MI 9 organizations responded to the changing operational scene and the outstanding successes achieved in the field of escape and evasion.

The organization of MI 9 in the Middle East area outlined in this chapter is sufficient for the purposes of this book. However, Foot and Langley in *MI 9: Escape and Evasion 1939–1945* cover the wider roles and more detailed descriptions of the organization admirably.

Chapter Ten

The Western Desert

THE POPULAR CONCEPTION OF A 'DESERT' invariably produces in people's mind a picture of huge tracts of land covered with soft sand and dunes. In reality, deserts have various surfaces. Only about a tenth of the Sahara is sandy, the greater part being a flat, barren, gravel plain from which the wind has blown the sand away and piled it up in the low-lying areas where dunes are found.

All deserts have certain things in common. Scarcity of water and great extremes of temperature are the outstanding characteristics. Rainfall is scarce, though in parts of the Middle East it may be heavy during the winter, but surface water is absent over great areas for months at a time. Desert areas are generally cloudless, and high winds prevail over the larger ones for much of the year, with resulting serious sand and dust problems. Plant, animal and human life is sparse and concentrated near the water sources. Large parts of the desert, however, are practically lifeless for long periods. The temperature range in the extreme desert regions is considerable, with freezing nights following extremely hot days, the temperature often dropping by as much as 30 to 40 degrees Centigrade.

In such inhospitable and arduous terrain, the first essential for aircrew who found themselves crash-landing or parachuting behind enemy lines in the desert was survival. Only those who had a thorough knowledge of the conditions likely to be encountered, and had made adequate preparations before take-off, were likely to survive – unless they were incredibly lucky. In Europe, food, water and accommodation were largely obtainable by some means or other, but disguise, documents and ethnic background were essential. In the

Western Desert, disguise was rarely necessary, but endurance, desert lore and physical fitness were the essential elements for success.

Once the British withdrawal from Greece and Crete was complete, and personnel from MI 9 were able to concentrate on other issues, increased attention was given to providing preventive training for those flying over the Western Desert. At briefings, aircrew were reminded of the importance of carrying their escape aid box and their blood chit written in various local languages. The importance of wearing the correct footwear was emphasized by the maxim 'Always fly in the boots you intend to use to walk home.' Aircrew were advised to travel mainly at night and to find some sort of shelter or shade by day, such as a cave, derelict transport or a hole in the sand with old abandoned material or camel thorn bush to keep off the sun. Before starting off on the trek to Allied lines, crews were advised to have a good rest, eat and drink as much as possible, and not to hurry, since it would lead to perspiration and dehydration. They were further advised to carry as much water as possible, sacrificing food if necessary, and to use water sparingly, even if it appeared that they had a good initial supply. It was also essential to establish a strict discipline of taking only sips sufficient to keep the mouth moist every hour or two.

Crews were regularly briefed on routes to take and areas to head for. This varied to some extent as the ground war fluctuated, but the general principles remained the same for most of the desert campaign. Arabs tended to live in the coastal strip and in the jebel areas, where the majority were friendly, and where there were wells and many derelict transport and food dumps. Crews were advised to travel north after landing and to look out for Arab encampments, and on no account should they head south into the desert. It was emphasized that it was better to accept the possibility of capture rather than the more probable risk of dying of thirst and starvation. It was also important to avoid the immediate vicinity of the main coast road and all the 'fortress' towns, such as Bardia, Sollum, Sidi Barrani, Matruh and others.

By early 1942, MI 9 had started to organize field sections to work behind enemy lines where the LRDG and the Western Desert Liaison Officers with the Eighth Army gave them great assistance. From the second invasion of Cyrenaica in December 1941, MI 9 had started to use the Libyan Arab Force, which consisted of Senussi Arabs, trained in Egypt by British officers who had volunteered to lead MI 9 patrols

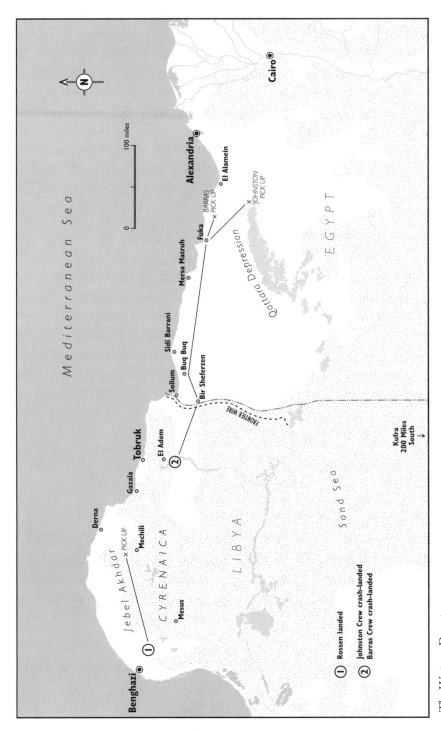

The Western Desert.

in the desert. Tony Simonds and his staff in Cairo had been steadily creating a Western Desert escape organization, and they were ready to launch their first operation in May 1942, the day before the second retreat from Cyrenaica began. This operation, the most sudden of the many moves and counter-moves in the Western Desert campaign, culminated in the Allied retreat from Gazala to Alamein, the latter being reached on 2 July.

The officer selected to lead the first MI 9 field section into the Western Desert was Captain P. Grandguillot, a French officer who volunteered for service with the British after the fall of France. He had lived in Alexandria for many years, and had considerable local knowledge. He left with six specially selected other ranks of the Libyan Arab Force on 26 May. His journeys from the time he left Cairo to the time he returned read like a desert exploration route. He travelled to Siwa, south-east of the existing Allied lines, with an LRDG convoy at the end of May, and established an MI 9 dump. He then travelled to the Mechili district, some 100 miles to the rear of the enemy lines, where he established a collecting centre for escapers and evaders. The MI 9 plan, implemented brilliantly by Grandguillot, is related in detail below, since it was this basic plan that was followed throughout the Western Desert campaign with local modifications.

The aim was to send an officer and wireless operator, and a selected number of Arab agents, to an area in the enemy rear, or on the flank of the battle area, to establish a dump of water and food. The surrounding area was divided into sectors, with an Arab agent allotted to each and a rendezvous point identified for him to visit at stated intervals. Each agent toured his area, dressed as a local Arab, to maintain contact with the local Bedouin tribes in the area, and to fix with them a rendezvous point where escapers and evaders were to be brought. The MI 9 officer in charge of the field section selected a different point for himself and his wireless operator as their headquarters, fixing a separate rendezvous to be kept with the LRDG or SAS patrols passing through the neighbourhood. They could be used to evacuate escapers and evaders who had been rescued, and when necessary, evacuate the MI 9 party. By this arrangement, none of the Arab agents knew the exact location of either the main food dump or the MI 9 officer and his wireless operator. If an agent was caught, he could not betray anything more than the location of other agents within his particular sector. The agents created a similar arrangement in their own sectors, so the local Bedouin could not divulge rendezvous points to other local Arabs and risk betrayal.

Grandguillot established himself near Mechili, and combed this area westwards into the jebel of Cyrenaica. He spent six weeks behind enemy lines before returning with a LRDG patrol to Kufra Oasis before returning to Cairo on 26 July. The first MI 9 expedition into the Western Desert resulted in the recovery of several evaders who would otherwise have been recaptured or died of exposure or thirst. It also established relations with the Senussi Arabs on a firm basis. Grandguillot's first operation was a great success, and he brought back valuable information that allowed MI 9 in Cairo to make more comprehensive plans for escape and evasion work. With the rapid retreat to Alamein, there were plenty of stragglers, units and individuals scattered over the desert who benefited from the newly established organization.

The situation after the withdrawal to Alamein was that both the enemy and the Allied lines extended southward into the desert as far as it was militarily feasible to carry supplies or obtain water locally. There was, therefore, permanently an open flank to the south. The LRDG, SAS and MI 9 operated on this open flank from bases well beyond the reach of either army. Before the retreat to Alamein, Siwa had formed this base until its occupation by the enemy. The LRDG base was then withdrawn further south into the centre of the Libyan Desert at Kufra. For the field sections, this involved laborious journeys across sand dunes and desert plateaux to reach the enemy-occupied regions in Cyrenaica and the Western Desert to the north.

MI 9 decided to make Kufra their main base as well, and dispatched 1,000 lb of stores to the oases by LRDG patrol on 13 August, followed by 250 lb of stores each week. These amounts may appear small, until the distances covered and the vehicles in main use – jeeps – are realized. Later in the campaign, transport aircraft were able to land at Kufra, allowing the amount of stores to be increased significantly.

On 15 August, Grandguillot, Sergeant Green of 'A' Force and seven other ranks of the Libyan Arab Force, with 2,300 lb of stores, left Cairo for Kufra. Green remained at Kufra with the main stores as Grandguillot made the long journey north to the Mechili area. After contacting all his agents in the region, and meeting with the local tribes, he travelled westwards to an area some 50 miles south-east of Benghazi, in the Mesus area, where he stayed for two months, establishing many dumps of food and water, and establishing a rallying point in the Benghazi area for escapers and evaders. He returned to

A patrol of the Long Range Desert Group near the Sand Sea.
(Imperial War Museum, London, E 12385)

Cairo via Kufra on 18 October. He was later awarded the MC for his outstanding work behind enemy lines.

The activities of this MI 9 field section have been outlined in some detail as they give some idea of the distances covered in the Western Desert, and the scale of MI 9 operations established to support escapers and evaders. Some of the crew of a 38 Squadron Wellington bomber were the very first customers to benefit from Granguillot's first patrol.

SAVED BY SENUSSI ARABS

Canadian-born Warrant Officer G. Rossen from Toronto was the second pilot of a 38 Squadron Wellington bomber tasked to drop mines at the entrance to Benghazi harbour. The six-man crew took off from Shallufa airfield near Suez at 8 p.m. on 21 May 1942 before heading west along the North African coast. As the aircraft left the target area it was hit by anti-aircraft fire and the captain ordered the crew to bale out. Rossen landed in the desert some 20 miles east of Benghazi and almost immediately met up with Sergeant J. Smith, the wireless operator.

Once the two men had collected their thoughts they salvaged some pieces from their parachutes before burying the remains under rocks. They set off walking in a north-easterly direction, using the moon as a guide. They travelled by night and sheltered in the shade of rocks by day for the next three days, but their only food was the survival rations in the escape aid box. They had no water and found the Horlicks tablets impossible to digest without water. On the third day they came across a small family of Senussi Arabs living in two small tents, who gave them food and water but made it clear that they must leave after taking a rest. They left at 4 p.m. after the Senussi had said a prayer over them and given them the direction to travel. They had also given the men some Italian Army clothes, a water bottle and some bread.

Rossen and Smith headed east for a day before they came across a well. By this time they had realized that the wells were generally to be found in hilly country. They strained the water using a piece of parachute material before drinking as much as they could manage before filling the water bottle. They continued walking east as long as they kept finding water, but turned north each time they went for a

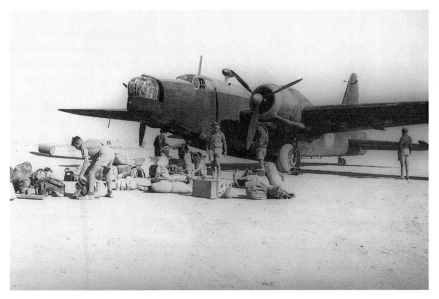

A Wellington bomber at an Advanced Landing Ground in the Western Desert. (Andy Thomas collection)

long period without finding a well. After a further eight days, three Senussi Arabs found them as they slept and took them to a cave where they were given food and shelter. The Arabs' camp was nearby, but they were not prepared to take them there for fear of the Italians discovering them.

Over the next few days, they encountered several Senussi parties who gave them food, water and clothing. Almost certainly, they had unknowingly made contact with the network of Senussi agents recently established in the area by Grandguillot. After 14 days of walking, a Senussi took them to meet two British officers 'who were working in the desert with the natives'. The officers were able to radio Cairo, who gave instructions for the two men to be taken to a lake south of Derna to be met by the LRDG. Two Senussi members of the Libya Arab Force took them to the rendezvous on camels, arriving too late to meet the LRDG patrol. However, two days later (about 8 June), two more Senussi arrived with Sergeant G. Armstrong, the Canadian observer of their crew.

Armstrong had been the first to bale out of the stricken Wellington, but he had failed to meet up with any other member of the crew. Despite injuring his ankle on landing, he walked due east for the next four days, initially travelling only at night, but as his desperation to find water increased he started to walk during the day. Eventually, he found a well, had a drink, and collapsed. When he woke up he found himself in a cave with three Arabs, who gave him eggs and goat's milk before he fainted again, eventually waking up in their tent. They were Senussi Arabs. He remained with them for the next six days, during which time his ankle and general health improved. On 2 June, an Arab collected him and they headed east for the next three days before he was passed to another group. Nineteen days after he had baled out, two Senussi took him to a lake about 70 miles south-west of Derna, arriving on 8 June, and there he met members of the Libya Arab Force. One of the corporals understood English and told him that he had recently seen 'an American and an Englishman', who had written their names in the corporal's notebook – they were Rossen and Smith from his crew.

After the missed rendezvous with the LRDG, Rossen and Smith were taken back to the two British officers, where, to their surprise and delight, they met Sergeant Ostram, the rear gunner of their aircraft, who had just been brought in by another party of Senussi Arabs. The following day, Armstrong was brought in. Eventually, the

Senussi Arabs gave a great deal of assistance to evading aircrew in the Western Desert. (Air Historical Branch)

four men were picked up by the LRDG and taken to their camp at Kufra, where they remained for four days before embarking on a 450–mile jeep journey to the Allied lines near the Siwa oases. They met a New Zealand patrol that arranged for an aircraft of the Desert Air Sea Rescue Flight to pick them up and return them to Cairo. They arrived 30 days after they had been shot down.

Rossen and his three colleagues arrived back in Cairo three days before Grandguillot's return from his first patrol to establish the network of dumps and Senussi agents. It is interesting to speculate whether they met, but the almost immediate success in bringing out the four aircrew must have been very gratifying for the MI 9 team in Cairo. Over the next few months, other aircrew would return as a result of the work and bravery of the Senussi Arab agents.

The official MI 9 report on Middle East activities written after the war paid a special tribute to the help and assistance afforded to Allied escapers and evaders throughout the Western Desert campaign by the Senussi Arabs. Even when the fortunes of the Allies were at their lowest, the Senussi never wavered in their support of the Allied cause.

Many were executed by the Italians, and reprisals in every form were taken on them whenever they were found giving assistance to the Allies. There were, however, few cases recorded of betrayal to the enemy. Even those who would not give active help maintained the desert laws of hospitality, and gave food and shelter to evaders passing through their area – the successful evasion of Rossen and his colleagues provides ample evidence of this.

Experience had shown that to carry out MI 9 work satisfactorily in the Western Desert theatre it was essential to have a staff officer with the Eighth Army Headquarters. No officer was available at the time, so Tony Simonds, and Major Crichton from his staff, paid frequent visits to the headquarters, from June to October, to coordinate escape plans and operations, including the use of forward patrols.

In addition to the field sections operating behind the enemy lines, use was also made of the Western Desert Liaison Officers with the Eighth Army, and to send Arab agents through the front lines to the areas immediately behind the battle area. After the Allied line was stabilized at Alamein, this method was greatly developed, and Arab camel patrols were organized throughout the Western Desert. Sectors were allocated to these camel patrols, which called at various water points, mostly near the coast, to try and contact escapers and evaders. Heavily involved in establishing this scheme and other clandestine activities was Lieutenant Colonel J. E. Haselden, a cotton merchant in Egypt before the war. He was killed during a raid on Tobruk on 13 September, a colleague describing him as 'a very remarkable man with a great influence over the Desert Arabs'.

There was one other scheme developed to assist evaders – the Qattara Depression Scheme. The southern flank of both armies at Alamein rested on the extreme easterly edge of the Qattara Depression. This was a vast area below seal level impassable to wheeled transport, and was rarely used by either side except by the occasional foot patrol. As the Depression extended some 150 miles behind the enemy lines, Simonds decided to make use of it. He sent Captain Prior and Sergeant Lewis, with some Arab agents, in September 1942 to establish dumps and collecting points along the line of the enemy's right flank. This was successfully achieved, despite the adverse climatic and physical difficulties, and resulted in the saving of many lives, particularly from thirst. The scheme continued until the Eighth Army had advanced beyond the area at the end of October.

Two Wellington crews successfully evaded capture as a result of assistance they received from these various initiatives. Needless to say, at the time they were completely unaware that they owed their success to the plans implemented by MI 9 staff in Cairo.

DESERT EVASION

When Montreal-born Flying Officer Christopher Hare RCAF lifted his Wellington bomber of 37 Squadron off the runway at Abu Sueir at 10 p.m. on 29 July 1942, he and his five-man crew could hardly have visualized what lay ahead of them as they set out to bomb Tobruk. Hare was a veteran of 30 bombing operations over Germany and the Middle East. Sitting alongside him was his Australian second pilot, Sergeant Alex Barras RAAF, who had recently joined the squadron, and was flying on one of his first operations. Observer and bomb aimer in the multi-national crew was another Canadian, Flying Officer Dan Chappell, who came from Windsor, Ontario. Three British RAF sergeants formed the rest of the crew.

As Hare settled the Wellington on its bombing approach to Tobruk at 9,000 feet, the starboard engine began to run very roughly, accompanied by a rapidly rising oil temperature. Minutes later, the engine seized, so the bombs were dropped on Tobruk airfield, as the crew jettisoned guns, ammunition and any loose equipment in an endeavour to maintain sufficient height for the long return journey to Egypt. However, it soon became apparent that a crash-landing was inevitable, and Hare selected a suitable area, turned the aircraft into wind and made an excellent landing 20 miles south of Tobruk. After destroying the sensitive equipment, the crew gathered the emergency rations from the dinghy, including an eight-gallon water tank, navigation equipment and the aircraft ladder. They headed south-east until dawn, when they stopped for the day to make plans for their attempt to walk back to Allied lines, some 350 miles to the east.

The crew established a marching routine, having teamed up as pairs, walking through the next three nights, when they achieved 12 to 15 miles each night. The water tank was lashed to the ladder and one team carried it on their shoulders. Another team carried the navigation equipment and the few stores, leaving the other two airmen to rest. Each hour they rotated the positions of the pairs in their efforts to conserve energy. On the fourth day they came across an abandoned British camp, where they were able to obtain some shelter from the fierce daytime heat. With weakness setting in as a result of the water supply running low, and a diet limited to Horlicks tablets, they discussed the idea of heading north to the area of perennial wells, but the sudden appearance of an Arab changed their ideas. He warned them of the presence of German and Italian troops, but promised to fetch some food. He returned two hours later with biscuits and rice before directing them to a well three miles to the east at Bir Sheferzen. They slept the night at the well, and remained the next day before replenishing the water tank to resume their night journey to the south-east.

Over the next three nights, they made good progress despite feeling weak, but the discovery of five wells that were all dry convinced them that they must head north towards the perennial well area near Buq Buq, halfway between Sollum and Sidi Barrani. They followed a northerly track, and just before dawn on the tenth day they found themselves on the coast road near an observation tower where they spent the day. Alex Barras went off to look for wells, and soon came across a large road-building party of Italian soldiers. He monitored their movements while remaining undetected, before returning to the rest of the party. Unable to replenish their water supply, they reduced the daily ration to one cupful each, with one Horlicks tablet as their only food.

At dusk they pushed on eastwards, keeping just to the south of the coast road. After five miles they noticed a single truck parked just off the road, and the two Canadians and Barras went across in the hope of draining the water from the radiator. As they approached, an Italian challenged them, and Barras's attempt to bluff him failed. More troops arrived, and in the general confusion the three airmen managed to get away. Barras returned to his three colleagues, but the two Canadians became lost, and they were not seen again. The others headed south-east into the desert, walking all night, with Barras taking over the navigation duties using the stud-type escape compass, which they checked nightly against the North Star. Early in the morning, they found a well and were able to replenish the water supply and get some sleep. A truck disturbed their rest, and it was clear that they were still in an area of considerable enemy activity, so they decided to continue walking throughout that day and the following night. For the first time, they began to feel that they might be lost, and as morning dawned they dropped down thirsty, hungry and completely exhausted, and quickly fell asleep.

How long the four airmen were asleep is not clear, but some time in the morning two Arab shepherds found them. After being informed that the crew were British, the two shepherds rushed off to bring back some goat's milk and a few biscuits. Barras asked them to direct the party to an Arab village, and after some persuasion they agreed to do so. After a rest, the crew set off, but it was not until the following evening that they found any Arabs. Despite their fear, the Arabs fed the crew magnificently. After Barras offered them a monetary reward, they allowed the four airmen to sleep in the village for the night. The next morning they were given directions for the next Arab encampment, which they reached two days later in an exhausted condition after a slow journey caused by their blistered and bleeding feet.

At this new village, the Arabs gave them biscuits and water and guided them into thick shrubbery about three miles away. During the day, they returned with more food and water. Barras talked with two of them during the day, trying to persuade them to guide the party back to the British lines. The 'conversation' took many turns and Barras had to make numerous promises in an endeavour to secure their services. Eventually, at 8 p.m., and after giving them all the Egyptian money the crew carried, Hamid Musterva and his son Abdullah agreed. They brought along a camel loaded with 16 gallons of water and some food, together with Arab robes. An hour later, the party set off.

With the Arabs guiding them, the crew headed south for about 20 miles before turning eastwards. The next few nights were uneventful, except for increasing foot and stomach trouble. The crew had difficulty digesting the hard Arab bread, and one or two were sick. However, despite their weakness, they were making about 20 miles a night and their spirits were high as they made good progress and began to feel for the first time that success was possible. Reaching a road in the Bir Abu El Heiran, and close to a depression containing about 80 abandoned British trucks, the Arabs made a camp on the crest of a small hill, and dug four shallow pits for the airmen to use as shelters before they took the sensible security precaution of moving on a few miles to make their own camp.

During the morning, Sergeant Warwick, the rear gunner, went to the nearby well to fetch water. As he reached it, he noticed the approach of a truck loaded with Italians, and he immediately returned to the camp to report that he did not think he had been seen. He brought two gallons of water and a .303 rifle and 15 rounds of ammunition found among the abandoned equipment. The airmen decided to stay where they were and hope that the Italians would soon depart, but the truck stopped to disembark 12 soldiers, who set to work to recover spares and wheels from the British vehicles. Two hours later, the truck returned and passed 20 yards from the airmen before stopping. Sergeant A. Jones, the front gunner, was in a trench some 50 yards from the others, and he had slept through the morning completely oblivious of the Italians' presence. Unfortunately, he stood up at that moment and was seen by the Italians, and one of them drew his rifle and started walking to him. Barras told the others to don their Arab robes as he drew his revolver. The Italian stopped a few yards away and stared at them. Realizing the danger, Barras shouted, 'Saeedee, saeedee', as he beckoned the Italian towards him, hoping to take his rifle and force him to call out to his comrades that all was well. However, at that short distance it was obvious to the Italian that they were not Arabs, and he turned and raced back, shouting to his comrades. The airmen picked up their water bottles, rifle and revolvers, and when the Italians came back up the hill firing at them, they fired a single shot from the rifle, which stopped the Italians advancing for a brief period. The airmen took advantage of the lull and headed over a small ridge, where they spotted a burnt-out truck a few hundred yards away, which they reached unseen. They lay in the truck for two hours, during which time they could hear the Italians searching for them some distance away.

Barras was very worried that the Arab guides would make off, so he decided he must try and find them. He climbed out of the depression, and seeing no sign of the Italians he called his colleagues and they set off in the direction they had seen the Arabs depart earlier in the day. After some three miles, they found them, quickly explained the situation, and told them that the party would carry on until nightfall, when they would stop and wait for the Arabs to join them. This they did. The Arabs explained that German soldiers had stopped them and warned them not to get involved, as they intended to wait at the well for the British party who had left their two-gallon container, so were expected to return. That night, the party put 20 miles between the well and themselves. They passed south of the German advanced

Sergeant Alex Barras RAAF on the day he and his colleagues were picked up by a patrol of the 11th Hussars. (Imperial War Museum, London, E 16340)

landing ground at Fuka, where they saw a great deal of activity, but they did not encounter further enemy troops. With their guides, they made good progress as the terrain became easier, although all of them had developed foot trouble. They were aware of some enemy activity in the Abu Dweis area, but this was easily avoided at night. On the 22nd day of their 350-mile trip, they saw a British armoured car, which drove over to them. It belonged to an advance reconnaissance group of the 11th Hussars. Barras took details of their two Arab benefactors before bidding them farewell. They were later rewarded for their valuable service.

After a night with the Hussars, the four airmen were driven to an advance RAF headquarters at Burg El Arab before returning to Cairo for medical checks and debriefings. The official report of their successful evasion concluded that 'the four members of the crew have shown great grit and determination and the highest praise is certainly due to them'. The authorities singled out the Australian, Sergeant Alex Barras, who had clearly been the leader and inspiration for the rest of the crew, for particular praise. The report concluded:

> It is noteworthy that the other members of the crew did not question the natural leadership of Sergeant Barras. In spite of the great hardship and sufferings that have left their mark on Sergeant Barras, his morale is completely unimpaired, and his sole desire is to return to operations. He is a particularly fine type.

A few weeks later, it was announced that he had been awarded the MM for his initiative and gallantry.

The successful evasion of the four airmen from the crashed Wellington graphically illustrates the overriding qualities needed for a successful evasion from deep inside enemy territory. The crew had a plan, which they stuck to. They travelled in the cool of the night, and rested during the heat of the day. They carefully rationed their meagre supplies of food and water, and they were able to obtain the assistance of local Arabs who knew the country. Barras had taken the trouble to learn some basic Arabic, which proved invaluable. The crew would be the first to acknowledge that they had also enjoyed some luck, but they displayed in abundance the most essential qualities for an evader – a 'never say die' attitude, and an utter determination to remain free. Their two Canadian colleagues were not quite so lucky in the desert, but over the next few months they, too, were to display the same qualities.

After becoming separated from the rest of the crew, Hare and Chappell travelled south. They met an Arab who gave them some water and food, with directions to another encampment. On the 14th day they were able to obtain an Arab guide, and set off for the Qattara Depression. Four days later they were seen by an Italian patrol and were captured. They were interrogated and held in Italian prison camps in North Africa before being transferred to Italy, where they ended up in the POW camp at Sulmona.

Hare and Chappell had been prisoners for 14 months when the Italians capitulated, culminating in the signing of an Armistice on 10 September 1943. The prisoners had high hopes that they would be released, but it soon became apparent that the German forces would take control of the camp. With their imminent arrival, the prisoners evacuated to the hills to the east of the camp. Many parties had no food, and returned to sleep in the camp overnight, when, in a surprise move, the Germans surrounded it and captured all those who had returned. They also scoured the foothills and recaptured another 800 prisoners. A group of 20 German soldiers armed with machine-guns surrounded the position where Hare, Chappell and other officers were hiding. Chappell escaped to the mountains with another Canadian, and Hare took cover in a bush where he remained undetected. At nightfall he escaped to the mountains, where he met up with Chappell and a party of six other escapers at a shepherd's hut, where they rested.

The escapers were sheltered and fed for six days by Italian woodcutters. They then moved on to the village of San Vittorino, where the group was split up among various houses to be looked after and well fed for almost three weeks by the local Italian population. Once they received a message that the Allied advance northwards was getting closer to their village, the party split into various groups to travel south. Hare and Chappell remained together and joined two other Canadians before travelling through the mountains, receiving a great deal of help from the local people. They crossed the Allied lines on 19 October, five weeks after their escape. After debriefings, they were flown to Algiers before continuing to Whitchurch, near Bristol, where they arrived on 30 October. A few weeks later, it was announced that both Hare and Chappell had been awarded a Mention in Despatches for their fortitude and determination culminating in their escape.

Christopher Hare returned to operational flying as a squadron leader in November 1944, flying Lancasters with 150 Squadron from Hemswell near Lincoln. In May 1945 it was announced that he had been awarded the DFC 'in recognition of gallantry and devotion to duty in the execution of air operations against the enemy'. He remained in the RCAF after the war, eventually becoming the Squadron Commander of 414 Squadron flying CF-100 jet night-fighters. He was awarded the AFC for his services, but tragically he was killed when his fighter crashed at North Bay in Ontario.

LATE ARRIVALS CLUB

Winnipeg-born Pilot Officer Brian Johnston of the RCAF was the wireless operator and only officer in Sergeant R. Carter's Wellington crew of 70 Squadron. As darkness fell on 7 September 1942 they took off from Abu Sueir near the Suez Canal in their Wellington 'T for Tommy' to bomb Tobruk. Just before midnight, the aircraft turned onto its final bombing run at 12,000 feet when it was repeatedly hit by anti-aircraft fire six miles to the west of Tobruk. The aircraft started to lose height and the bombs were jettisoned just before both engines failed. The captain and his second pilot, Sergeant Dennis Bebbington, managed to restart the starboard engine, and they turned the aircraft onto a south-easterly heading into the desert. All available loose equipment was jettisoned, and an SOS was sent with an approximate position. Sergeant Carter switched the landing lights on when it became obvious that a crash landing was inevitable. The two pilots completed a perfect landing in the desert, and all the crew walked away uninjured.

During their preparation for the crash landing, the two pilots noticed some tracer fire a few miles to the north, so elected not to burn the aircraft, as this would undoubtedly attract attention. They destroyed all the sensitive equipment, such as the bombsight, the IFF, radio and codebooks. Johnston assumed command of the party, and they worked quickly to collect the survival equipment and emergency rations. They also salvaged the navigator's compass, a Very pistol, some first-aid supplies, local maps, and survival aids taken from the dinghy equipment. The water tank in the aircraft was taken out and every possible receptacle was filled with water. The crew drank the rest so that they were able to start their trek fully hydrated. Owing to the possible proximity of the enemy, they decided to move away from the crash site immediately.

The actual position where the aircraft landed was much farther south than they had calculated, and so they decided to walk north to strike the coast and pinpoint themselves. After an hour's walk they decided this was not a good plan, and returned to the aircraft before striking off into the desert in a south-easterly direction. They walked until 5.30 a.m., when they decided to rest for the remainder of the night in some scrub. As dawn broke, they saw an abandoned truck, which allowed them to rest underneath in the shade. During this first day, Johnston devised a scheme to make the rations and water last for six days.

At nightfall they headed south, and once again found a derelict lorry that provided shade on the following day. During the morning, three Arabs appeared and took them to their encampment, where they were fed and given some supplies before returning to their truck to rest in the shade. They moved south the next day when they found a waterhole before intercepting a track, which turned out to be the El Adem–Bir Sheferzen road. They were able to follow it in a south-easterly direction, and on the fifth day it took them to the frontier wire between Libya and Egypt, where they rested for the night in the lee of a derelict staff car. The next day they came across some Arabs who gave them some water and biscuits. They were not prepared to escort the party to a town, so the crew continued towards Bit-el-Khireigat, where they were able to replenish their water bottles and rest the night before continuing eastwards.

For three days they walked in the direction of Bir Enba, but the going became difficult, and Sergeant Croiseau, the rear gunner, started to suffer considerable pain from his badly blistered and strained feet. The crew decided to head due north to get near the main road in case he could go no further, and had to surrender. On the 13th day they found a well and rested. Since the gunner's feet were getting worse and food was becoming short, they decided to make an attempt to capture a lorry, with a view to driving east. Johnston and Bebbington went on a reconnaissance and found a small hill, from which they had a good view of the surrounding country, and the traffic moving on the main road in the distance. The day was spent at the well, and in the afternoon the whole party moved to the hill, where they had a meal. At dusk, with Johnston in the lead, the party set off in the moonlight towards the road, which they came across after an hour when they turned in an easterly direction. After two hours they saw two lorries parked 50 yards apart a mile ahead of them. They stopped to devise a plan to capture one of the vehicles. They moved forward to nearby sand hills, and two of the crew remained there with the kit as Johnston, the two pilots and the injured gunner moved to the lorries. The latter was taken because he had fought during the Spanish Civil War and had some experience of mounting ambushes.

Johnston and Croiseau approached the driver's cab as Bebbington and Carter went to the rear in an attempt to capture the occupants, using their one revolver. Johnston had to strike the driver, who was shouting, but troops from the second vehicle were alerted and started to arrive. A short gunfight developed, and Johnston shouted for the crew to retreat back to the hill, as he and Carter ran into the darkness. Bebbington had got into the back of the truck, where he lost his hat, and where he was mistaken for one of the Italian soldiers. He then joined them in the search for the 'bandits', slipping away into the darkness as soon as he could. In the meantime, Johnston and Carter had rejoined the two other members of the crew and headed off into the desert. Bebbington met an Arab who gave him some water. Having filled his bottle and drunk as much as he could, he found a quiet place to sleep. The following morning, he headed south, saw his colleagues in the distance, and he was able to rejoin them. They did not see Croiseau again. (He was taken prisoner and released after the war.)

Over the next few days, the crew met small groups of Arabs who gave them water, and on one occasion they were taken to an encampment where they were given great hospitality and a meal. They were advised to travel only at night and departed the encampment at midnight heading in a south-easterly direction. On the 18th day they came across a herd of camels, and met the camel driver, who took them to his village where, once again, they were able to replenish their water. All were suffering from desert sores and many bites from sand flies and various bugs, and their feet were causing problems. Nevertheless, they stuck to their plan to walk by night and covered almost 20 miles the following night.

After a night at an Arab encampment at Ben Nasarra, they made east for a series of wadis, but found the going extremely difficult so headed south. Before dawn they saw anti-aircraft fire and searchlights in the distance, which proved to be the German landing grounds at Sidi Heneish. They made a wide detour to the south and east until dawn, when they rested. The next day, their 24th since starting their great walk, they came to a small village 10 miles south of Fuka, where they were well received but where no-one was prepared to take the risk of guiding them to Allied troops, although Johnston offered the villagers £100 per man. They left the village at dusk and walked for the next 24 hours with short rests only. Two days later, their water was getting low, but a torrential storm broke. Not only did they get soaking wet, but the rain swept masses of gravel over their kit and provisions, which they fortunately were able to recover once the storm had passed.

Early on the 27th day they reached the northern edge of the Qattara Depression, where they carried on walking south-east along salt marshes. After 18 hours they stopped to rest until daybreak, when they met some Arabs who provided them with some food, water and a blanket in exchange for the last of their money. One of them – almost certainly one of the agents established behind enemy lines by MI 9 – took the crew to Lake Magre, where they rested throughout the day under a palm tree. Exhausted, they slept through the night. Just after dawn on the 29th day, they were woken by the sound of vehicles. They attracted the driver's attention, and a short while later, two officers and two soldiers of No. 4 South African Armoured Car Unit arrived in two jeeps. Their ordeal was over.

They were taken to an oasis at Bir Nahid and given breakfast before being taken to the unit's headquarters. Transport then took them across the front line to a rear headquarters of a tank unit, where they spent the night before being taken back to Seagull Camp in Alexandria to recuperate.

This remarkable feat of endurance and determination was one of the great escape stories of the Western Desert campaign. The

Pilot Officer Brian Johnston RCAF (centre) and his crew at Seagull Camp, Alexandria, the day after their arrival following their epic 29-day walk. (Mrs P. Bridgewood)

Wellington crew had been behind enemy lines for 29 days and had walked a distance of no less than 340 miles. They had followed their survival training to the letter, having devised a plan, which they stuck to, rationed their water and travelled at night, resting during the heat of the day. The 22-year-old Canadian had brilliantly led them, but every man in the crew had played a key role. Their unknown Arab helpers had made a major contribution to their successful evasion. The establishment of the network of Arab agents in the Qattara Depression just a week or two earlier had undoubtedly ensured, perhaps guaranteed, their ultimate survival.

Johnston was recommended for the MC, but it was subsequently discovered that a recommendation for the DFC had been submitted just before he had been shot down. The authorities decided to combine the two citations, so he was denied a specific award for his gallantry and superb leadership behind enemy lines. Many would agree that he should have received both. The absurdity of the situation was graphically highlighted when it was announced that Sergeant Bebbington and Sergeant Davies, the navigator, had been justifiably awarded the MM. The joint citation concluded: 'Pilot Officer Johnston acted as leader throughout, being excellently supported by Sergeants Bebbington and Davies. This officer and airmen displayed resolute courage and fortitude throughout the hazardous period.' Sadly, Dennis Bebbington was lost on operations over the Mediterranean the following March on his last bomber operation before going on a rest tour. He is commemorated on the Runnymede Memorial.

In addition to their awards, the five evaders were enrolled into a unique club, 'The Late Arrivals Club'. Squadron Leader George Houghton, who worked as a Public Relations Officer in Cairo in 1941, had written a brief newspaper story of a pilot who had been shot down in the desert before spending a few days walking back to rejoin his squadron. He described the pilot as a 'late arrival', and the story prompted other aircrew with similar experiences to write to him with the idea of creating an informal club. Houghton designed a certificate and a small badge showing a winged flying-boot, which some aircrew wore unofficially on the sleeve of their uniform. The idea became popular, and almost 500 certificates and badges were awarded before the end of the Western Desert campaign.

Late Arrivals Club

(Founded Western Desert, June 1941)

THIS IS TO CERTIFY, that
    FLIGHT SERGEANT R.W. JEFCOATE
of   62   Squadron
is hereby nominated a member of the

Late Arrivals Club

IN AS MUCH AS HE, in   INDIA

on AUGUST 1, 1942
when obliged to abandon his Aircraft, on the
ground or in the Air, as a result of unfriendly
action by the enemy

SUCCEEDED in returning to his Squadron,
on foot or by other means, long after his
Estimated Time of Arrival.

IT IS NEVER TOO LATE TO COME BACK

An example of the Late Arrivals Club certificate. (ACA Archives)

Chapter Eleven

Greece

IN A BULLETIN ISSUED BY Advance Headquarters 'A' Force, the Greeks were described as 'probably the staunchest allies we have in all the occupied countries. They are not merely friendly to the Allied cause, they regard themselves as in the war on our side.' Aircrew were reminded that there would inevitably be a few who were traitors and spies, and so they must exercise caution, but the overwhelming majority, particularly in village and farm districts, were likely to give active assistance. Following the withdrawal of British forces from Greece and Crete in May 1941, air activity over Greece and the adjacent Aegean Sea was very limited for the next two years. However, many soldiers and airmen remained at large and successfully evaded capture. To rescue some of these men, MI 9 soon established a fleet of caiques (local sailing ships) to transfer evaders to the west coast of Turkey. Key to the establishment and success of the sea escape lines were the British Naval Attaché in Istanbul, Commander V. Wolfson, and his assistant in Smyrna (Izmir), Lieutenant Commander Noel Rees. Rees built up a clandestine naval base on the peninsula to the west of Smyrna, and even managed to get it declared a prohibited area. As early as 1942, MI 9 established fuel and food dumps on many of the islands in the Aegean to assist evaders and the caiques patrolling in the area and *en route* to the Greek mainland for clandestine operations. Helpers were maintained on all these islands on a 'reward basis', being rewarded for any evaders they helped.

As air activity in the Aegean Sea increased in 1943, and following the abortive Dodecanese campaign in the autumn of 1943, the caiques were used extensively to evacuate surviving forces, land agents on the various islands, and to pick up evaders. They were remarkably successful in rescuing over 700 people, including a number of aircrew, and it was this network of sea escape routes that became the main method of recovering aircrew shot down in eastern Greece, the Aegean Sea or from one of the many islands. By the middle of 1944, MI 9 had a fleet of 32 caiques operating in the Aegean Sea, with Smyrna as the main reception port in Turkey, and Cyprus providing the main repair base. The successful evasion and pick-up of a Wellington crew is typical of the operations mounted by the caiques.

AEGEAN SEA PICK-UP

The six-man crew of a 38 Squadron Wellington bomber took off from the desert airfield at Berka, near Benghazi, at 8 p.m. on 7 November 1943. At the controls, and captain of the aircraft, was Flying Officer R. Adams of the RCAF, and he and his crew had been detailed to search for shipping around the island of Naxos in the Aegean Sea. Two hours after take-off they arrived off the island, where they spotted a ship in the main harbour. They descended to 60 feet to begin an attack from the south. As they approached the target, the aircraft was engaged by heavy anti-aircraft fire, which disrupted the attack and caused the bombs to miss the target. Adams decided to carry out another attack, and after a further 30 minutes he commenced another low-level approach to the ship. Again, the Wellington was engaged, but the Australian bomb aimer, Warrant Officer T. Faulkiner, released the bombs, which the crew were certain had hit the ship.

As Adams and his second pilot, Flying Officer John Spencer, turned the aircraft out to sea, it was obvious that the bomber had sustained serious damage in the starboard wing and engine from the anti-aircraft fire. They managed to gain some height before the engine failed, but it soon became clear that they had no chance of returning to base as the aircraft suddenly started to lose height. Adams turned the aircraft into wind, and carried out a perfect ditching on the calm sea. All the crew clambered out of the sinking bomber safely and climbed into the dinghy, which had inflated successfully. They started to paddle towards an island they could see in the distance, and just after midnight they landed on the island of Sifnos. After recovering the various survival aids, they destroyed the dinghy and found themselves a hiding place in the lee of a wall.

Next morning they were found by a small girl who took them to her father who lived close by. They told him their identities, and were able to ascertain that there were no German forces on the island. They left him and headed towards a village near the centre of the island, which they reached in the afternoon, and where they were fed and made very welcome. That evening a man who could speak English came to see them, and he took the crew back to his house on the edge of the village. They were introduced to the local Chief of Police, a sergeant major in the gendarmerie, and to the priest of the island. It was agreed that the six men would go to the nearby monastery to be sheltered by the priests, who looked after them very well.

The Chief of Police was aware that a patrol of six British 'soldiers' were on the nearby island of Serifos, and he agreed to make arrangements for Adams and his crew to be taken to the island by local caique. During their three-day stay at the monastery, the crew were visited by many of the islanders, and their presence became so public that the first boatman refused to take them, particularly since most of the villagers wanted to give the crew a send-off. Since German soldiers were based on another nearby island, he expected them to find out about his involvement and he would be punished.

Two days later, they finally set sail from the island at 6 a.m. heading for Serifos with another Greek boatman. He also was very nervous, and instead of taking the party to the north of the island, he dropped them on the southern end, leaving them to find their own way to the British patrol some miles to the north. After spending the night in the open, they headed across the island. They soon met the local inhabitants, who gave the party all the help they could, including directions to the monastery that they had been advised to contact by the priests who had sheltered them earlier. On arrival later in the day, they were made very welcome, and it was here that they met the patrol of the LRDG led by Lieutenant Gibson who had been carrying out clandestine operations among the islands, and were waiting to be picked up at the end of their tasks. The Wellington crew joined the patrol to spend the next three weeks living with them in a series of caves.

The patrol was due to be picked up on 25 November by a large motorized caique operated by the Royal Navy's Levant Schooner Flotilla based in Beirut, but it was delayed. The caique was on a month's patrol in the Aegean Sea gathering intelligence and supporting the numerous LRDG patrols operating on the Greek

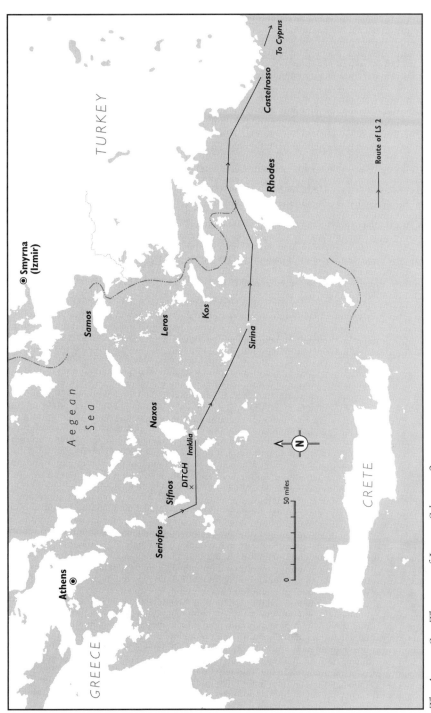

The Aegean Sea. The route of Levant Schooner 2.

Islands. The presence of Adams and his crew on the island had been radioed to the captain of the caique, so he was expecting to have six extra passengers, but bad weather delayed his arrival for three days. The food had been rationed on the basis of the original date, so the local inhabitants immediately came forward and fed them. An attempt to airdrop additional supplies failed because of high winds and bad weather.

Just after midnight on 28 November, LS 2 (Levant Schooner 2) anchored in the rendezvous off Serifos, and the captain, Lieutenant Alexander McLeod RNVR, went ashore in a rowing boat to meet Gibson and Adams. Arrangements were made to take the 12 men to LS 2 in the hope that the caique would sail that night. Unfortunately, the weather became worse and the vessel had to move to a new anchorage, where the camouflage netting was rerigged. Finally, the vessel managed to sail under the cover of darkness at 6.15 p.m. the following day, and headed off in a south-easterly direction towards the island of Iraklia.

LS 2 entered Spelia Cove on Iraklia in the early hours of the following morning, and Lieutenant McLeod berthed and camouflaged the vessel against a rock face. He was hoping to meet another LRDG

A Levant Schooner Squadron motorized caique lands stores on one of the Aegean islands before collecting men of the SBS and aircrew evaders.
(TNA: PRO HS7/272)

patrol and two RAF aircrew who had been picked up off Naxos, but arrangements to meet them failed to materialize. The caique remained concealed throughout the day, and with fuel and food running low McLeod decided to head back for a forward base off the Turkish coast. As soon as darkness fell, LS 2 left the cove and headed eastwards. After three hours of sailing, the engines started to malfunction, so the caique headed for Anidros. The crew spent the next day rectifying the engine problem, and the captain took advantage of the delay to carry out a reconnaissance of the island.

At 5.30 p.m. LS 2 left in the twilight and headed east at seven knots, but the engine continuously broke down, and McLeod was forced to take cover off the island of Sirina, where he distributed food to local people who had assisted shot-down aircrew to escape. Sailing at night, LS 2 limped towards an advanced supply dump at Loryma, arriving in the early hours of 3 December. After taking on board 50 gallons of fuel, LS 2 sailed down the island chain inside Turkish territorial waters heading for Castelrosso and on to Port Vathy, where a rendezvous was made with a Special Boat Squadron (SBS) supply caique early on the morning of 5 December. Sailing later that day, LS 2 hugged the coast of Turkey until dusk, when it altered course for Cyprus, entering Paphos harbour at noon. There the Wellington crew were disembarked and taken for debriefing before being flown back to Cairo and more detailed debriefings at Air Headquarters.

~

As the war progressed, Greek partisan groups proliferated, and they were supported by SOE agents, members of the British Raiding Support Regiment, and by forces drawn from the SBS and the LRDG. All had to deal with the complex, and at times hostile, dealings of the various Greek political parties, who often appeared to be working to very different agendas. Fortunately, the various schemings and intrigues between the parties did not prevent them having a common hatred of the occupying German forces.

Once the Allies had a firm foothold on the mainland of Italy following the invasion in September 1943, it was possible to establish airfields and to deploy large air forces. From airfields on the eastern coast of Italy, air operations could be mounted over the Balkans in support of the numerous partisan organizations. In the autumn of 1944, the Germans started to withdraw from Greece, using the main railway lines to evacuate their forces north towards Yugoslavia, and so presenting a major target for Allied light bombers and fighter-bombers.

SHELTER WITH THE GREEK PARTISANS

Twenty-year-old Dennis 'Mac' McCaig travelled from his home in Fiji to join the RAF 'as a fighter pilot', an ambition he achieved in 1943. After completing his training, he was sent to Italy, where he joined 249 Squadron based on the Adriatic Coast. Shortly after his arrival, the squadron re-equipped with the powerful, long-range Mustang III fighter.

As dawn broke on 8 October 1944, he and a colleague took off from Brindisi airfield to attack trains on the main coastal railway route west of Salonika in Greece. After transiting over the Adriatic Sea, the two Mustang pilots descended to low level over Greece before heading for their targets. On arrival in the target area, no trains were seen, so the two pilots attacked road transport with their cannon, when they encountered light anti-aircraft fire. Shortly after passing the small town of Polykastron, McCaig noticed a stream of white vapour coming back over the cockpit canopy. It was the dreaded sign of a leak of the essential engine coolant, indicating that it was only a matter of a few minutes before his engine failed. He called his leader and immediately turned for home, started to climb, and headed to the distant hills where he knew he had a better chance of evading capture. With the leak getting worse, he climbed through 10,000 feet when the engine stopped. He rolled his Mustang (HB 933) onto its back, opened the canopy, undid his straps, and fell clear. His parachute opened and he drifted in silence towards the hills. He was knocked unconscious and damaged his knee as he landed heavily in scrub in a small ravine in the foothills of the mountains.

When he came to, he gathered up his parachute and dinghy pack before setting off up the ravine. He noticed a young boy and girl staring at him, and they were soon joined by a tough-looking group of armed men. As soon he was able to make them understand that he was an 'Ingleese pilot', he was embraced in a great bear hug, and he knew he was safe among friends. The leader indicated that it would not be long before a German patrol arrived to search for him, so the party set off into the hills. After a few hours of climbing, they arrived at the small, primitive village of Kegala Livadia, where he was given a warm welcome by the very poor, but friendly, villagers.

Shortly after his arrival at the village, a man with a basic knowledge of English arrived, and he was able to tell the leader of the group that he wished to be put in touch with the British Mission. He was assured that this would be done, but not before they had visited the crash site of his aircraft, which was a few miles away. McCaig indicated that he was unable to walk any further, but after two glasses of the local 'firewater', a meal of dubious content, and the friendly persuasion of his hosts, he relented and they set off during the afternoon. It proved to be an arduous journey. On arrival at the crash site, he stood in disbelief as he looked at the tangled wreckage of what had been his new, gleaming Mustang resting in a 15 ft crater. However, it also became obvious why the partisans wanted him to accompany them to the wreckage. Their sense of honour dictated that they could not take the valuable materials that remained among the tangled wreckage, but they had to be formally 'given' the aircraft, which McCaig was pleased to sanction. By the time the party had returned to the village, he was totally exhausted, and was soon asleep on his inflated dinghy and wrapped in his parachute in a damp, but safe, cellar.

After two days, a big rugged-looking man with a soldier's bearing arrived. He was armed and exuded authority, and, in broken English, told McCaig that he would take him to the British Mission. The headman of the village was pleased when McCaig gave him all his survival equipment and parachute, but the unexpected gift of his .38 revolver and ammunition pouch brought a great beam of delight to his rugged face, and another bear hug. As he left with the guide, McCaig turned to wave to the people who had saved him and provided him with shelter and food.

The guide set off along a mountain track at a fast pace, which McCaig found exhausting. With only brief stops to drink from the mountain streams, they walked all day until it was dusk, when they arrived at a group of tents in a pine forest. He was shown to a tent in the centre of the partisan camp, where he collapsed with exhaustion onto a camp bed and waited for further developments. Shortly afterwards, a well-built American burst into the tent and announced that he was called Hank, was a member of a US Ranger group, and had arrived to escort him to the British Mission. His delight was tempered by the announcement that they would be leaving immediately in order to get down the mountain before daylight.

Greek partisans and their mules negotiate the harsh terrain.
(Imperial War Museum, London, E 29964)

Hank gave him some American rations before leaving to arrange a new guide and two mules for the onward journey.

Plans were soon made, and McCaig found himself sitting astride a wooden saddle on a mule. Not long after the three men set off, a light persistent drizzle began and they were soon soaking wet and cold. The journey was nearly all downhill, causing McCaig to slip forward against the iron-hard saddle which gave him great discomfort. The jarring of the mule's uncertain step as it struggled downhill in the black night added to the agony. McCaig described this gruelling journey as 'unreal, a kind of nightmare of misery and insecurity in an enveloping wet blackness'. The hours slipped away until his senses started to spin and slowly slip away. He heard distant voices and felt a hand shaking his shoulder, and then gently slapping his face. He had fallen from the mule in an exhausted faint. After a brief rest, they continued into the black, wet night. As dawn broke, they walked into a sleeping village beneath Mount Paikon, stopping in front of a house. Within minutes, a major of the British Raiding Support Regiment greeted him with a cup of tea. McCaig had finally arrived at the headquarters of the British Mission. The uncomplaining Greek guide who had walked the whole route down the mountain lifted him from the saddle, and led him into the comfort of a warm house.

The major lodged in the house where the owners soon made McCaig welcome. The wife insisted on washing all his clothes after she had prepared a bed for him. He removed his sodden clothes, and fell into the bed under the coarse blankets and animal skins. He slept for the next 20 hours. When he finally woke, something quickly shattered his drowsiness. He had been molested by bed bugs, and his body was covered in rashes, causing an indescribable itch. After a liberal sprinkling of bug powder, he joined the major, who arranged for a wireless message to be passed to Cairo announcing McCaig's safe arrival.

Over the next few days, McCaig accompanied the major to inspect a flat area where an airstrip was being prepared for a Dakota resupply flight at night. It was about 1,000 yards long and 50 yards wide just below the foothills. The area was being levelled and cleared, with piles of brushwood gathered at regular intervals along the sides. When lit, these provided the beacons to mark out the landing area. The radio operator for the mission was a half-Greek/half-Egyptian called Andreas, who was in daily contact with Cairo, and McCaig soon moved into his house. Time passed slowly without news of a pick-up, but the boredom was interrupted when the major asked McCaig to give a talk on the war situation to the villagers, with Andreas acting as the interpreter. With many references to the loyalty of the fighting Greeks, of Churchill, and the role of the RAF in attacking the Boche, the talk was assessed as a great success.

After more days of waiting, the message finally arrived announcing the arrival of the Dakota. That night, the men of the Raiding Support Regiment and the American Rangers gathered at the airstrip with the leaders of the Greek partisans to await the arrival of the Dakota loaded with arms and supplies. A defensive ring of partisans patrolled some miles from the airstrip to intercept any German patrols, as others stood by each brushwood pile ready to fire up the flare path. Eventually, the steady throbbing of aircraft engines broke the calm of the bright moonlit night. The aircraft flashed the correct identification letter and circled as the fires were lit. It completed its circuit and lined up with the crude flarepath before losing height to come over the edge of the field to land alongside the first flares, breaking to a standstill just before the end of the field. It quickly turned back along the runway, where willing hands soon had all the freight unloaded onto horse-drawn carts, which rapidly dispersed.

As the pilot restarted the engines, a number of Rangers clambered on board, and McCaig turned to thank the major and Andreas before he too climbed into the Dakota. He found himself sitting next to Hank, who commented that it was a more comfortable journey than their night mule ride through the mountains. The Dakota roared off down the bumpy strip and headed for Italy, arriving at Bari in the early hours of the morning. McCaig was taken to a reception centre, where he was debriefed and given a new uniform before being sent to a rest centre near Naples for two weeks. Just a month had passed since he had been shot down. During this time he had been sheltered and befriended by some of the poorest people in Europe, who steadfastly refused to allow the occupation of their country to undermine their efforts to gain their freedom. What little they had to offer they willingly shared with their unexpected visitor who was helping them to achieve their aim.

Dennis McCaig pictured the day after his return to Italy. (D. McCaig)

McCaig returned to 249 Squadron and continued on operations. On 26 February 1945, he took off for a reconnaissance along the Dalmatian coast, where he discovered two German patrol boats anchored in the harbour at Fiume. He and his number two turned to attack at low level through a curtain of anti-aircraft fire. After strafing the targets, he pulled away to sea when he noticed the deadly stream of glycol fluid. His engine had been hit. He started to climb as he headed out to sea, but it was soon apparent that he would have to bale out again. This time he was not so lucky. He was soon picked up by a German launch, and taken ashore for immediate interrogation before travelling by train to Germany, where he spent the rest of the war as a prisoner. On release, he remained in the RAF to complete 20 years' service, during which time he was awarded the MBE as a staff officer, and an AFC for his work developing the Swift fighter aircraft. He was also mentioned in despatches for anti-terrorist activities in Cyprus.

Chapter Twelve

Italy

WITH THE EXCEPTION OF BOMBER COMMAND'S occasional sorties to Milan and Turin, the air war did not arrive over Italy in any great force until the invasion of Sicily in July 1943. Thereafter, the Allied air forces mounted very large-scale operations over the country, and the majority of casualties fell to the intense light and medium anti-aircraft fire – the majority of the *Luftwaffe's* fighter force had been withdrawn to the Russian front.

Until the Italians negotiated an armistice soon after the Allied landings, evading capture in Italy was virtually impossible. The population were the enemy, German and Italian troops were based throughout the country in large numbers, and the only realistic route to freedom involved crossing the almost impenetrable barrier created by the mountains of the Alps. One who succeeded was Flight Lieutenant Tony Snell.

FROM SICILY TO SWITZERLAND

The Allies launched the invasion of Sicily during the early hours of 10 July 1943. Spitfire Vc aircraft of 242 Squadron operating from Malta provided cover for the amphibious landings near Gela on the south coast of the island. Leading one section of the fighters was Flight Lieutenant Tony Snell, a veteran of the North African campaign. Over the beach area he was attacked by Messerschmitt Bf 109 aircraft, and his engine was badly damaged and caught fire, forcing him to crash-land in a small clearing a few miles north of the Allied positions. He

Italy.

quickly vacated the aircraft and ran for cover towards a small stone building a few yards away. The German fighters turned in to strafe the crashed Spitfire and the building, where Snell discovered a Sicilian farmer lying on the floor.

Once the German fighters had flown off, the farmer took Snell to his home, where they looked at his escape maps to try and pinpoint his position, which they assessed to be some 10 miles inland from Gela. Snell was anxious to leave and get away from the area of his aircraft as quickly as possible. Thanking the farmer he left to work his way through scrub to the top of a hill in order to fix his position in relation to the coast. He was just about to emerge from the scrub when he discovered that he was on the outskirts of an Italian military camp. He retreated and decided to rest until it was dark before attempting to reach the Allied lines.

As it was growing dark he moved on, having decided to travel along the sides of the hills whenever possible in order to avoid radar sites and observation posts positioned on the top of the hills, and also to avoid roadblocks in the valleys. At one point he saw the silhouette of a sentry barring his way, so he retreated, knowing that he had no alternative other than to cross a meadow. He found a stick and hobbled slowly across the meadow with the stoop of an old man, hoping to be mistaken for a peasant.

Having walked for about two hours he arrived at what appeared to be a hut in a clearing with a large tree. He was considering how to avoid it when he saw the outline of two men rise up to a crouching position, followed by two flashes as they opened fire in his direction. He dodged behind a tree and returned their fire with his .45 automatic pistol. He started running, but came under fire from another direction, which he returned. Realizing that he was in a very dangerous situation, he shouted out, 'Comrade'. The firing stopped as eight or ten Italian soldiers approached him. He started speaking quickly in French, despite his limited knowledge of the language, but in the hope that they understood less. One of them asked in French if he was a friend of Italy, to which Snell replied that he was with the Vichy forces and was fighting with the Italians. With this remark, he put his pistol back in the holster with a flourish, but kept his hand on it as he gesticulated with the other. They appeared to believe him, and offered him a drink from a bottle of wine. He asked them for the direction of the enemy, the British and Americans, before ambling off feeling very uncomfortable as he turned his back on them. As soon as he was clear he reloaded his pistol before turning south to head for the coast.

As he headed south, he could tell by the flashes of gunfire that he was getting close to the front line. Having walked along the sides of the hills, he was aware that he had probably headed too far to the west, but he kept a constant check of his heading by reference to the Pole Star and his escape compass. He reached the coast road, which he was just about to cross, when a deep guttural voice from the darkness called, 'Halt!', but he continued walking slowly, which promptly generated the command, 'Hands up!' In the dim light he saw two men standing near a concrete pillbox about 10 yards away. He put his hands up with his pistol concealed in one, and began speaking in French. Suddenly, he was aware of a tinkling sound on the ground, which started to get uncomfortably closer. He leapt to the side of the road to dash away just as a grenade exploded, followed by gunfire. He took cover in some scrub, and held his fire in order not to give his position away. After a pause, he cautiously worked his way back across the road in the hope that they would expect him to escape in the first direction he had taken. The ruse worked and he was able to slip away.

When he had time to review his situation, he concluded that he had travelled too far to the west, and beyond the area of the beach-head. He worked his way further east where he could see gunfire, but it soon became apparent that he was in a defended area as he encountered fenced-off areas, trip wires and a minefield, which was marked out with tapes – a hazard he managed to carefully avoid before continuing to the east. As he approached a rise near the sea, he could see tracer firing in a northerly direction, which was soon countered by firing from the north. He concluded that the tracer must be from the Allies, and headed towards a copse near the position. He waited until the firing stopped, and then listened intently until he heard some twigs snapping. Thinking this must be an Allied patrol, he followed the noise, but was taken by surprise when he discovered he was on the edge of an airfield with fighters parked with equipment, which he mistook to be American, stacked close by.

He was moving very cautiously to try and determine if he was in Allied territory when he saw two sentries standing 20 yards away. They looked like Americans by the outline of their helmets, so he stood behind a bush and called out the password 'Desert Rats'. There was no reply, so he stepped out expecting an English-speaking challenge. Instead, two Germans stepped out with their light machine-guns pointing at him, and beckoned him forward. He tried his French trick again, but an officer arrived on the scene and marched him across the airfield with his hands above his head and the two guards a few paces behind. As his bluff had failed, he told them in English who he was. He was searched, but managed to transfer items from one pocket to another as he pretended to assist them. He was able to retain his silk escape map by using it as a handkerchief.

On reaching a wooden hut, his name, rank and number were taken and he was searched again. He was told that he was to sleep in the hut before meeting the Commandant in the morning. It was frustrating for him to see the movements of the Allies on the beachhead clearly, and it was also obvious that the Germans were very agitated. Suddenly, he was marched off to a clearing with an officer and two soldiers, each carrying a machine-pistol. He was ordered to kneel down, which he didn't understand until he was told again. He squatted and was looking at them wondering what they were going to do when a blue torch beam was shone on him, and he saw the shining barrels of the pistols pointing at him. He realized that he was about to be executed.

He instantly leapt to his feet, and immediately felt the impact of a bullet in his right shoulder, which knocked him sideways, but he did not fall. He ran as a fusillade of shots rang out, and there was a flash and bang behind him as a grenade exploded. He fell down a rocky slope, but got to his feet and continued running as more shots rang out and grenades exploded. He fell heavily again, this time into a crevice between two large boulders, unable to get up. He was in great pain, and he knew he had been hit many times, but he was particularly aware of the blood pumping from a vein in his shoulder. Fortunately, the Germans did not bother looking for him, but as the minutes passed he became weaker and thought he would die. Suddenly, his will to survive overtook his pain, making him determined to try and get to the Allied lines. He felt he had nothing to lose. Struggling to sit up, he discovered that his left arm was just usable, so he tore off his blood-soaked shirt to bind into a tourniquet, holding it tightly twisted under his right shoulder as he gathered his limp right arm in the crook of his left. He blacked out as he got to his feet, but managed to stumble a short distance to a better resting place, where he blacked out again.

He carried on in this manner until dawn, his rests getting longer as he became weaker, until he saw a guard post ahead. He realized that he would not survive much longer and must get help. He hoped they might be Allies as he stumbled forward before collapsing in the road. The guards had seen him, and called for a stretcher, but he was disgusted to see that they were German. He was placed on the ground when an officer arrived to say that the Commandant had ordered that he was to be shot for 'spying on the airfield'. Snell reminded him who he was and that his possessions and identity cards had been taken the night before, and he insisted on seeing the Commandant. A firing squad was assembled as the officer left, to return a few moments later with his identity card, and announcing that he was to be taken to a field hospital.

He was given a blood transfusion at the hospital, where he was soon operated on for the removal of a number of bullets and pieces of shrapnel. Two bullets had shattered his right shoulder, two had passed through his left arm and another had chipped his spine, coming to rest near it. Fifteen pieces of shrapnel were removed from his body and legs, with one piece severing the radial nerve of his left wrist. After two days, he was taken by ambulance to a hospital in Catania, where he stayed for six days. As the Allies advanced in Sicily, the hospital was evacuated, with the wounded being taken by hospital ship to Leghorn in northern Italy before being transferred to a hospital at Lucca, near Pisa, where he arrived on 23 July. He remained there until 26 September, when the Germans, who by then had taken control of the hospital after the Italian Armistice on 10 September, decided to take all the patients to Germany by train.

During his time in the hospital, Snell realized that the best chance of avoiding a transfer to a German POW camp once he had recovered was to abscond from the hospital. During the time he was at Lucca he hoarded all the concentrated food he could get hold of. He managed to obtain a binocular case from an Army officer, and he packed this with Horlicks tablets, chocolate, Marmite tablets, etc. He modified the case to fit on the strap of his water bottle, and he accumulated a store of ointment and dressings for his wounds. When he was strong enough to get up and walk, he walked round and round the hospital gardens every afternoon, gradually increasing the distance in his efforts to regain his strength and get as fit as possible.

Early on the morning of 26 September, all the patients were taken by ambulance under guard from the hospital to the railway station to board a hospital train. The carriage was laid out with three-tier bunks, and Snell chose one at the end, conveniently close to a large window that appeared to be open. There was a German guard with a rifle who spent most of the time in the middle of the carriage opposite the toilet. Snell agreed with Captain Huff of the USAAF that they would jump from the train together once it was dark.

A diversion was set up as the train slowed, and Huff jumped. Just as Snell was about to go, a German patrol entered the carriage, the window was slammed shut, and Snell regained his bunk without attracting attention. He immediately made arrangements for another attempt with Captain F. Lewis MC, and they waited for the train to slow again. As the train slowed, two other Army officers engaged the guard in conversation, and Snell climbed through the window clutching his water bottle and a Red Cross parcel. He steadied himself on the outside, and then jumped, being thrown over by the impact. He picked himself up and headed up the line, where he soon made contact with Lewis. After congratulating each other, they headed away from the lights of a nearby town, which they later discovered was Mantova.

They spent a miserable night in the open getting very cold and wet before setting off south across the Po Valley towards the lines of the advancing Eighth Army. After another miserable day they decided to approach a farm for food and shelter. They selected one without telephone lines, which Snell approached as Lewis kept watch. He was able to convince some farm workers that he was English, and they sent him to another farm, where the farmer proved willing to help them. He gave them food and shelter for the night, and the next morning, he provided farm labourers' clothes to put over their battledress, some food, and directions for the best route south.

For the next three days they followed the same routine, receiving help on each night, until they came to the River Po. Sentries guarded all the bridges, but a fisherman took them across in his boat. Eventually they came to an isolated farmhouse on the edge of the village of Fabrico. The farmer gave them blankets to sleep in a barn, and later in the evening, he invited them to listen to the BBC news. Both men were beginning to suffer from the effects of their wounds and asked to stay another night. They were fed and a friendly barber came to shave them. Just before they sat down for lunch, a man arrived with a typewritten note which said: 'Stay where you are, you are among friends. Tonight you will be taken to a place of safety'.

Two men arrived that evening to escort Snell and Lewis to the home of one of them, where clean dressings were put on their wounds, and they were given a good meal. They were then transferred to a larger house, to which they were admitted once they had proved their identity. Here they were introduced to a number of people who were in the Italian Resistance movement. They were given sumptuous food and wine and provided with excellent accommodation for the next three days. They were given new clothes, which transformed them from 'peasants to gentry'. A journey to Modena by train was arranged for them, accompanied by a member of the organization. A prearranged signal identified their next contact, Mario Luglui and they followed him at an interval of 50 yards to a house where they were concealed for the next month. Towards the end of the period two British soldiers and two South African majors joined them.

Shortly after arriving in Modena, Snell was approached by the leader of the local Resistance movement who told him that he had a special job for him. He wanted him to go to the mountains with him to inspect a high plateau with a view to using it as an airfield for landing arms and supplies for the partisans, and for evacuating escaped POWs. He met a young partisan leader who took him on a six-hour bus journey into the mountains south of Modena. He showed him his concealed automatic pistol and said he would use it if anyone attempted to capture them. The bus arrived on the outskirts of the village of Sestola where the young man lived, but thick fog prevented them from going to the site for the next two days. Eventually, the party was able to leave early in the morning of the third day to climb to the site near the summit of Mount Cimone, which proved totally unsuitable as a landing ground, but was ideal for receiving supplies by parachute. Supplies could be taken away by mule packs for a mile or two to an area where there was a track suitable for woodcutters' tractors and lorries. Before leaving, Snell measured the site and drew a plan.

The partisan leader explained that he wanted sufficient arms of all descriptions to equip 10,000 men who were available to attack the Germans once the Allied armies' advance reached the area. Back at Modena, Snell drew up an elaborate plan of the situation, including full information about the use of reception parties and signals to be used. He included his sketch map of the dropping zone.

After a month at the first house in Modena, the evaders were moved to Silvio Baschieri's flat. His daughter Anna stole some identity cards from the town hall and had them made up with false information. During this time plans were drawn up to get the four men out of Italy. After three more weeks, the two South Africans reached Switzerland successfully, and the Resistance leader announced that they planned to send Snell and Lewis by the same route. They were provided with 40,000 lire each and appropriate clothing.

On the night of 1 December, they were escorted to Modena railway station and they met the leader's two brothers, who took them to Milan, where they met the guide for the next stage of the journey. At 7 a.m. the next day, they left with him on a long train journey, during which time they had a narrow escape because their tickets

Anna Baschieri who stole identity cards to assist Tony Snell's evasion. (A. Snell)

were at fault. After a meal at the guide's house, they set off with another young man who escorted them to a cottage where they spent the night. Next day he took them by train to a small hamlet just west of Tirano on the Swiss frontier, and they spent the afternoon in a cowshed there.

That night they met two guides who were to accompany them over the mountains and across the Swiss frontier. They waited all night, but the signal that the frontier was clear did not arrive until dawn on 4 December. The path up the mountain was long and very arduous for the two men, as they were still recovering from their serious wounds. They finally reached the frontier after a five-hour climb, and said goodbye to their Italian helpers. They walked to the nearest Swiss village, where they were put in touch with the British Consul, who arranged for them to go to Berne. Snell remained in Switzerland for four months recovering from his wounds and arduous travels before returning to England in October 1944.

Tony Snell's bid for freedom is one of the most remarkable efforts by RAF aircrew in the Second World War. Escaping death by a firing squad by a split second, and evading capture despite his serious

Tony Snell (left) with his friend Bob Large shortly after his return to England and still recovering from another operation on his left arm. (R. Large)

wounds, required courage and fortitude of the very highest order, not to mention great presence of mind and alertness. After the war, the full details of his escape came to light, and in July 1946 it was announced in the *London Gazette* that Tony Snell had been awarded the DSO, one of the very few awarded exclusively for escaping from the enemy.

⌒

Following the armistice, the attitude of the Italian population changed dramatically, and with few exceptions they were prepared to assist escapers and evaders. Partisan groups became established in the north of the country, and this provided some support for those who chose to head for neutral Switzerland. There were two other alternatives. Evaders could head south and hope to meet up with the advancing armies, although this involved a long trek as the advance slowed, followed by negotiating a route through the battle area and the German front line. Others headed towards Rome in anticipation of its capitulation, but they too were disappointed until June 1944. However, in September 1943, Major Sam Derry had escaped from a train taking him from Italy to a POW camp in Germany, and had made his way to Rome, where he contacted the British Minister in the Vatican City and was invited by him to coordinate the activities of Allied escapers and evaders who were arriving in Rome in increasing numbers. Shortly afterwards he established the 'Rome Organization', and he has recounted his remarkable activities in his book *The Rome Escape Line*.

Derry's activities in Rome had been brought about by the escapes made by Allied POWs from the Italian camps left unguarded following the armistice. Many POWs expected their release to follow the Italian surrender, but the sudden arrival of the German troops to transport them to captivity in Germany prompted many escapes from the Italian camps, and later from trains carrying the unfortunate prisoners north.

Within a matter of days of the Italian surrender, Advance Headquarters 'A' Force issued a new directive to aircrew operating over Italy. The most important point was to remind them that the Germans would treat Italy as an occupied country and would therefore institute all the rigorous systems of control on the population, including identity cards, a system of travel control, the guarding of key control points and borders, and the inauguration of a native police force of their own selection. In effect, the conditions prevailing in Italy would be exactly the same as those in force in other occupied countries such as France, Holland, Belgium, etc. This approach by the Germans did have one advantage for the evader – the vast majority of the local population could be considered friendly.

Since the Allied armies were advancing north through Italy, aircrew were reminded of the importance of constantly being aware of the position of their own front lines and the bomb line. This would be particularly important for those evaders who chose to travel south to meet up with the Allies. As in other European countries, aircrew were recommended to avoid towns and to approach poor farmers in isolated hilly areas. With so many POWs escaping from the Italian camps, it was recommended that evaders should not travel in groups, and should be aware that the Germans were using low-flying light aircraft for searches. They had also put agents, posing as escaped Allied personnel or Italians, throughout occupied areas of Italy in an attempt to find who were helping evaders and where they were being hidden. German reprisals were as vicious as those in force in other occupied countries.

Specific advice was given for those who approached the battle zone, an area that evaders should approach in daylight so that the movements of enemy troops could be observed. The 'front' consisted of patrols, gun positions and small concentrations, and Germans were likely to shoot people in the area. With the Germans retreating, it was important for aircrew to be aware that they could encounter groups of the enemy behind the front in small, probably well-hidden groups. This created considerable fear among the local people, making it more difficult to make contact with any helpers. Reaching safety across the battle zone was a difficult and dangerous business.

THROUGH THE ITALIAN BATTLE ZONE

Twenty-three-year-old Flying Officer Jim Cole was the navigator/bomb aimer in the crew of the deputy leader of a formation of 12 Baltimore light bombers of 55 Squadron detailed to attack a road junction north-east of Mignano, 15 miles south of Cassino, on 20 October 1943. He was lying in the nose of the aircraft, having just released the bombs, when there was a very loud bang followed by a vicious yellow flash, which came down the side of his position. An anti-aircraft shell had burst on the starboard side of the aircraft very near the pilot's cockpit and blown the aircraft apart.

Cole was hurled forward as he experienced a terrific blast, followed by complete peace as he found himself floating through the air. He immediately pulled the ripcord of his parachute, but was alarmed when it came away in his hand. He managed to locate the end of the wire and release cord, which he pulled. To his relief, the parachute opened. On the way down he saw another parachute, but was unable to attract the attention of the survivor. He made a soft landing on his back with his parachute hooked up in a tree. The explosion had scorched his hair and blown off his wristwatch, left flying-boot and leather helmet. Fortunately, the radio lead of the latter had become entangled round his left ankle, a very lucky break for Cole, as he was able to improvise and make it into a shoe, which he wore throughout the time he was evading the enemy.

After landing and gathering up his equipment, he ran into a wood at the foot of a hill on the side of a valley, where he collapsed exhausted and crawled into a bush and hid. Within a very short time, German soldiers came past and scoured the hillside looking for him, keeping up their search for over four hours before moving on. However, they were very much in evidence over the next few days,

Baltimore bombers on an Italian airfield are prepared for another raid on German targets. (Air Historical Branch)

although their failure to find him gave Cole confidence that his hiding place was good, and he decided to remain for three days to allow the search to subside. During this time he lived off his emergency rations.

At dawn on 24 October he decided it was safe enough to start walking south towards the Allied lines. His progress was painfully slow, as he soon discovered that there were many German trenches and gun positions, so he dared not cross any territory that he could not survey first. He worked his way higher up the hill where boulders and bushes gave him some cover, and gave him a better view of the route ahead. Apart from the German positions that were close by, his main concern was a lack of water, and his attempts to locate a spring or a mountain stream failed. On the fifth morning he decided to utilize the dew. He found that by wiping the long grass with his handkerchief he could pick up enough moisture to squeeze into his water bottle. It took him an hour to half-fill the bottle, and although it looked muddy it tasted excellent after a few days without anything to drink. For food he experimented with eating young grass and acorns, but found them unpalatable.

During the daytime, Cole stayed under cover and used the time to observe and memorize the positions of guns, trenches and anti-tank traps. He also saw soldiers mining the approaches to a bridge. There was very little traffic during the day, but it increased considerably at night. (Owing to the extensive daylight bombing campaign of the road and rail systems by Allied bombers, German transport was forced to move almost exclusively at night.) He travelled southwards at dusk and at dawn, but found the nights when he was resting very cold. By the sixth night he was beginning to feel desperate, and decided that he would have to descend to the valley to try and get more water. He took an energy tablet before setting off in search of food and water. He found six figs on a tree, and a stream provided him with some brackish water, which he purified with his Halazone tablets. This made him feel better, so he decided to carry out a reconnaissance of the immediate area in the hope of finding more food and a better resting place.

During his search, he discovered that what appeared to be haycocks in the fields were, in fact, machine-gun pits with moveable lids. There were also cunningly concealed infantry trenches under most of the hedges. It was during this search that he was almost discovered. While moving his hands under a bush to see if there was any fruit, he discovered that it was a camouflaged tent whose occupant was snoring. In his hurry to get away, he tripped and alerted a guard standing less than 20 yards away. He had seen the silhouette of the guard, but since the German had stood perfectly still, he initially mis-identified him as a tree. Fortunately, Cole managed to slip away. Later that night, he was looking for some grapes when he heard heavy footsteps approaching. He immediately froze with his hands held above his head in an attempt to look like the silhouette of a tree. The two German soldiers passed within a few feet!

The following morning he went back to the cover of the hills. He was not feeling well as the effects of the energy tablets wore off, so he remained in his hiding place in bushes for the next 36 hours. On the eighth morning, he heard some Italian voices and discovered that they belonged to a family who appeared to be living in nearby caves. He watched them all day before deciding to approach them to ask for food and water. He identified himself with his blood chit, and asked for their help. He received a very warm welcome and was given soup, meat and bread, with as much water as he wanted. When he had finished, they gave him a bottle of water, some bread, cold meat and a blanket before pointing up the hill, indicating that he would find more Italian peasants. That night he slept well under the cover of the rocks, wrapped in his blanket.

On the afternoon of 29 October he met a peasant boy who was looking after a flock of sheep and goats. The boy went to fetch his father, who told him to remain under cover during the daytime. That night he came to fetch Cole and hid him in a mud hut. After a meal of vegetable soup and dry bread, he slept by the fire with three peasants, their wives, about 15 children and two goats as his companions. It rained hard that night, and he was thankful that it was the first night that he had managed to rest under a roof. The next day he hid in the fields, but returned in the evening for a meal, which he had just finished when one of the peasants rushed in to tell them that German troops were on their way up the hill. Cole hurried out to hide in a thicket a mile away, where he had to spend the night in torrential rain. His Italian helpers brought him some bread and water in the morning, but it was the last time that he saw them. The next day the Germans arrived and destroyed the hut.

Cole spent the next day and night in his uncomfortable thicket, while it continued to rain as the temperature fell. Having no food or water, he decided to move on, but he soon came across the first evidence that the advancing Allied armies were approaching, so he resolved to find a new hiding place and rest as soon as possible. After a mile he came to a ravine, where he met two Italians, one of them being a man he had met at the mud hut. They showed him a new place to hide and provided him with food and water. Within two days he found himself in the crossfire between American and German artillery forces. As long as the shells kept dropping short he felt safe, and as the day progressed he was able to judge the approach of the bomb line as the Allies advanced.

On the morning of 3 November he saw an American advance patrol moving forward into the ravine, so he crept forward from his hiding place to meet them and warn them of the camouflaged machine-gun pits and mines that lay ahead. He contacted the patrol and was being escorted to meet the officer in charge when the German forces opened fire on them. The group scattered and managed to lose contact with each other. Cole decided to climb up to the ridge behind the ravine, and there he found himself under the trajectory of the shells from both sides.

Later in the day, he met two Italians who were working for the American intelligence organization, and they took him to two

American soldiers who had been cut off from their advanced forces while setting up a forward observation post. The group decided to make a dash for it, and they scrambled through rocks and scrub, taking cover whenever they heard the scream of shells. They got over the high ridge, and after two hours they managed to get to the valley floor. They headed for the American lines, making contact with them west of the village of Presenzano. Cole was able to identify himself before being taken to the main headquarters, where he was able to give details of the defences he had encountered along the Mignano Valley. He was soon driven away from the battle area to be handed over to Captain de Villiers of the Grenadier Guards. A few days later he was driven to Foggia, where he rejoined his squadron for a few days before being flown to hospital in Tunis to spend three weeks recovering from his ordeal. On 17 December, two months after he had been shot down, he arrived at Prestwick to start some leave.

Chapter Thirteen

Poland

POLAND FORMS PART OF THE NORTHERN PLAIN of Europe, and except for the Carpathian Mountains in the extreme south, it consists of rolling country, with many forests, especially in the south-east.

In 1939 Poland was partitioned by Germany and Russia. The Germans incorporated a large part of their share into the Reich itself, the remainder being formed into the so-called General Government. There was, however, little distinction between the two parts of German-occupied Poland. German control was complete wherever they were able to make it effective, but they did not dare to venture into the forests of southern and central Poland, which were largely under the control of Polish and Russian partisans.

Until the Mediterranean Allied Air Forces (MAAF) established airfields in Italy towards the end of 1943, air operations over Poland were minimal, but it was not until the middle of 1944 that any significant operations took place. With the advance of the Russian Army westwards in the spring, the resupply of Polish partisan groups who were harassing the rear areas of the German Fourth Panzer Army became a regular activity for the long-range Special Duties squadrons equipped with Halifax and Liberator aircraft. These sorties, often involving a round trip of 1,750 miles, most over enemy-held territory, were some of the most hazardous of the war, and losses were very high. During the extensive operations to support General Bor and his Polish Home Army's uprising in Warsaw, which started on 1 August, Polish, Royal Air Force and South African squadrons based in Italy flew 181 sorties over a 22-night period, losing 31 aircraft – a loss rate of over 17 per cent. Sadly, their efforts were in vain. With the Russians watching from just a few miles across the River Vistula, Bor and his brave Polish patriots were finally crushed at the beginning of October.

Throughout the autumn of 1944, the Russian Army continued to advance westwards, and the Polish partisans were involved in numerous major battles as the Germans retreated. The forested area to the east of Krakow witnessed the fiercest battles waged by any underground army during the Second World War. Fighting alongside the Polish partisans were large forces of Russian partisans. Air supply to the Poles continued throughout the period until the Russian armies had swept on towards the German frontiers.

There were many problems facing aircrew shot down over Poland. MI 9 had been unable to set up escape lines, and evaders had little choice but to head for Russian-held territory. There were many different factions and groups among the Polish and Russian partisans, and there was the ever-present threat posed by a retreating German Army. Despite their position as one of the Allied Powers, Russia had its own agendas, and formal arrangements to assist escapers and evaders were difficult to create. Even where they existed, the Russian armies were so vast that agreements reached at the staff level often failed to permeate to the front-line commanders. In the forests, apart from Polish and Russian partisans, there were numerous independent bandits who would shoot any wanderer just to get his boots. An additional hazard was low-flying aircraft, which flew regular patrols looking for the large bands of partisans.

By the summer of 1944 specific briefings on evasion tactics in Poland had been prepared. Aircrew were reminded that the most valuable aid to an evader in Poland was the loyalty and patriotism of the population. As in other areas, aircrew were advised to approach only poor and isolated farms and to avoid towns, lines of communication, and large rivers. Almost inevitably the country people would be able to put evaders in contact with the partisans.

Both Polish and Russian partisans were well organized, and they controlled most of the huge forested areas in the south and east of the country. The two groups worked alongside each other, but did not cooperate very closely. The chief necessity when in the hands of the partisans was for evaders to be able to identify themselves, and it was essential to carry the blood chit to help overcome the inevitable language difficulties. Aircrew were advised to retain their weapons, 'as proficiency in their use makes a great impression on the partisans'. It was inadvisable to talk politics with either the Poles or the Russians, and with the latter it was very important to obey all instructions. There was very little scope for the Poles to evacuate evaders, and aircrew were advised to ask to be passed to the Russians, who had radio links to Moscow, allowing identities to be checked with the British Mission.

The Germans rarely ventured into the forests, but they bombed and machine-gunned them every day, particularly in areas where the partisans were known to be living. Living conditions in the forests were very uncomfortable – aircrew were even advised to carry de-lousing powder as part of their escape kit. There was also a warning about the strength of the vodka, a drink consumed by both the Poles and Russians. Although considered a very useful protection against the cold, it was very strong. The Polish variety was 45 per cent alcohol, whereas the Russian version was about 90 per cent, and it was advised that both should be heavily diluted and drunk while taking food. Finally, aircrew were told that once they were in the hands of the partisans, it was very unlikely that the Germans would capture them, since the partisans would keep them out of harm's way. However, if there was a risk of capture, it was better to fight to the death, because the Germans would not hesitate to use torture in order to obtain information.

WITH THE POLISH AND RUSSIAN PARTISANS

Warrant Officer Tom Storey and his crew of seven took off from Brindisi in their 148 Squadron Halifax IIA aircraft at 7.30 p.m. on 23 April 1944. They were on a Special Duties operation to deliver arms and supplies to the Polish partisans in the Lublin area. On the outward journey, Storey had to shut the port inner engine down as it overheated, but he decided to press on. The aircraft was approaching the dropping zone at low level when the port outer engine suddenly failed. Storey jettisoned the load, but he found that he could no longer control the aircraft, so he ordered the crew to bale out. As he left the aircraft, he saw another one immediately behind the four-engine Halifax. The flight engineer, 21-year-old Sergeant Charles Keen, remembered seeing a Junkers 88 night-fighter just before he baled out, and it seems probable that it shot the supply aircraft down.

All the crew baled out successfully but were scattered on landing. Storey was the last to leave, by which time the aircraft was very low, and his parachute had only just opened when he hit the ground hard, injuring both legs and suffering concussion. When he recovered consciousness, he found himself on the edge of a field, where he buried his parachute and life-jacket. He had great difficulty walking, and quickly realized that he would need help, so he limped towards a nearby village, where he unsuccessfully knocked on a number of doors. One building was lit up, but as he approached from the back garden, he saw a German sentry on the gate, and he retreated as quickly as possible. He learned later that the building was being used as a barracks for eight soldiers and two members of the Gestapo.

He went to another house and was just about to knock on the door when it opened and a youth came out. Storey grabbed him before he could make a noise and whispered 'RAF, English' in his ear, managing to convince the youth, who then took him to a farmer's cottage next door. Storey had a modest knowledge of German, and he was able to explain who he was and his situation to the farmer, who offered to give him shelter for the night, but he would have to give him up in the morning as German troops were staying only a few doors away. Storey said that he would leave straight away in that case, but if the Germans subsequently caught him, he would tell them that the farmer had helped him. This prospect worried the farmer, who immediately fetched his son. Two more men were summoned, and together with the farmer and his son they discussed the situation, finally agreeing to help him. Before dawn, the group carried him to a nearby wood. The Poles had an intricate system of signs, passwords and sentries, all of which had to be negotiated before Storey and his helpers reached a camouflaged dugout, which turned out to be the headquarters of the local partisan group.

Storey remained under guard at the dugout for the next 36 hours. On the morning of 26 April, Lieutenant 'Grom', the Group Commander of the region, arrived and greeted Storey with a 'Heil Hitler!' Storey promptly advised him that he was English and spoke German because it was the only common language with his helpers. 'Grom' then invited Storey to write down the names of all his crew and the serial number of his crashed aircraft. This satisfied him, and later that afternoon, Charles Keen was brought to the dugout.

After baling out, Keen had landed in a marshy area south of Tarnow not far from the wreckage of the Halifax. He found travelling across country difficult in the marshland, and was forced to walk along a road. He had lost his boots during the parachute descent, and this

Some of the Polish partisans heavily involved in the rescue of RAF aircrews shot down over Poland. Zygmunt was killed a short time later. (C. Keen)

slowed his progress as he tried to get as far away from the crash sight as possible. He called at a house in an attempt to get food and some boots, but the old lady was too frightened to open the door. He walked along the country road all through the night, passing through numerous woods. Just as dawn was breaking, he heard footsteps and he threw himself into a ditch just before three German soldiers passed. He remained in the wood all day and resumed his journey as darkness fell. He found a woodcutter's cottage and again tried to get some food and boots, but was warned that there were many Germans in the area, and he had to continue walking. During his walk through a wood the following night he met two teenage Polish boys, when he was able to explain his predicament. One of them ran off to return sometime later with food and an old pair of boots. By pointing to his watch, the boys indicated that they would return later in the morning, at which point Keen fell asleep. He woke at noon to find two men with revolvers drawn standing over him. By repeatedly saying 'RAF' and showing his uniform and identity discs, he made them understand that he was English. They gave him some paper and told him to write down the names of his crew. They then took him a very short distance to the dugout, where he was delighted to meet his pilot, Tom Storey. During his sleep, Keen had been in the same wood a few hundred yards away.

Over the next two nights, the partisans tried to move Storey and Keen across the River San, but the appropriate coded torch signals were not received from the other bank, and the attempt had to be abandoned. Acting as the courier between the groups was 16-year-old 'Nina' Mierzwinska, who travelled large distances on horseback in order to carry messages. On the night of 27 April, Flight Sergeant Pat Stradling and Sergeant Jim Hughes, the two air gunners, were brought to the dugout.

Stradling and Hughes had landed either side of a railway line south of Tarnow. They both headed for a nearby wood to spend the following day under cover. By a fortunate coincidence, they had chosen the same wood and they soon met up with each other. At dawn they saw a German Fieseler Storch observation aircraft flying low over the area, and they decided to stay in the wood until it was dark, when they headed off in a northerly direction. Two days later, they saw a group of Polish farm labourers working in the fields, and they watched them all day, intending to approach them once it got dark. Late that night they went to the nearby farm, where they were given some food and hidden in a loft. Shortly afterwards, two men arrived and the two evaders were able to convince them of their identity. They were then asked to describe the appearance of Storey and Keen. Twenty-four hours later, they were taken to the dugout, where they rejoined their two colleagues.

Throughout the four days since the Halifax had crashed, the

Germans had brought in an extra 300 troops to the immediate area to reinforce the extensive search for the crew, which included regular sweeps at very low level by the Fieseler Storch. They had also taken 50 hostages from the neighbourhood. In addition, very large German forces were massing in the area against a 7,000-strong Polish partisan force. Therefore, once the four men had joined up, 'Grom' decided that he must move them away from the area as soon as possible. In an attempt to avoid the Germans, 'Grom' decided to travel across an area of treacherous marshes and away from the forested area. With the young 'Nina' leading the way on her horse, and with an escort of partisans, the airmen travelled through the marsh area by horse and cart for another attempt to cross the River San. Following the earlier abortive attempt, 40 partisans from the Zamosc Group, led by Second Lieutenant Kmicic, crossed the river from the north to augment the local group in case it proved necessary to fight their way across the river. In the event, this proved unnecessary and the river crossing was successful. Kmicic was given the responsibility of safeguarding the four airmen until they could be evacuated, and he led the group well away from the area to Bilgoraj in the Ulanow district, where the four evaders were sheltered in farmhouses and woods.

There were numerous groups of Russian partisans in the area who received regular supplies by parachute. Storey asked to be taken to one of the Russian groups, where he met the commander, Lieutenant Kunicki. 'Nina', who was bilingual, accompanied him to act as the interpreter. He agreed to assist them, and the four evaders were handed over by Kmicic and his Polish colleagues, who had done so much for them. Kunicki's young radio operator, 'Valentina', contacted Moscow and forwarded details of the four men. Over the next few weeks, the four airmen lived rough in the woods with the Russians. Storey and Kunicki went out almost every day looking for suitable fields for a transport aircraft to land. After three weeks, a Russian aircraft dropped supplies, firearms and an agent onto a field selected by them. The agent's job was to select and prepare a field suitable for a Dakota. A large cornfield was assessed to be suitable, and it was flattened while the group waited for radio confirmation of an aircraft's arrival. Eventually, on the night of 6/7 June, the group moved to the field to set out a landing strip. The Dakota arrived, and after an exchange of coded signals the flarepath of hand-held torches was lit and the aircraft landed. Arms and supplies were unloaded before wounded Russian partisans were loaded into the aircraft, together

With the Russian partisan leader, Lieutenant Kunicki, and his radio operator, Valentina. The RAF aircrew are left to right, Keen, Hughes, Storey and Stradling. (C. Keen)

with some women and children. The four RAF evaders made their farewells to Kunicki, 'Nina' and their helpers before boarding the aircraft to take off on the next stage of their journey to freedom. Within days of their departure, the Germans, with a force of 40,000 men, launched a massive attack against the Polish and Russian partisans, the biggest battle in Europe against a partisan force. A number of the helpers who had assisted the RAF men were killed, including the young Russian radio operator, 'Valentina.'

The four men were taken to Kiev, where they spent seven days in a hotel at the headquarters of the Ukrainian partisan movement as the guests of Lieutenant Colonel Vicktor Khrapko, the officer in command, who treated them most courteously. A woman interpreter offered them a bath, their first for two months, an experience that allowed them to feel as if they had rejoined the human race. Charles Keen recalled that 'she also offered food, drink and a woman . . . in that order'. They left Kiev on 13 June and were flown to Moscow, where they were met by a Russian General accompanied by Air Commodore Roberts and some of his staff from the British Mission. They were taken to the headquarters of the Mission, where they were

Storey and his crew in Kiev with Lieutenant Colonel Vicktor Khrapko and a female interpreter. (C. Keen)

formally handed over by the Russian General. They found themselves treated as celebrities since they were the first RAF aircrew to have been flown back to freedom from behind German lines in Poland.

After two weeks recovering in Moscow they were put on a train for Murmansk, a journey that took four days. They spent two days in the Intourist Hotel before boarding HMS *Matchless* to sail for Scapa Flow, arriving there on 8 July. It was the end of a journey that had started in southern Italy 10 weeks earlier.

After recovering from their ordeal, Tom Storey was posted to St Athan as a unit test pilot, and Charles Keen left for Canada, where he flew with the Transatlantic Ferry Unit. The two gunners did not return to flying duties. A number of the Polish partisans lost their lives in the great battle of June 1944, but 'Grom', Lieutenant Kunicki and Second Lieutenant Kmicic all survived. So too did the daring young 'Nina', who later married an Englishman and settled in Southampton.

SHOT DOWN OVER WARSAW

The aircrews of the Special Duties squadrons made desperate efforts to drop supplies to the Polish Home Army during the Warsaw Uprising of August and September 1944. Flying at very low level and slow speed to ensure that the supplies landed in the very small dropping-zones, the aircraft made an easy target for the anti-aircraft defences, resulting in the loss of many aircraft. The majority of aircrew were killed, but some managed to parachute to safety, and a few evaded capture.

Flight Lieutenant Allan Hammet DFM RAAF from Melbourne was a wireless operator and a veteran of bomber operations over Germany when he was posted to Italy to join 178 Squadron, equipped with the four-engine Liberator bomber. At 6 p.m. on 16 August he and his crew took off from Foggia to drop supplies to the beleaguered Poles in Warsaw. The dropping-zone was found and the big bomber emerged unscathed from the intense anti-aircraft fire before turning south for the long flight back to Italy. South of Warsaw, the aircraft was attacked by a night-fighter and set on fire. Just before he died from bullet wounds, the pilot gave the order to bale out. Wounded in the arms and legs, Hammet was the only member of the crew to escape before the aircraft crashed in flames. He landed in a field 15 miles east of Krakow, and immediately buried his harness and life-jacket before heading north-east.

He walked for the next two nights, hiding in woods during the day, but on the third day he realized that he must get help and have his wounds attended to. He approached an isolated farm, where he was made comfortable before a nurse arrived accompanied by a member of the local partisan group who was able to converse in French. He was given food and had his wounds dressed before leaving at 3 a.m. on a horse and cart to a house on a large estate. He was visited by a doctor, given some civilian clothes and taken to join a group of partisans at Slaboszow. He remained with them for six weeks, living in the woods and regaining his strength.

About 20 September he took part in his first operation with the partisans when they mounted a raid for arms, ammunition and clothes, which they obtained from a small group of German soldiers without a fight. Three days later they raided a sugar factory. Eight Germans were killed and the group removed all the sugar, which was later distributed to the local population. A week later he learnt of a Miss Walker who was in Warsaw, and he was taken by the partisans to try and locate her, but his 10-day search was unsuccessful. By the end of October he had rejoined the partisan group. Within a few days he was involved with them in the shooting down of a Fieseler Storch observation aircraft by machine-gun and rifle fire, killing the pilot. The Germans sent out a reprisal force of about 100 Ukrainians from the nearby German garrison. A partisan force, including Hammet, met and opposed them, and in the fierce fight that followed, eight of the enemy were killed for the loss of eight partisans, including two escaped British POWs. Hammet was not aware of their involvement until after the event, and was unable to obtain any details of their identity. A few days after this engagement, news came that three of the Ukrainian soldiers were hiding in a peasant's hut nearby. Hammet led a small party to attack the hut, and threw a Mills bomb into the room they occupied. He did not wait to see the results, but learned later that they had been killed.

In November he was taken to a house where he was sheltered, during which time two British soldiers joined him, and they stayed together until the Russians arrived in mid-January 1945 to liberate them. The three men were moved to Czestahowa in February, where Hammet met Flying Officer Wlodzimierz Bernhardt of the Polish Air Force, who had gathered together almost 500 Allied POWs, and set up a reception centre.

Bernhardt was the bomb aimer of an all-Polish crew of a 301 (Polish) Squadron Halifax that had taken off from Brindisi, also on 16 August, to drop supplies near Warsaw. They had completed the sortie successfully and were heading back to Italy when three Junkers 88 night-fighters attacked the aircraft 40 miles east of Krakow. With the aircraft crippled, the crew baled out, and Bernhardt landed in a tree. Sadly, his wireless operator, Warrant Officer Bachanys, was shot and killed as he was descending in his parachute. Bernhardt soon established contact with a local civilian, who took him to his home, where he fed and clothed him before putting him in contact with the local partisan group. After his identity had been checked, he joined another group and spent the next two months taking part in their attacks. Their work consisted mainly of attacking road convoys, shooting Gestapo officials, and rounding up and disarming small German posts and storage sites. The group were in wireless communication with England and Italy and were able to inform the authorities that he was safe.

In October, Bernhardt was wounded during an attack, and he was taken to live with a family who sheltered him for a few weeks until arrangements were made for him to go to a rendezvous to be picked up by an aircraft. Unfortunately, bad weather prevented the aircraft landing, but Bernhardt was pleased to see that four other members of his crew were also at the rendezvous. He returned to stay with another family, where he remained with two of his crew, going out on 'many anti-Nazi patrols' until the Russians arrived on 6 January 1945. On their arrival Bernhardt and his partisan colleagues hid their arms and were disbanded. He then assumed the identity of a Polish workman who had never left the country, having obtained the appropriate forged documents.

Towards the end of January the Polish Militia arrested him, but thanks to a deputation by the local inhabitants, he was released with apologies. He left for Krakow on 1 February in an attempt to get back to his squadron. On arrival he assumed the identity of a French-Canadian, again with the appropriate papers, and soon discovered a large group of Allied POWs. It appeared that nothing was being done for them, so Bernhardt made contact with the Polish YMCA. Together with another Polish airman, also posing as a French-Canadian, he set up an organization with contacts in the YMCA to house and feed a group of 115 men, with a further 50 sheltered in private houses. He established an office to coordinate the operation, and a regular Staff Sergeant of the British Army gave him a great deal of help with the administration. They were able to obtain money and food from the Polish underground movement to run the organization.

Towards the end of February he was called to a conference with the Russians, who told him that arrangements were being made to repatriate the POWs and that transport would soon be available. Food and accommodation was promised, but it was never forthcoming. Eventually, on 23 February, a party of POWs and evaders arrived from Czestochowa under the command of Flight Lieutenant Hammet, and the two groups combined under his command. The party grew to almost 800 over the next three weeks before they were finally put on a train for Odessa on the Black Sea, where they embarked on the SS *Moreton Bay*, arriving in England at the end of March.

Of all those living under German occupation, few suffered more than the Poles, but their faith in the Allies never diminished, and they made great sacrifices to help Allied escapers and evaders. That Poland did not achieve its freedom at the end of a bloody conflict, which started with the grotesque rape of the country by Hitler's Panzers, remains one of the greatest tragedies of the Second World War.

PART FOUR

The Far East

Chapter Fourteen

Introduction

SOME MONTHS BEFORE JAPAN ATTACKED PEARL HARBOR, it was decided to establish an MI 9 organization in India Command. The task was entrusted to Major W. R. P. Ridgeway, who worked in a particularly secret sub-section of the General Staff (Intelligence) Branch, GSI (d), in the New Delhi Headquarters, which was responsible for deception in addition to the MI 9 and MI 19 roles. In March 1942 it was decided to form an independent section, GSI (e), with Ridgeway in charge of a staff of six officers, including a flight lieutenant. In addition to this, Lieutenant Colonel Leslie Ride, an escaper from the garrison in Hong Kong, formed an MI 9 operational organization, known as the British Army Aid Group (BAAG), in China. The remarkable exploits of Ride and his team are not covered in this book, but the reader is recommended to consult Edwin Ride's *British Army Aid Group – Hong Kong Resistance 1942–1945*.

During 1942 the main emphasis of GSI (e) work was on the MI 19 – prisoners of war – side, and little was possible with the staff available to undertake more than basic training and the issue of a limited number of aids and devices for evasion to RAF units in Bengal Command. Early in 1943 GSI (e) was reorganized, creating a clearer definition between evaders and the needs of POWs in Japanese camps across South-East Asia. However, lack of experienced staff prevented any major developments, and in an attempt to offset this handicap, the organization's activities were modelled on the experiences of MI 9 in Europe and the Middle East. It took some time to recognize that circumstances were very different, and further modifications were necessary in order to carry out successful operations.

The turning point came in the autumn of 1943, when Lord Mountbatten arrived as the Supreme Commander of South-East Asia Command (SEAC). A study identified the need for more personnel, and also recommended that MI 9 and MI 19 should operate separately, albeit maintaining a close liaison. With the increased activity of the United States forces in the SEAC area, the experiences of Europe highlighted the value of a joint organization of MI 9 and the American MIS – X. It was agreed that the two organizations should be integrated on the lines of the European system, and to be called 'E Group' South-East Asia and India Command. (In the event, the two never established the same relationship that existed in Europe and the Middle East.) E Group was formed on 6 April 1944, when its responsibilities were outlined in a charter as:

1. All preventive training of ground, sea and air forces.
2. The organization and implementation of all arrangements for contacting and effecting the release of prisoners of war and evaders from enemy territory.

In the fulfilment of its escape and evasion tasks, E Group was tasked to maintain the closest contact with the Air Sea Rescue Service, and with clandestine organizations such as the Arakan Coastal Forces, Force 136 and V Force, who were also operating in the areas of E Group's interests. Where possible, it was intended to use such assistance as could be provided by the various clandestine organizations, but the arrangements were not intended to place restrictions on E Group recruiting its own agents to employ on purely MI 9 duties.

The main E Group headquarters was established in New Delhi, with an advanced headquarters at Colombo in Ceylon (now Sri Lanka). An E Group Training School was established in Ceylon to train MI 9 agents and RAF and Fleet Air Arm aircrew. An office was also set up in Calcutta to brief aircrew, issue escape aids and to produce a bulletin giving the latest information to aircrew. Finally, an E Group Training Camp, commanded by Squadron Leader D. Vint, was established at Cachar Hills in Assam to train agents for operations in Burma, and to run courses for RAF aircrew in jungle lore and evasion. The new E Group organization, under the command of Lieutenant Colonel R. C. Jackman, was a great improvement and recognized the increasing needs created, in part, by ground advances by the Army, and a considerable increase in air operations, particularly at long range. However, the organization was dogged by a shortage of manpower, and it took some months before the establishment was brought up to strength.

A number of major factors influenced the work of MI 9 in the Far East. Few people appreciated the vast distances involved, and a post-war report graphically highlighted a comparison with Europe. The three main headquarters of E Group were situated at Delhi, Calcutta and Colombo, and would compare on a geographical scale with a headquarters established in London, Vienna and Tunis. During the latter stages of the war, when E Group was operating in French Indo-China, it was the equivalent of a headquarters in London detailing an advanced headquarters in Vienna to mount an operation in the Caucasus. The report went on to highlight that even short journeys in Burma 'which were a few inches on a map took weeks on the ground owing to the difficulties of mountain and jungle travel'.

A very big factor with a large bearing on the success of any MI 9 operation was the amount of help that could be expected from local inhabitants. It was not until the later stages of the war that there was any appreciable underground movement in any country in which MI 9 was operating, and the local inhabitants themselves, through fear of the very harsh reprisals meted out by the Japanese, were not inclined to give any assistance in the majority of cases, although there were some notable exceptions in some areas of Burma.

Another great difficulty to confront MI 9, not only in the mounting of operations, but also in the evacuation of British and some Commonwealth evaders, was the virtual impossibility of moving a white man through a country without everyone becoming aware. It was known that the presence of a white man was almost always immediately reported to the Japanese, but it was also known that it took time for action to be taken on such a report. Therefore, provided the evader could keep moving and was able to vary his route, he stood a good chance of keeping ahead of the enemy. This continual movement was not, however, possible when it was necessary for clandestine forces to establish a 'safe area' behind enemy lines. In practically every operation mounted, at one stage or another, work was hindered by the enemy's efforts to capture agents and evaders, entailing taking extensive precautions to get warning of the enemy's approach. Safe areas often had to be abandoned just as they were ready to receive evaders.

Finally, the difficulty of survival in jungle territory was the major factor that affected MI 9 agents, clandestine groups, escapers and evaders alike. As far as MI 9 parties operating in enemy-held territory were concerned, it meant a constant and regular air-supply programme, which was often interrupted by severe monsoon weather conditions. Few Europeans were able to live off the country in the jungle for any prolonged period of time, and the limited scale of rations in aircrews' escape aids soon created various complaints of malnutrition, which in turn would inhibit travel and resistance to disease. The uncertainty of the reactions of any local people merely compounded the difficulties. The primary aim of any evader in the Far East was first to ensure survival, then consider evasion.

All the factors mentioned above combined to make MI 9's task in the Far East extremely difficult. It was only with experience that it was realized how each one of these difficulties demanded that the methods which were so successful in Europe and the Middle East had to be modified, and in some cases abandoned, in the Far East theatre. It is not surprising, therefore, that the results, based on the number of personnel returning from behind enemy lines, cannot compare with those in the other theatres. However, in judging the success or failure of MI 9 in the Far East it is important to appreciate the value to morale generated by MI 9's teaching and work – something that could never be measured, but which undoubtedly improved the efficiency of those flying over such inhospitable terrain.

Chapter Fifteen

Environment and Training

IN THE EARLY DAYS OF THE FAR EAST WAR, little consideration had been given to the need for aircrew to understand 'jungle-craft' in all its aspects of practical training, specialized equipment and literature. After they had seen the unbroken and inhospitable jungle stretching beneath them to the horizon, it is not hard to understand how the imagination of aircrew direct from Great Britain or the Commonwealth flying training schools was taxed with many fears and uncertainties. There was no real information available to educate aircrew on the true significance of each and every unpleasant, and imagined, feature likely to be encountered in the jungle. Allied to the lack of appropriate survival and escape aids, aircrew slowly came to regard the jungle as an infinitely more formidable enemy than the Japanese.

Information of successful evasions that trickled through to the squadrons was not encouraging, and merely increased the feeling of hopelessness that the task of evasion presented. The few aircrew who did return were in very poor physical shape, and were usually unfit for further operational flying. The lack of survival aids and food might have been overcome had shot-down aircrew known where to seek food and shelter, and not been panicked by fear of the jungle surroundings. Unfortunately, the value of the experiences of the few evaders was lost to others since there was no system for a detailed debriefing, and what information was collected was considered to be secret, and not permitted for open distribution! Almost all were immediately posted out of the theatre of operations, taking with them their valuable experience.

As highlighted in the previous chapter, survival was the key to a successful evasion in the harsh weather and terrain of the Far East. To have any chance of survival, an evader had to carry certain essential equipment such as a map, a compass, a hunting knife and some medical aids. However, most important of all was a practical knowledge of how to live a 'Robinson Crusoe' existence, allied to an assumption that he would have to rely entirely on his own personal prowess and physical endurance to survive at all. Only when he appreciated and understood how to take advantage of what his surroundings offered could he start to undertake the difficult task of walking back. He could not place any reliance on the goodwill of tribesmen, nor expect any assistance from clandestine organizations. In the event, help was sometimes available, but the assumption had to be that an evader would have to survive by his own initiative and wits.

In early 1943, the first items of survival equipment began to be distributed to squadrons. The issue consisted of a money belt containing coins worth almost 100 rupees (about £9), a kukri jungle knife, and a tin containing a food concentrate in pill form. A few medical aids were included, but the wrappings proved ineffective. Over the next two years, the quality of survival and escape aids improved significantly. One of the first officers to recognize the need for improvements in survival aids and in training was Squadron Leader C. V. Beadon, who arrived to join the Air Training Branch at Air Headquarters in New Delhi in March 1943, having completed a tour of bomber operations against Japanese targets during the early phases of the war in Burma. One of the first issues to attract his attention was a file with the enlightened heading of 'Spartan Training – Aircrew'. It contained remarkably few enclosures, so action was initiated along three distinct lines:

1. The compilation of literature.
2. The development and production of a suitable jungle-kit.
3. The establishment of a special school, manned by experienced instructors.

The first booklet to receive wide circulation was edited by Flight Lieutenant Braithwaite, who had served with the Burma Forestry Department. It was written for aircrew based on the author's experience gained during his retreat from Burma in 1941 and other information that he had gathered. The title of the book was *Under the*

The jungle survival kit. (TNA: PRO AIR 23/4297)

Greenwood Tree. A second publication, produced by the RAF Welfare Department of 222 Group, appeared a short time later, and was called *The Jungle Hiker.* Both gave invaluable tips in a very readable format.

Beadon also recognized that the clothing worn by aircrew was entirely unsuitable for flying over jungle terrain. The existing

European pattern of flying clothing was too hot and heavy, and aircrew had taken to wearing shorts and a light shirt. Many wore soft suede or desert boots that proved totally useless in the jungle. Beadon decided that he would design a lightweight flying overall in khaki drill, which would meet the three basic requirements of:

1. Protection in the air against fire.
2. Protection on the ground.
3. Providing a means of carrying survival and escape aids.

The overall had to be capable of carrying a much-enhanced range of survival and escape aids. These fell into four categories: a comprehensive range of medical, marching, and survival aids, and the jungle flying-overall itself.

Fitting the overall with sufficient pockets to take the small containers of aids solved the problem of stowing them in a convenient place in the air so that they were not left behind when the aircraft was abandoned. Beadon incorporated a satchel, which fitted into the back of the suit with webbing shoulder straps and a belt, and could be detached once on the ground. Normally, the aids were carried in flight in the pockets, and on landing they were transferred to the satchel, which could be carried comfortably as a small haversack. For aircrew flying bomber and transport aircraft, a small haversack with snap fasteners was added into which the bulk of equipment was packed and kept close at hand in the air. In an emergency it was clipped onto a belt or the parachute harness. The flying-overall was officially known as the Mark III Kit, but it was universally known as the 'Beadon suit'. To enhance their chances of survival and evasion once on the ground, aircrew were strongly advised to wear British Army marching boots whenever they flew.

The establishment in mid-1943 of training schools in Ceylon and Assam for jungle survival was a significant development. The practical instruction in survival was combined with briefings on the more secret aspects of MI 9 training, as well as instruction in the use of special equipment. Over 2,000 people, the majority RAF, received instruction at the schools, qualifying them to give local instruction and lectures on return to their units. One method of disseminating information that developed rapidly was the preparation and issue of various types of bulletins. Some were classified for issue to intelligence officers who used them for their own lectures, and to give instruction

The Squadron Commander of a Hurricane fighter-bomber squadron briefs his pilots before take-off. They are each wearing a Beadon suit. The haversack can be seen clearly. Some pilots are carrying kukri knives and revolvers. (Imperial War Museum, London, CF 197)

on any aspect of preventive training. Others were of a more general nature for wider distribution, and some were of the 'stop press' variety, giving local conditions on the various battlefronts.

The lectures and briefings given to aircrew stressed the important aspects of survival and evasion unique to the region. Although some of the initial actions to be taken by downed aircrew were similar to those in other theatres – such as destroy sensitive equipment, delay parachute opening if baling out, bury the parachute and get away from the immediate landing area – the jungle presented different issues and priorities. It was important to find a hiding place quickly, but in jungle terrain it was often not necessary to travel very far from the landing area to be safe from being followed. It was essential to lie up, rest, check survival and escape aids and formulate a plan. Any plan had to establish a direction of travel, include a routine of hours for marching with rest periods, and a strict food and water-rationing policy. In areas occupied by the enemy it was essential to get to the hills for cover and avoid the plains. Enemy troops were often thinly scattered in most areas, and even in the most heavily occupied districts, it was likely that they would not penetrate far into the hills

One of the survival publications The Jungle Hiker *produced for aircrew. (R. Jackson)*

THE
JUNGLE HIKER

when they held the valleys and plains in strength. In the hills, therefore, there was a better chance of meeting friendly natives who were far less in fear of the savage reprisals taken by the enemy on individuals, families, and sometimes, whole villages known to have assisted Allied personnel.

The actual process of making contact with a native in the hope that assistance would be forthcoming was recognized as 'one of the trickiest projects facing the evader'. Aircrew were advised to travel unaided as far as possible, and only attempt contact with natives when it was impossible to proceed without assistance. The golden rule was to contact a male native only, and one who was alone, and to approach him after spending some time observing him. One useful method was to wait on the far outskirts of a village close to a stream where someone would inevitably arrive sooner or later to draw water. The best time to try and make contact was just before dusk. If the attempt was unsuccessful, the half-light and subsequent darkness offered the best chance for the evader to get away. On the basis that the native would be more surprised and frightened than the evader, a smiling greeting and a salute before displaying the silk blood chit gave the evader the best chance of a friendly response. If a native indicated that he must return to his village for further help, it was essential for the evader to wait outside the village and to move his position so that he could observe those that returned. If he had doubts, he could quickly retreat back into the jungle. Once a reliable contact had been made, it was good practice to offer a small reward, and show the headman the blood chit and promissory note bearing the Royal Coat of Arms carried in the money purse, and tell him that the British authorities would reward him for any assistance given.

The final obstacle for an evader was to make contact with Allied troops successfully. In the Far East war, fixed battle lines were rarely established. The difficult terrain often formed natural barriers, and this, allied to the vast distances and dense jungle, tended to create isolated areas of intense active operations with routes leading back to areas of civilization and non-combat support areas. These 'lines of communication' offered the best opportunity for an evader to make contact, since the activity in the actual combat zone would be very fluid and well guarded by alert sentries and patrols. The final approach had to be made very slowly, with frequent stops to observe air and ground activity in order to determine the location of friendly troops. Once the evader had made his mind up that he had reached a friendly area, he was advised to 'step out boldly into the open with hands held high and displaying the Union Jack on the blood chit. Under no circumstances hesitate or having come out into the open try to regain cover.'

Owing to a combination of the alien terrain, vast distances and the brutality of the Japanese – aircrew were treated as war criminals, and many were summarily executed at the point of capture – few aircrew succeeded in evading capture. However, the advances made by the escape and evasion organization, the availability of better survival and evasion aids, and the improved training given to create a better understanding of how to live and travel in the jungle created a greater awareness and belief among aircrew that it was possible to return.

The final paragraph of the first edition of an E Group Bulletin summarized the advances made by the escape and evasion organization when it stated: 'What is encouraging is that returning aircrew are suffering less and coming back quicker because they are using their special aids and carrying out the lessons learnt by their predecessors and passed on by E Group briefers and Squadron Intelligence Officers'.

Chapter Sixteen

Burma

AFTER JAPAN'S SWEEPING GAINS IN MALAYA, Singapore and the Dutch East Indies, it was decided that all remaining Allied resources would be devoted to the defence of India, Ceylon and Burma. Initially, the Japanese had few aspirations towards Burma, but quickly realized the value of the port facilities at Rangoon and the Burma Road that carried supplies to the Nationalist forces in China led by Chiang Kai-shek. Attacks were launched in February 1942, and by the end of May, Japanese forces occupied the whole of Burma. Initially, the RAF presence in Burma was just a handful of squadrons, but as the three-year war ebbed and flowed before final victory, the size of the RAF presence built up greatly, culminating in a total of 66 RAF and Commonwealth squadrons by July 1945.

Burma is a large country with a central plain dominated by the Irrawaddy valley. The river rises in Tibet and flows south to be joined by the Chindwin south of Mandalay. The lower Irrawaddy pursues its way southwards to form the vast delta with the capital and main port, Rangoon, to the east of the delta. East of the Irrawaddy and running parallel is the River Salween, which rises in the Shan Hills. The region is surrounded by jungle-covered barriers, with the mountains of Tibet to the north, and in the west the Arakan Yoma, the Naga Hills and the Chin Hills, whose ranges vary from 3,000 to 8,000 feet, with occasional peaks over 10,000 feet. In the east the Shan Hills border Yunnan in South China and reach heights of 8,000 feet. The whole mountain system is traversed almost entirely by tracks only, with the exception of the Burma Road running east from Mandalay over the Shan Hills to China.

The other major feature that influenced air operations was the weather. The 'campaigning season' was usually restricted to the eight 'dry' months from October to May. During the period of the south-west monsoon, which normally established itself in May, air operations were curtailed because of the violent weather and the unserviceability of all but a few all-weather airfields. As much as 200 inches of rain falls in some areas of Arakan. However, despite the difficulties, ground forces had to be supported, almost entirely from the air, and operations often continued in the most appalling conditions when mud and swollen rivers were guaranteed. One former RAF pilot who spent three years flying on operations over Burma was quoted as saying: 'There were three enemies in Burma, the weather, the terrain, and the Japanese – in that order!'

'The people will certainly not eat you' was the opening sentence of the paragraph dealing with the attitude of the population outlined in the Burma section of the *MI 9 Bulletin*. It went on to say that if a small gift was offered, and a smiling evader treated them with an understanding of their customs, the natives would treat an evader kindly. As a general rule in Burma, a village situated in the hills was more likely to provide help than those on the plains and valleys. This was born out by experience, and the Chins, Nagas and Karens gave valuable support to evaders and to E Group organizations.

E Group Establishment 1 had specific responsibility for the Burma region, and had very close links with Headquarters Fourteenth Army. An advanced E Group headquarters at Comilla in Assam controlled the operations of four forward headquarters, each located with an Army Corps – the one located with XV Corps had a special section to deal with evacuations by sea. Each forward headquarters organized a system of village watchers and guides within its sector who were responsible for contacting any evaders who came into their area. Once in the hands of these field sections, an evader was taken to a prearranged rendezvous point before being evacuated down a 'rat line' through the enemy lines or to a rough airstrip for evacuation by a light aircraft. Also available were two teams of trained and well-armed agents, led by an officer, who were prepared to rescue, by force if necessary, POWs held in forward areas or evaders in a dangerous situation. In the period 1 February to 31 July 1944, 675 escapers and 119 evaders, including 17 aircrew, succeeded in reaching Allied lines. Arrangements made by E Group with their watchers and other clandestine organizations were responsible for the rescue of 10 of the aircrew.

Linked to the watchers and guide scheme was a reporting system that became known as the 'Rescal Service'. Air Force units and formations reported all losses of aircraft behind enemy lines to HQ 224 Group at Comilla who were in direct communication with the nearby E Group Headquarters. On receipt of a 'rescal', the E Group operations staff, who knew the locations of all clandestine parties working behind enemy lines, took action to pass on the message to one of their field parties or to the forward troops most suitably placed to render assistance. A monthly review showing the number of 'rescals' received, the action taken, and the number of aircrew recovered was prepared and given the widest distribution. Although this did much to raise the morale of aircrew, it was also apparent that there were comparatively few cases where an aircraft came down where help was immediately forthcoming. Two further steps were needed to assist aircrew who crashed where no clandestine field parties were working. The first was the provision of 'searcher' aircraft – usually a Beaufighter – to locate and report on survivors, and the second was a team of parachutists on standby to be dropped at the scene and to guide survivors to safety. By the end of the war, E Group had virtually created an Air Jungle Rescue Service organized on similar lines to the well-established Air Sea Rescue Service.

The three narratives that follow highlight most of the features and methods described in this chapter on Burma. They also graphically illustrate what could be achieved by those well prepared and possessing an absolute determination to succeed. Some did, and their stories are remarkable.

WALK OUT OF THE JUNGLE

By March 1944, the Japanese Fifteenth Army had advanced into northern Burma and was attacking across the Indian border near Imphal. A number of airstrips had been constructed in the Imphal valley in north-east Assam, including an all-weather strip at Palel, which was the home of 34 Squadron equipped with Hurricane IIc fighter-bombers. Flying Officer Ray Jackson had recently joined the squadron, and on the afternoon of 22 March he prepared to take off on his fifth operational sortie. Six aircraft were tasked to bomb and strafe a target near the village of Kuki on the Japanese lines of communications just across the border in Burma.

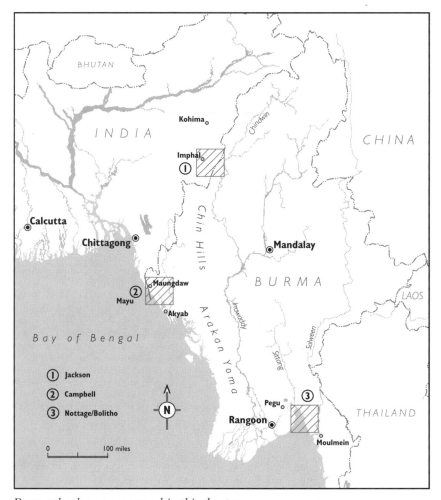

Burma: the three areas covered in this chapter.

The formation took off at 2.50 p.m. and headed for the target, which Jackson bombed in a shallow dive. As he was easing out of the dive, he heard a dull thud in the port wing, and noticed oil pouring out. He realized that the engine would soon fail, so he started to climb and turn towards the Lahkazi Valley, knowing that he would soon have to bale out. After making a quick call on the radio, he disconnected his radio lead and oxygen mask, stuffed some maps in his pocket and undid his straps. At 1,500 feet the engine seized and caught fire. He rolled his aircraft onto its back, pushed the control column forward, and was thrown clear. He opened his parachute and tried to steer it towards a small clearing on the side of a wooded hill. On landing, his parachute caught on a small tree, so he tried to haul it in, since it

Hurricanes bomb a bridge on the Tiddim road in Burma. (Imperial War Museum, London, CF 175)

would provide valuable material for his survival. However, he had to abandon his attempts as he heard shouts, which forced him to head off into the trees.

Jackson was wearing a Beadon suit, but the pocket containing his food had been ripped off as he left the cockpit of his burning Hurricane. As soon as he heard the voices, he moved up the hill, using his folding machete to cut through dense undergrowth, to a cave where he rested to sort out his survival kit. He stayed there until it was nearly dark, when he became aware of several fires starting below him. There was a breeze and he realized that the fires would soon reach his position. He thought it was a deliberate attempt to force him up the hill, so he decided to traverse along the hill as close to the fires as possible until he reached a clearing, where he heard voices. He kept very still as two Japanese soldiers passed him within touching distance. Once they had disappeared he moved away from the area, and found some undergrowth, where he collapsed into a deep sleep.

When he woke the following morning he decided to head north-west towards Jessami, where he knew there was an army outpost. He filled his chargal (canvas water bottle) as soon as possible, but noticed footprints, which he recognized as a Japanese army boot, so he decided to avoid the streams and head towards a ridge. He walked all day, covering about nine miles before he came to a clearing where he decided to stay for the night. He cut several bamboos and covered them with ferns before intertwining saplings and leaves to make the shelter waterproof. He lit a fire to dry his socks just before a violent thunderstorm broke. He crawled into his shelter and fell asleep, only to be awoken by something wriggling near his feet. He lay still as a four-foot snake curled up alongside him – he eased away from it!

The following morning he continued in a north-westerly direction until he found a Naga village, which he avoided. However, he found an isolated basha where he found some grains of rice and corn. He was attempting to grind the corn when an old Naga appeared, and her cry of surprise attracted a man to his position. Jackson saluted and greeted them in the recommended manner, and they indicated that he should follow them. As he entered the village he noticed two Japanese soldiers, so turned and ran as fast as he could to hide in some bamboo, recognizing that he had made a basic error in entering the village before observing it carefully. He expected to be attacked, but nothing happened so he travelled through the night to get clear of the area.

Over the next seven or eight days, he made slow progress heading to the north-west, taking compass bearings from time to time on features, and using his watch to check the position of the sun to assess directions. The whole of this part of his journey was in dense jungle, often involving climbing and descending steep hills. During this time he established a daily routine of walking from 6 a.m. for three hours before taking a 20-minute rest. He then moved again until noon, when he rested for an hour. He repeated the same routine in the afternoon until he stopped at 6 p.m., when he made himself a shelter. He soon learned the importance of preparing a shelter for the night well before dusk, and to make a bed raised above the ground whenever possible. He did not experience any great hunger but rationed himself to small pieces of melons that he found, corn from a cob, and nuts that he saw 'baboons' eating. He drank a tin of water every day, but his attempts to fish were unsuccessful.

On the ninth or tenth day he camped near the junction of two rivers. He washed and dried his feet and socks, and treated some blisters with sulphanilamide from his escape kit. He dressed the blisters daily and they soon recovered. The following day he had great

*Ray Jackson (right) with a
fellow Hurricane pilot.
(R. Jackson)*

difficulty crossing a fast-flowing stream, and the struggle to get to the
far bank left him feeling exhausted, so he decided to rest for the day.

Mosquitoes and leeches were regular nuisances, and ticks and
vicious black ants also bothered him. He had no major problems with
wild animals until the 11th day when he had just entered a clearing.
He heard a rushing and crashing sound coming from the far side, and
a large, black, hostile animal appeared, which he thought was a black
panther, and came towards him quickly, veering off at the last minute
and disappearing into the undergrowth. He kept his revolver close to
hand for the next few hours.

By the 12th day he was feeling exhausted and his lips were very
swollen and cracked. He reached a stream and used his last water-
purifying tablet. He also noticed what looked like a potato, which he
tried to eat. As he bit into it, he felt a stinging sensation and his lower
lip and tongue started to swell, and became so large that he could
hardly swallow. Despite rinsing with lots of water, he could not reduce
the pain and burning sensation. He decided that he must get some
help, and set off in the direction of a village that he could see in the

distance. He sat to rest when a Naga woman appeared and screamed at the sight of him. This attracted others, and Jackson made gestures of greeting, and was very relieved to see that they acknowledged his smile. He was clearly in a distressed condition, and the Nagas gave him something to drink together with rice and berries.

Slowly, and with great difficulty, he eventually reached the village, where he met an excited crowd, including a small boy who knew a few words of English. The boy said that he would escort Jackson to Jessami, a two-day walk, once he was rested. A meal was provided and the elders of the village discussed the situation, at which point he learned that a strong Japanese force was established to the west. After a comfortable night, two boys led Jackson towards his goal. In his pack was some rice and pork wrapped in a huge banana leaf. After two or three miles, the elder boy was suffering from acute pains and could not continue. He pointed the way ahead and Jackson found himself alone again.

A day or two later he was nearing Jessami when he heard gunfire, which forced him to divert to the north. Eventually he came across a village, which he approached with some apprehension, but he had a friendly welcome from the headman and villagers. He spent the night there, but started to suffer from dysentery, almost certainly brought on by the lack of water-purifying tablets. He moved on using a wider track before resting in an old basha, where he discovered evidence of recent British occupation. He soon encountered two young Nagas, one carrying a recently slaughtered pig on his back. Having discovered that he was British, the two youths urged him to follow them back along the track to the basha, where they recovered some buried tins of fruit. They left quickly and soon arrived in the large and important village of Phakekedzumi, where he discovered that one of the men was called Acheppo and the other was a Christian pastor. They immediately fetched a schoolteacher who could speak some English.

The villagers had noticed that Jackson was walking badly, so the pastor's young wife bathed his feet, and he was very touched by the tenderness of this simple Christian family. The village schoolmaster arrived to explain that the Japanese were near the village and had been behaving very badly, including taking all the food, hence the arrival of the dead pig. After a good night's sleep, Jackson was given a blanket to wear and a spear to carry, and six young Nagas, attired in the same way, escorted him on the next stage of his journey. After a day's march they reached another village where he was given food and shelter, and this process was repeated over the next few days as he headed north.

In one village he treated a boy with jungle sores, and this news, together with the fact that he was a Christian, travelled before him; after a warm welcome he was expected to conduct a sick parade. In one village he was sitting by a fire when a man who said that he had been a missionary's cook approached and asked if he would like to eat, whereupon he was given eggs and bacon!

Late one evening he was in another village when a panting Naga youth came up to him and gave him a note and a box. The note informed him that it was known that he was in the area and a patrol would come and get him. In the meantime he was to enjoy the American 'K' rations included in the box. The note had come from Major David Henchman, the commander of a British V Force team. V Force was one of the SOE organizations that operated behind enemy lines on sabotage and intelligence-collection work, using native troops led by British officers. The following day, Jackson and his guide set off to meet the major and his group. After a brief greeting and instructions on the way ahead, they parted and Jackson moved on to rendezvous with a six-man patrol who had been told that he would need carrying to safety. It was 16 April, almost a month since he had been shot down.

Jackson said goodbye to his faithful Naga friends and set off with the patrol for the V Force base camp. On arrival they were surprised to find just two men guarding the place. Apparently a Japanese attack was expected, so the camp had been abandoned. Once again, just as he thought he was safe, Jackson discovered that danger was still around him. The patrol immediately pressed on in the dark until they reached the remainder of the force, who were preparing a defensive position. Jackson offered to assist with the defence, but the medical officer gave him some pills, and he remembered no more until he awoke the following morning.

He spent a few days with the column in the defensive position on a ridge. He was well fed and given various medications as he slowly recovered. A Dakota arrived to carry out a resupply airdrop before the column left to pursue the Japanese. Jackson was left in charge of a small group of sick soldiers, and was given instructions to head for the Allied lines. More Naga men were provided as guides, and they carried one of the wounded soldiers on a bamboo bier. Two days and a few villages later, they came to a metalled road and had just turned a bend when a medical jeep appeared. The wounded man and Jackson

The letter delivered to Ray Jackson after he had been in the jungle for almost three weeks. (R. Jackson)

were collected, and the jeep headed for the main British positions. They had been travelling for a few miles when they encountered a small airstrip with a number of Hurricanes parked in dispersals. On approaching an airman to enquire about the identity of the unit, Jackson was startled by the greeting from an amazed airman, 'F*** me – it's Mr Jackson!' It was his own 34 Squadron, but he was barely recognizable in his cloak, jungle boots and with a few weeks of beard. His CO rushed to meet him, and he was soon at the Army General Headquarters, where he was debriefed by the staff. A few hours later he returned to the squadron and many happy reunions.

During the 30 days that Ray Jackson had been in the jungle, he had followed the jungle survival rulebook almost perfectly, and he was one of the few aircrew to return from the jungle through enemy lines. He had devised a plan, followed sensible routes and made a good shelter whenever possible. He had taken care of his feet, preserved his rations and water, and used his survival aids correctly. After his initial mistake, he avoided villages until he was sure they were friendly, and then he approached with traditional courtesies. Like so many evaders, he discovered that the local people in the remote villages were prepared to risk their lives to help him. Above all, he had kept his head in a very alien environment and stuck to his plan. It was no surprise when it was announced that he had been awarded the MC for his outstanding achievement. He spent the rest of the war as an instructor at the RAF's School for Jungle Self-Preservation Training in India, where he instructed aircrew on the techniques of jungle survival.

SEA EVACUATION FROM THE ARAKAN

From the autumn of 1943 the Hurricane IIc aircraft of 258 Squadron had been tasked regularly to fly night 'Rhubarb' sorties during the moon period. These were low-level flights along the rivers of Burma looking for river traffic to attack with the aircraft's powerful 20 mm

A cannon-armed Hurricane takes off from a makeshift airstrip. (ACA Archives)

cannon. It was for such a sortie that Warrant Officer J. R. L. Campbell took off from an advanced airfield near Cox's Bazaar, south of Chittagong, at 9 p.m. on 3 April 1944. He flew inland to pinpoint the Kaladan River before turning south towards Akyab, where he saw some lights on the water, which he attacked. As he left Akyab, he turned to fly up the Mayu River, where he saw a light on the western bank. He was flying at very low level above the water in bright moonlight when there was a loud explosion and the cockpit filled with bright light and smoke. The Hurricane hit the water and sank in seconds, coming to rest on the river bottom some 10 feet below the surface.

Campbell quickly recovered his senses and pulled the cockpit hood back, undid his straps, released his parachute and floated to the surface 200 yards from the shore of a sandbank on the eastern side. He noticed considerable wooden wreckage around him, including what appeared to be half the keel of a small boat. His aircraft had almost certainly collided with the mast of the boat, and they had demolished each other. He swam ashore on his back, kicking gently and not using his arms, to prevent attracting attention. After 10 minutes he reached the shore with all his kit intact. The banks were a very thick mud, and Campbell found it difficult and tiring to get on to firmer ground. He buried his helmet and oxygen mask before trying to walk away, but the mud hindered his progress, so he decided to swim across to the main peninsula. After swimming a short distance, he thought better of this and decided to rest until daylight, when he could review his situation. Just after midnight, he took off his sodden Beadon suit, and spread it across the mud before lying on it in an attempt to get some sleep. Throughout the night he heard voices and the sound of paddles from a number of sampans as they searched the area. Later, he was able to determine that he had crashed near Rathedaung.

The next morning he checked his Beadon suit, only to discover that all the rations and medical aids had been lost in the river. He decided to rest during the daytime, when he saw a number of natives on the other side of the river, but he stayed out of sight. He had nothing to eat and decided that the water was too brackish to drink without sterilizing tablets. At sunset he started walking north and soon decided to abandon his Beadon suit, leaving him wearing a shirt, slacks and boots – he kept his revolver and kukri. He also had his escape aids and decided to keep his flying goggles. Once he was in a remote area he slipped into the river to swim to the peninsula. After

30 minutes he began to think that he would not make it, and considered jettisoning his revolver and kukri, but he decided to keep them. He had been in the water for almost one hour when his feet touched the bottom of the river, but he had another 200 yards before he could drag himself across the mud to firm ground, where he collapsed exhausted.

He found an animal track heading inland, which he followed until he came across a village and heard voices. A child suddenly appeared and screamed before running off to the village, whereupon many men started shouting. Campbell decided not to risk entering the village since he was still reasonably close to the crash site, and the locals sounded very agitated. He headed for the hills, where he eventually found some bamboo near a chaung (a stream-filled gully). He chopped some of this down to make a bed, but had difficulty in sleeping.

Early next morning he lay on the bank and watched a number of sampans taking vegetables to the south in the direction of Akyab. He had not had any food or water since the crash, and seeing a clean-shaven native on the other side of the chaung, decided to swim across and seek help. After reaching the opposite bank, he attracted the attention of the native and indicated that he needed food. He was taken to a nearby hollow and told to wait. The native returned with an unpleasant-looking individual, and they spread out a blanket and started to cook rice. Once it was ready, they invited Campbell to start eating, at which point the two men attacked him, taking all his

Pilots of 258 Squadron. J. Campbell is second left in the back row. (via N. Franks)

possessions before running off. Campbell grabbed the remains of the rice and ran into the hills. He found a stream and climbed up the bed until he found clear water for his first drink. He then continued to clamber up the steep hill to the ridge. Eventually he had to abandon the stream and follow an animal track to the top of the hill, after which he walked along the ridge in a north-westerly direction. At sunset he came across a completely deserted village, so hid in a ditch and tried to get some sleep.

Next morning he felt very weak and decided that if he was to make any progress he would have to move during the daytime. He came across a village where he noticed that the men were carrying rifles, so decided to avoid the place and carry on northwards. He found a stream and sucked up some water before rolling into a ditch with chest pains and feeling very weak. He forced himself to continue after a rest, soon locating a small road, where he found plenty of evidence of an earlier withdrawal by British troops. An hour later he saw two natives ahead. With all his equipment lost or stolen, and without food and water, he felt that he had no choice but to risk meeting them. He waved and saluted in the approved manner, and he was relieved to see them wave back in a friendly way. He approached them and indicated that he was looking for food, at which they pointed to a nearby village. He made a cautious approach to the edge of the village, and lay down to observe it until sunset. About his time, he saw an old bearded man standing outside a basha, and he decided to go across to him. As Campbell appeared, there was a momentary look of fear across the man's face, and he immediately grabbed the pilot and dragged him into the basha, where there were three children and a woman. By a combination of sign language and a few words, Campbell tried to make the family aware of his situation, and to the sound of sympathetic noises they gave him rice and water.

As he was eating, some younger men arrived and made signs that they would send word of his arrival to the British forces at Maungdaw, which Campbell initially understood to mean that they would take him to the town. Later that evening they took him from the basha to a clearing near the beach, where they told him to hide. He remained in this clearing for the next four days, until 10 April, during which time the old man brought food to him twice a day, and also told him that the Japanese had been to the village to make enquiries about him. On the night of the fourth day the villagers moved him to a place they had prepared in the foothills, since they had discovered that the Japanese had started searching along the beach. His new shelter was in a small concealed clearing that they had covered with dry grass. He was to remain there for the next 11 days.

On 14 April he received a note brought by a native messenger which read, 'Hello RAF. Shall do my best to get you out tonight. Chin up and keep smiling. Stay where you are. From Holmes, V Force 11/4/44.' This note cheered him up a great deal, but when he asked the villagers who brought him his food when he would be rescued, they always replied, 'in two days'. Three days after receiving the note, there had been no further word of rescue, and Campbell began to worry. He acknowledged that he 'had to take a good grip on myself to avoid becoming hysterical'. The villagers were very vague about any rescue, and the Japanese were still in the beach area, making it very difficult for a clandestine sampan to arrive. In addition, he was beginning to worry about his health, and the loneliness was beginning to affect his morale, which was at its lowest since his crash 14 days earlier. The old man continued to bring two packets of food and tins containing two or three pints of water each day.

After a further two days, Campbell wrote a note, which he addressed to 'Major Holmes, V Force', and gave it to a native to take. In it he said:

Much cheered by your note received 14/4/44. Locals now say escape by sea impracticable as too many Japs on beach who look likely staying there. Can you send me some stuff to darken my face and hair, also a guide if possible, though I expect the people here will help. If this can be done then I can walk out alright. I can swim river no difficulty. It's pretty bloody lying up here with nothing to do but lay and hope. But I am still quite fit so can manage journey. Trusting in you. Campbell RAF.

There was an understandable note of optimism and desperation in his letter, since he was in very poor physical shape to undertake some of the options he had outlined. There was further frustration for him the next day when the old man visited him with more paper and a pencil, asking for his name and those of his helpers to be written down with a view to a reward for their assistance. Campbell readily agreed. On 22 April a second note arrived from V Force saying: 'Hello RAF. Have tried damnedest to get you out by sea but all I can offer you is a V Force boat and some stout lads of mine. Take this, it's your only chance. D. C. V. Holmes. Major, V Force.'

Campbell was overjoyed. Instead of the usual 10 yards that he put between his hideaway and the place where he answered the call of nature, the next time he walked only three yards away, so sure was he that rescue was imminent. He remained awake all night listening for the sound of a boat, but nothing happened – he was bitterly disappointed. Late the following afternoon a young native he had not seen before, called Ali Amud, arrived with another note: 'Hello RAF. Very sorry, we tried very hard last night but struck a rock. Everything went wrong. Will try again. What is your rank, name and number? Keep your spirits up. Holmes. V Force.' This messenger said he was going back to radio to Maungdaw, and that he would return with a motorboat and take him out to sea. He told Campbell that he expected to be back in about four days' time.

Two days later Campbell left his hideaway for the first time in 11 days, when the villagers took him a short distance away to a rise in the ground where he spent a most uncomfortable day without shade, and being eaten by voracious ants. At about midnight a native came to him and whispered that a sampan had arrived for him. He followed him down the hill, where he met other men that he had not previously seen. One of them approached him and gave him 200 rupees to give to the old man who had looked after him throughout his stay. Campbell sought him out to say goodbye and to thank him before moving down to the beach, where he saw a sampan, and where Lieutenant Lothera, an Indian officer, met him with a warm welcome. All the party boarded the sampan, which headed off for the sea. Once clear of the beach area they encountered very bad surf and breakers, and the native troops had to bale continually to keep the boat afloat. The sea was so rough that one of them fell overboard and had to be rescued before they finally reached the open sea. The lieutenant told him that they would be making a rendezvous with a small steamer in two hours' time, which duly arrived. On board he met Major Holmes and a number of other officers who had been involved in his rescue.

At 8 a.m. on 26 April, the steamer arrived at Kappagaung a few miles north of Maungdaw, where the party was met by a jeep that took them to the headquarters of 25th Division. Campbell met the senior officers, who offered him every kindness before he departed with Holmes to his V Force headquarters. Later that day he was flown back to his squadron to meet his squadron commander, Squadron Leader Neil Cameron (later Marshal of the Royal Air Force Lord

Cameron), and to start a series of debriefings and medical checks before going on a period of recuperation from his ordeal, which he had borne with great fortitude and patience.

LIGHT AIRCRAFT PICK-UP

Shortly after dawn on 26 April 1945, Wing Commander George Nottage AFC, the Commanding Officer of 177 Squadron, and his navigator, Pilot Officer Norman Bolitho, took off from Chiringa, south of Chittagong, in their Beaufighter. Their target was a radar site on the island of Bilugyun on the eastern side of the Sittang estuary east of Rangoon. Three hours after take-off they were approaching the target from the west when they encountered very heavy rain, which obscured the target. Near the island they saw an enemy lugger carrying cargo and Japanese troops, which they attacked with cannon. After six attacks, during which heavy small-arms fire was encountered, the lugger was seen on fire heading for the coast.

As the Beaufighter pulled away from the target, Nottage noticed that the oil pressure of the starboard engine had fallen to zero, and he immediately headed for the coastal plain. The engine caught fire, and the aircraft started to lose height, making a forced landing inevitable. Nottage put the stricken Beaufighter down in a paddy field near the small town of Thaton. He and Bolitho scrambled out of the aircraft, taking with them their survival equipment and escape aids. They heard natives approaching, so immediately headed away from the crash site in a northerly direction. After about two hours' walking they found a heap of sugar-cane stalks on the edge of a paddy field, and they decided to hide and rest to take stock of the situation. They were 200 miles behind enemy lines.

Both were wearing Beadon suits and Indian Army boots. They each had a kukri, escape aids and various survival aids in the pockets of the Beadon suits. As dusk approached they set off toward the town of Thaton, taking great care to cross the road and adjacent railway line just to the south of the town. Once clear, they headed for a gap in the hills. They crossed a small river and filled up their water bottles before heading into low-lying hills, where they decided to rest once it became light. During the day they made plans for their march. They were not sure if they were in friendly Karen territory so decided to head north to cross the Bilin River before turning west towards the

Sittang River to contact British patrols working behind enemy lines. At their final briefing before taking off, they had been given the last known positions of these units. They decided to walk by night, and estimated that the journey would take 14 days – they later revised this estimate to 21 days.

Throughout the day, they could hear voices so remained hidden. Just before dark they ate some Horlicks tablets and their 'K' rations, but George Nottage was just recovering from dengue fever and had difficulty eating. They started walking as darkness set in, avoiding small villages where the dogs could be very vociferous and give their presence away. Progress was very slow through the jungle, and they had to stop when Nottage started to feel ill. The rest of the night was spent under a pile of bamboo, but this did not prevent them from getting very wet when heavy rain started. Despite the rain getting more intense, they pressed on as soon as dawn broke, but the going became very hard as they traversed through hilly, wooded country, intersected by many small and flooded ravines. Progress was slow so they changed their plan to travel by day, and over the next two days they made progress north despite the continuous, heavy rain.

On the sixth day they had a very unpleasant experience. After walking all day in the rain, they camped under some trees on a hill near a pagoda. They filled their water bottles, added the purification tablets, and were able to make some tea. However, the rain continued and they got very little sleep since they found that they had bedded down on a termite nest. They awoke to find themselves and their clothes smothered in termites. A breakfast of Horlicks did little to lift their morale as they set off along some bullock tracks.

The first thing they did on the eighth morning was to climb a small hill, when they were able to pinpoint their position by identifying the southern bend of the Bilin River to the north. They found that the area was more thickly populated than they had anticipated, and they had to take great care as they passed through some small villages, although the natives took no notice of them. At one point they came across an old garden where they were able to collect some pineapples to supplement their meagre diet. In the pouring rain they traversed a number of rubber plantations, and suffered from the attention of leeches as they crossed a valley. The leech sticks in their survival kit dealt with them effectively.

At 3 p.m. on the ninth day they reached the steep banks of the wide and fast-flowing Bilin River. This appeared to be a formidable obstacle, but luckily they saw a young man herding some buffalo. Using sign language, they asked him how to cross and he immediately took them to a better stretch, took their kit on his head and waded across with the two airmen following. They rewarded him with three rupees and some cigarettes from their survival pack, with which he was delighted. Across the river were sugar-cane fields, and they soon found a hut used for pressing the cane, so they decided to stay the night. They had a meal of 'K' ration biscuits and chocolate, and George Nottage was able to eat a small amount as he was beginning to feel better. They slept well for the first time since their arrival in the jungle.

A small boy found them in the hut the following morning, and indicated that he would take them to his village to get some food. They followed him and met other children, but stopped on the edge of the village to wait and see if it was safe. Once the children had gone, they moved their position to observe the place. Four men appeared with food and the headman made his dislike of the Japanese very apparent. He showed them a safe route out of the area, and they left the village. They soon crossed the main road between Bilin and Papun, when they had a ringside seat of ten Mosquitoes bombing and strafing positions in Bilin. By mid-afternoon they had found a little-used bullock track heading north-west, and they were able to make good progress. They found a pool of fresh water and decided to camp for the night. There was a ledge well covered by bamboo, so they decided to build a decent shelter, which included thatching the roof with fern. This was the best shelter they had made, but it was the first night without rain! They slept well after a meal of stew.

Early in the morning, they set off in a north-westerly direction over fairly open country, which gradually got thicker and more difficult, making progress very slow. In the afternoon, they met an elderly Burmese who gave them a greeting but passed on. They decided to rest, have some food, and wash their socks. Shortly afterwards, the elderly man returned and sat next to them. He produced a leaflet dropped by an Allied aircraft, which told of the Japanese retreat and advising the villagers to head for the hills. He asked the crew if this were true, and they confirmed it.

The elderly man kept saying 'chow' with appropriate hand movements to his mouth, and led them to a small village in a coconut grove, where other men collected some of the fruit for them to drink the nourishing milk and eat the flesh. They were also given salt crystals, some 'chugri', a soft sugary sweet, and some green tea. They slept the night on the veranda of the old man's house. The following morning after more tea, their host led them to a bullock track, telling them to go north and keep clear of the west, where the Japanese were patrolling. They had to cross two swift-flowing rivers before continuing on the old bullock cart track. As they rested at lunchtime, they suddenly saw about 10 men on a small ridge pointing rifles at them. Nottage immediately recognized the rifles as Lee Enfields, which gave them some hope that they were friendly natives. Their leader came down, recognized that they were white men, and called his men down. Soon it was all smiles: the airmen had been found by loyal Karen tribesmen. Language was a problem, but with lots of sign language and the use of the blood chit, they discovered that there were other white men in the area. They set off at a fast pace to a village where they noticed a basha with a pair of boots hanging out to dry. They entered the basha to be greeted by Major Lucas of Force 136 and two of his men, a clandestine force operating behind enemy lines, together with Captain Pierce working for E Group. The two exhausted aircrew were fed and able to rest.

On the 13th day (8 May), they left early in the morning on a six-mile climb to the team's base camp at Pete-Atet, where they met more members of Force 136, and where a wireless message could be sent to Calcutta. Plans were discussed for their return to British lines, since their presence was a nuisance for the Force 136 team, who had various sabotage jobs to complete. Discussions centred on levelling a landing strip to enable a light aircraft to land and pick them up. Nottage accompanied a party back to the village to talk to the headman about the possibility. He selected a flat area and arranged for some of the villagers to level the bunds (ridges) that separated the fields, and estimated that the job would take four days. The party returned to their base camp to send a wireless message requesting a pick-up. They were informed that a Lysander would be sent when all the arrangements had been made. In the meantime, a Dakota was sent to parachute supplies to the party. During this period, a young Indian soldier, Ali Mohammed, arrived. He had been forced by the Japanese to join the Indian National Army, but had managed to escape.

By 14 May, the airstrip was ready and a wireless message was sent, but it was two more days before two Lysanders arrived. The first landed too fast and tipped onto its nose, damaging the propeller. The pilot was carrying a Force 136 man as a passenger. The second

Lysander had to be waved away. This landing accident presented Major Lucas with an unexpected, and very difficult, problem. The aircraft had to be hidden, and more food had to be found for the extra men. Nottage went with a party to a monastery near Malabu to discuss the food problem with the monks, and they agreed to supply pork and rice. There was also some concern among the local people, who were aware that the Japanese were asking difficult questions about the increased air activity. On 19 May most of the party returned to the airstrip to make improvements, but they had not been there long when they were warned that a Japanese patrol was moving towards them in an attempt to encircle them. They set off back to the camp when they suddenly found themselves face to face with a small patrol. The British party dived off the path, and the Japanese disappeared. However, Nottage and the Lysander pilot had become separated from the rest of the party. They saw some movement, which they soon recognized as their own party, but they were concerned about how best to identify themselves, so Nottage started to whistle the tune to 'Colonel Bogey', and they were able to rejoin the others safely.

Major Lucas decided to move base camp and hide all the heavy equipment in the jungle. Another signal was sent to Calcutta suggesting that L.5 Sentinel light aircraft should be used to pick up

L.5 Sentinel aircraft flown behind Japanese lines to pick up George Nottage and Norman Bolitho. (Imperial War Museum, London, NYF 23230)

Norman Bolitho (left) and George Nottage arrive back after their 31 days behind enemy lines. The Indian soldier, Ali Mohammed, who was rescued with them, looks on. (N. Bolitho)

the passengers. Force 136 were training and arming loyal Burmese of the Burma Defence Army, and they arranged for a detachment to guard the airstrip. For the next two days, the party waited for rescue, but no aircraft arrived.

On the 31st day (26 May), four L.5s, led by Flight Lieutenant John Dunbar, the CO of 221 Group Communications Flight, took off from Pegu, 50 miles north of Rangoon, with a Spitfire squadron acting as escort. Just before arriving at the airstrip, the Spitfires left and the L.5s dropped to treetop height as they approached at 11 a.m. Signals and flares were lit and the four aircraft landed safely. It was then that they discovered that there were five, not four, men. The Indian soldier was devastated to be left behind, but Dunbar rushed over to him and told him to hide in the bush and he would try to return for him. Nottage, Bolitho and the two men from the Lysander were then lifted out by the L.5s and flown back to Pegu. Dunbar's aircraft was rapidly refuelled and he returned to the strip without an escort. A very happy Indian soldier jumped into the back of the light aircraft and Dunbar was airborne in a few moments. It was a very courageous act, as the Japanese might have been waiting at the airstrip for him – he was subsequently awarded the DFC.

George Nottage and Norman Bolitho returned to 177 Squadron

within a few days, and received a great reception, but they were not allowed to return to operational flying. A few months later, it was announced that George Nottage had been awarded a DSO for his long period in command, and his unique evasion. Norman Bolitho was awarded the DFC in recognition of his outstanding service. Sadly, there was a price to pay. Shortly after their rescue, the Japanese assumed that local Karens had provided help, and the headmen of the nearby villages were beheaded.

A measure of George Nottage and Norman Bolitho's achievement can be understood when it is noted that in the seven months up to March 1945 a total of 176 aircrew were forced down over enemy-controlled territory in Burma or in the jungle, and 166 disappeared without trace. Just 3 of the 10 to return evaded from Japanese-held territory.

Chapter Seventeen

South-East Asia

BY THE TIME OF THE SURRENDER OF SINGAPORE on 15 February 1941, and with it the loss of 140,000 men, most of the surviving aircraft of RAF and Commonwealth squadrons had flown to airfields in Sumatra, where the Japanese gave them no opportunities to settle and develop any coherent air plan. The loss of personnel and equipment, the lack of a command and control system, and the spartan support facilities available left each squadron fending for itself. The Japanese harried the depleted forces from the outset, and the remnants of remaining squadrons retreated to Java to try and carry on the fight. With the Allied fleets driven from the sea between the Philippines and the Dutch East Indies during the February battles, and the RAF, Commonwealth and Dutch air forces destroyed, there was nothing to stop the Japanese from occupying Java. Against overwhelming odds, the squadrons fought until they were effectively destroyed. Formations and men were cut off and a few ships tried to escape through the Sundra Strait, but many were caught and sunk. The overcrowded SS *Kote Gede* managed to reach Ceylon with the remnants of one or two squadrons. A handful of other ships arrived in Australia, but the great majority of personnel were captured, to spend the rest of the war in the miseries that prevailed in Japanese POW camps, many never to return. An example of the great losses is graphically illustrated by 258 Squadron's experience. In the four weeks following their arrival to reinforce Singapore, just six of the original 22 pilots were saved during the hectic evacuation from Java. Other squadrons and units all had similar experiences.

Although British SOE officers had managed to establish an escape line from Singapore through Sumatra to the west-coast port of Padang, from where some 2,000 personnel sailed for Ceylon and India, there was no time to organize an effective evacuation. The very few others who did manage to evade the rapid Japanese advance did so as a result of their own efforts, initiative and courage. An epic voyage, under the command of Wing Commander John Jeudwine was one of the few to succeed.

OPEN BOAT TO AUSTRALIA

As the Japanese advance into Malaya and Singapore gathered momentum in January 1942, reinforcements were sent from the Middle East, including 84 Squadron equipped with Blenheim IV bombers. Wing Commander John Jeudwine, a regular officer, had just assumed command, and his first job was to take the squadron to Palembang in southern Sumatra, where it arrived at the end of January. Jeudwine and his crews flew many bombing sorties, but were unable to stop the Japanese advance towards Sumatra, and the squadron was forced to redeploy to an airfield in north-west Java, where it continued operations with its depleted force of Blenheims. As a Japanese invading force arrived on the squadron's airfield, Jeudwine was ordered to destroy his aircraft and equipment, and take his men to the port of Tjilatjap on the south coast of Java to await evacuation. By commandeering any vehicle that could be found, he was able to move many of his men to the Dutch-controlled port.

On arrival at Tjilatjap it soon became apparent to Jeudwine that the situation was chaotic and evacuation was extremely unlikely. He immediately tried to requisition a Dutch corvette, but the local commander refused to cooperate, and an excellent opportunity to evacuate his men was denied. He searched the coast for other ships, but his efforts failed to find anything suitable. On his return, he was told that orders had been issued to send his men to an inland town, and many had already left. Sixty of his squadron remained in Tjilatjap, and he was given permission to try and evacuate them. A search of the local docks produced two ship's lifeboats salvaged from an old liner, and a small motor launch. The men scoured the area for any useful equipment and supplies. A sextant and ship's compass were found, together with an old Bartholomew's school atlas. In addition, a good supply of food and water was obtained.

The plan was for the motorboat to tow the two lifeboats, each carrying 30 men, out to the open sea until it ran out of fuel, when it would be abandoned, and the lifeboats would sail south to Australia. With the docks under attack, the small convoy departed at 11 p.m. on 6 March 1942. The launch soon got into trouble, and it was also clear that the lifeboats were overloaded and could not be sailed in such a state. In heading for a small cove to reassess the situation, the motor launch was wrecked and one of the lifeboats was badly holed on a reef. Jeudwine anchored his boat as the supplies were salvaged from the other two before beaching the boat. He was now faced with a major dilemma.

In the short, but very turbulent, time since Jeudwine had taken command of 84 Squadron, he had shown that he was a man able to assess difficult situations before making firm and clear decisions. After discussions with his men, he decided that the remaining boat, with a crew of 12, should try to make the trip to Australia, alert the authorities, and arrange for a ship to be sent to rescue the remainder. Selecting the crew was a difficult job, but Jeudwine decided to take Squadron Leader K. Passmore as his second-in-command, Flying Officer C. Turner, the only navigator, and Flying Officer Streatfeild, who, apart from Jeudwine, was the only man with any sailing experience. Jeudwine decided that the rest of the crew should be the fittest among the Australians who had volunteered to fight with the RAF, and he gave them first refusal: seven accepted.

It was estimated that it would take about 16 days to reach the nearest point on the north Australian coast near the small town of Roebourne, 950 miles away. The 30 ft boat, named HMRAFS *Scorpion*, after the squadron's badge, finally set sail at dusk on 7 March. The following day it was becalmed when a Japanese submarine, the I-56, surfaced a mile away before approaching to within 100 yards. The captain and some crew, including a gunner manning the machine-gun, could be clearly seen. Expecting to be machine-gunned, the crew held their breath, but were relieved to see the submarine depart after completing a circle around their boat. They took this act to be a good omen. A breeze sprang up and they sailed on, beating for most of the way against headwinds.

The crew soon discovered that the rudder was damaged, and it proved to be a constant problem throughout the voyage. Sergeants Corney and Lovegrove had to make emergency repairs almost daily, and the ultimate success of the voyage was in no small part due to

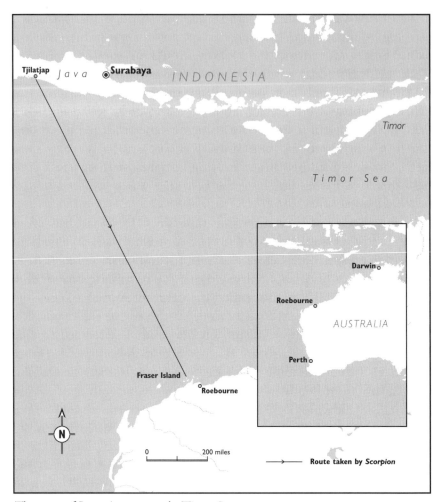

The route of Scorpion *across the Timor Sea.*

their initiative and courage in constantly entering the water to effect repairs. Passmore was in charge of the boat routine and rations, and he set the daily ration as nine ounces of bully beef or camp pie, six biscuits, half a pint of water and a can of beer. Some delicacies were saved for the Navy custom of 'Saturday night at sea' and for special occasions.

A routine of two watches was soon established, with Jeudwine and Streatfeild sharing the steering. Sleeping space was very cramped, and shelter from the burning sun was very limited, causing most to suffer from painful sunburn. Only modest progress was made in the first week, when the boat was often becalmed, but this was interrupted by a violent storm during which the rudder failed again – taking many

The original log of the Scorpion *kept by the navigator C. Turner. (G. Moore)*

hours for the two sergeants to effect repairs with makeshift tools. The crew also discovered that some of their water casks had been contaminated with salt water and another had been spilled, leaving them with insufficient for the rest of the voyage. Fortunately, another heavy thunderstorm allowed them to replenish all their casks, but it was a timely reminder of the great care needed to safeguard their most precious commodity for survival.

On 21 March they ran into another storm, accompanied by a very heavy swell. The boat had to heave to as it was shipping water faster than the crew could bale out and was becoming waterlogged. Once again, the rudder broke, and the two sergeants had a daunting task to lash it together in the mountainous seas. By late morning, the wind abated and the boat was able to make headway, achieving some six knots east of south. Within a few days, the fickle weather changed again, and this time the crew were becalmed for almost a week. Clothes were dried, games invented and the daily sun sighting indicated that they were drifting back north. It was at this time that they had to reduce their daily food allowance. The voyage was taking longer, but more worryingly they discovered that the constant waterlogging of the boat had damaged much of their food supply.

As a breeze developed to signal the end of the calm, another hazard loomed. A 60 ft whale surfaced some 200 yards away and started to circle the boat, eventually coming alongside with its tail on one side and its head on the other. One flick of the tail would have capsized the boat, with catastrophic results, but after a short period, it sailed off to join an even bigger companion.

On the morning of 16 April, Sergeant Corney was on watch, and he declared that he could definitely smell spinifex, a native Australian shrub. The crew had also seen an increasing amount of seaweed, suggesting that they might be near the coast. However, hopes were dashed when Jeudwine discovered that his watch had lost time, probably making their sun sightings inaccurate. He immediately ordered a reduction in the food and water ration. Optimism soon returned the following day when a butterfly was sighted, and a new species of jellyfish. On 19 April they thought they heard a motor, and daylight the next day gave them their first sight of land. They went ashore on an island, and a plate on a beacon told them that they were at Fraser Island, 50 miles west of Roebourne. After 44 days at sea they went ashore, but all kept falling over, finding it difficult to balance and stand up. During the afternoon they sighted a flying-boat, but it appeared not to see them, so they set sail to the east along a chain of islands. They beached in the evening, when they caught and cooked some fish – their first fresh food for 45 days. They spent the night ashore, when they rediscovered the joy of lying on a stationary bed.

The following day they were sailing north-east when another aircraft appeared. They attracted its attention, and after a circuit of the *Scorpion* it alighted. Jeudwine swam across to it and was able to explain who they were and their situation. The aircraft was a US Navy Catalina of Patrol Squadron 101. It took three men off the boat before getting airborne. The *Scorpion* sailed on, its crew intent on reaching Roebourne under their own sail. At 12.30 p.m. the next day, the Catalina reappeared with orders to take off the remaining men. To the disappointment of the crew, their protests that they wanted to sail the boat into port were ignored, and they climbed aboard the Catalina and set the *Scorpion* adrift.

So, after 47 days at sea, and sailing almost 1,500 miles in a leaking boat with a lash-up for a rudder, the 12 men were safe. The crew of the *Scorpion* spent the night on the USS *Childs*, where they were shown great hospitality. The next day they were flown to Perth, where Jeudwine alerted the authorities to the plight of those he had been forced to leave behind. Arrangements were made for a US Navy submarine to go to Java, but it found no evidence of the other men. It transpired that they had run out of food on the day that the *Scorpion* sighted land, and they were forced to give themselves up to spend the rest of the war as prisoners of the Japanese.

After the voyage, Jeudwine paid a handsome tribute to his crew

The epic voyage of the Scorpion *and its crew was given much publicity in the Australian press.* (G. Jeudwine)

AS THEY REACHED AUSTRALIA a few days ago after an epic voyage from Java in ship's lifeboat, unshaven, barefooted and bandaged. The same R.A.F. men are shown below . . .

Spent 44 Days In Open Boat

. . . after being issued with new uniforms. Picture taken yesterday at their Melbourne hotel. From left: Pilot Officer Streatfield, Wing Commander Jeudwine, Pilot Officer Turner, Squadron Leader Passmore.

when he said, 'I would not, if the opportunity again occurred, alter one of the crew. They were magnificent.' The crew reciprocated the feeling, one of them saying, 'He always led from the front and constantly inspired those under him by his example. I have met very few COs with his qualities.' Notwithstanding the remarkable achievement of getting the *Scorpion* to Australia, John Jeudwine showed his true feelings when he wrote: 'I think the worst tragedy of the whole show was that the other crews whom we left off Tjilatjap had gone when help reached them. It takes away any satisfaction I might have felt on making the boat trip successfully.' For his outstanding leadership during the voyage of the *Scorpion*, John Jeudwine was awarded the OBE. He later commanded bomber squadrons in North Africa and in Bomber Command, when he was awarded the DSO and the DFC. Tragically, he was killed in a flying accident just after the war had finished.

~

The Japanese advance into the south-west Pacific was remorseless. The capture of Singapore and the Dutch East Indies was followed by the conquest of the Philippines. By July 1942 the Japanese had occupied most of Papua New Guinea and taken the Solomon Islands, posing a direct threat to Australia, which was then in range of Japanese bombers. American and Australian reinforcements were rushed to the area and the advance was halted. Over the next six months, some of the bloodiest battles were fought and eventually won by the Allies, with the turning point coming at Guadalcanal in February 1943. With Papua and the eastern Solomon Islands secure, the American-led Allied forces were able to start their advances to regain the huge amount of territory occupied by the Japanese in the south-west Pacific. Prominent in all these operations were the squadrons of the Royal Australian Air Force.

RESCUE FROM PAPUA NEW GUINEA

At 7.20 a.m. on 3 November 1943, Wing Commander Bill Townsend and his RAAF navigator took off from Goodenough Island, off the east coast of Papua New Guinea, in their 22 (RAAF) Squadron A-20C (Boston) twin-engine bomber. Townsend, the Squadron

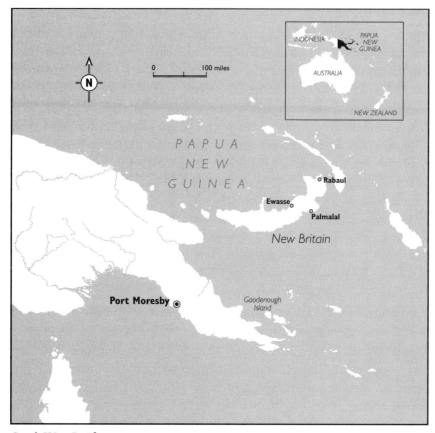

South West Pacific.

Commander from Victoria, was leading a raid to bomb Japanese barges that were massing at Palmalmal on the south-east coast of the Japanese-occupied island of New Britain. As they approached the target, a squadron of Beaufighters strafed the area with their cannon as the Bostons started their low-level bombing run. Just as Townsend released the bombs, the aircraft received a direct hit from anti-aircraft fire, cutting off the fuel supply to the engines and causing a fire. Too low to bale out, Townsend immediately ditched the aircraft, which settled on a coral reef. The dinghy was released from the port wing, when it automatically inflated, and Townsend and his navigator, Flying Officer David McClymont of Sydney, clambered aboard and paddled furiously for the nearby shoreline 150 yards away. Fortunately, the jungle came right down to the water's edge to give them cover from the searching Japanese, who arrived soon after the two airmen had headed into the jungle.

Once ashore, they quickly gathered their emergency supplies together, which included a jungle knife, ground sheet, and 15 days of emergency rations, consisting mainly of dehydrated meat, vegetables and fruit. During the briefings on survival procedures, they had been warned to head inland before contacting natives since there was the possibility that those living on the coast might be under the influence of the Japanese. They proceeded on a compass heading of north-west until nightfall, when they stopped to eat and prepare a shelter with the groundsheet. Torrential rain fell overnight, and this taught them to stop travelling at about 4 p.m. each day to allow time to build a substantial lean-to shelter to keep them dry.

The two men continued their trek through the mountainous terrain for the next 10 days, until 13 November, when they came to a village where they soon discovered that the natives were friendly. By the use of a phrase book of the local 'Pidgin' language they were able to make themselves understood. A young boy was able to tell them that there was a 'Captain belong English'. He was referring to Captain Ian Skinner, who was the leader of a group of 'Coastwatchers', a remarkable group of Australians, New Zealanders and men from the British Solomon Islands who carried out immensely valuable work in Japanese-occupied territory reporting by radio the movement of enemy forces.

The villagers looked after the two men well. After a few days they met a native wearing an Australian slouch hat, who paddled a canoe towards them calling out, 'Me friend belong Australia true.' He was Golpak, the 60-year-old chief of the Mengen group of villages, and he was to be the airmen's 'number one' for the next month. He was a colourful and brave character who did a great deal of good work for the Allies, and he immediately started work to build a shelter for the two men. Over the next few weeks, he provided an excellent diet of fish, chicken, fruit and vegetables, but during this period, there were numerous times when Golpak's informers alerted him to the presence of the Japanese, and Townsend and McClymont had to hastily head for the jungle or to nearby caves to hide. On one occasion when they heard shooting, Golpak and the two Australians had to rush to the jungle, where they hid in a waterhole with the water up to their necks. It was only after they clambered out that Golpak informed them that the waterhole was infested with crocodiles. Eventually, the men thought that they were endangering Golpak and his natives, so they sent a message to Skinner seeking approval to join him, and he agreed.

The two Australians left Golpak and his courageous and kind villagers to head towards the centre of the island, where they met Skinner. They arrived at the rendezvous on 20 December, and the following day Skinner led them on a six-hour march to his unit's radio station, where they were to spend the next six weeks with members of the Coastwatchers, and where they were introduced to Lieutenant Fred Hargesheimer of the USAAF.

Early in December, Skinner had learned from his native contacts that an American pilot was living with them on the north coast, and he made arrangements for him to be brought to the station. He was Fred Hargesheimer, a photographic reconnaissance pilot who had been shot down six months earlier. His was a remarkable story of courage and an absolute determination to survive. For over a month he lived on nothing but snails and bamboo shoots before natives found him, took him to their village, and saved his life. He had suffered badly with dysentery and malaria and his body was covered in sores. He had been forced to move into the jungle to hide whenever Japanese patrols arrived, but the courageous villagers gave him food and helped provide shelter for him. Once Skinner became involved, Hargesheimer was kept supplied with food and information, and he was able to assist the Coastwatchers' radio operator, Sergeant Matt Foley, in sending messages about Japanese air and ground activity. On one occasion they were able to alert the Allied forces that a large formation of Japanese dive-bombers were heading towards them, and as a result of their warning the attack was intercepted by Allied fighters, with heavy losses to the Japanese attackers.

Shortly after Christmas the two Australians and the American had to leave the Coastwatchers' camp in a hurry. A native had arrived to warn Skinner and his second-in-command, Lieutenant John Stokie, that a Japanese patrol had landed on a beach eight miles away and had started looking for the airmen. With two native guides and a supply of food, they headed into the jungle in torrential rain. They spent a miserable week in makeshift shelters before Skinner was able to get a message to them that it was safe to return. It took them three exhausting days to reach the main camp.

On 30 January 1944, a radio message was received by Matt Foley, which read, 'Airmen can be evacuated.' The message went on to give a time and the latitude and longitude of the rendezvous. Unfortunately, the position had been corrupted, and when it was retransmitted, the maps were found to be out of date! Early the next

Wing Commander Bill Townsend bids farewell to the Australian 'Coastwatcher', Sergeant Matt Foley. (RAFES)

morning, a RAAF aircraft flew overhead to drop a message with all the necessary details. They consulted their maps and found the position of the rendezvous – the Korinindi river. It was only 13 miles north-east of their camp as the crow flies, but on foot through the thick jungle it would be two or three times further. There were just four days to complete this crucial route to safety for what was almost certainly the only chance of rescue.

The three airmen said their farewells, and led by their native guides they set off into the jungle, relying entirely on the skill of the guides. They soon encountered a ravine, which took four hours to negotiate, and their spirits fell when they realized that they had covered such a short distance in overcoming the obstacle. They had to make a detour along a ridge, where they found a track that branched off in two directions after a mile. The guides were unsure and guessed which one to follow, only for the party to find themselves back at the fork one hour later. Shortly after taking the second fork, they stumbled across a village where they rested for the night, wet and very dispirited after such a strenuous day making a very short distance.

They left with new guides early next morning, but soon encountered difficulties. They had to skirt another deep ravine and make a wide detour, which brought them to a torrent of brown water that was impossible to cross. After another detour, they came across two deserted huts where they rested for the night. Another early start was made the next morning, and after a three-hour march they arrived back at the village they had left two days earlier. Shortly afterwards, two natives arrived with a message from John Stokie telling them that the rendezvous had been brought forward 24 hours. Desperation began to set in.

The following morning they set off with a hill native guide and numerous carriers. The rain finally stopped, and they were able to cross the river that had halted their progress the day before. They soon encountered an even bigger obstacle, but the carriers used a large fallen tree to make a crossing point and the party moved on as fast as possible. Next, they had to navigate through the second-largest swamp in New Britain. Following a slow-moving river, and occasionally fording small tributaries, they came upon a huge tree that had fallen across the water. Once across this makeshift bridge, they made their way through a rotting, evil-smelling swamp before finding a place to make a shelter for the night, surrounded by crocodile-infested swamp. The next morning, 5 February, they had to move early with the rendezvous time approaching, and they were forced to wade through waist-deep swamp before finally hitting the coast at 11.30 a.m.

At the coast they had a one-mile walk along a narrow track before arriving at the rendezvous point, where a native policeman met them – the leader of another Coastwatchers group had sent him. They discovered that the final pick-up point was across the wide bay, a two-day trek if they walked round it, which would have resulted in them missing their rescue. The only alternative was to board a native war canoe with outrigger and sail, and cross the bay. They left at 3.50 p.m. and a strong breeze allowed them to make good progress. Halfway across they sighted another sail, which one of the natives suggested could be a Japanese patrol, and they devised a plan in case the boat came across to investigate them. The three airmen were to hide in the bottom of the boat, and once the boat was close enough, they would emerge with their four carbines, two pistols and one revolver and give the Japanese a broadside! Fortunately, they did not have to implement the plan.

For the final part of the journey they had to paddle furiously to make the fast-approaching rendezvous time. They completed the crossing of the bay just as it was getting dark at 7 p.m. They had deliberately aimed to be dropped short of the final rendezvous in order not to disclose the precise pick-up point. They said goodbye to their native friends who had risked their lives and worked so hard, before setting off with the policeman for the final short section of their journey. They had speculated on how they would be picked up and agreed that the most probable method would be by Catalina flying-boat. They were nearing the pick-up point at midnight when they suddenly saw in the moonlight the conning tower of a submarine. They broke into an excited run, which was halted abruptly when a number of natives armed with spears emerged to block their way. But these were a guard force placed to cover their departure.

Within minutes, two rubber boats were seen, and an Australian commando in charge of the covering force signalled the submarine by torch. The boats turned for the beach, and there was a joyful rush through the breakers to board them. In a few minutes the three airmen were being helped aboard the USS *Gato,* where they scrambled down the conning tower to a welcome from the captain, Lieutenant Commander Bob Foley. They were treated to hot baths, food and a warm bed as the submarine submerged to head for safety. Three months had elapsed since the two Australians had unexpectedly arrived in New Britain, and Fred Hargesheimer's ordeal had lasted nine months.

After the war, Golpak was made a Member of the Order of the British Empire for his courageous service to the Allies throughout the war. When he died in 1959, a memorial was erected in his memory near to the scene of his first meeting with Townsend and McClymont. Bill Townsend was a regular officer, and he rose to the rank of air vice-marshal to become the Deputy Chief of the RAAF Air Staff. He was President of the Australian Branch of the RAF Escaping Society and died in 1987. Ian Skinner was awarded the MC for his wartime activities. Fred Hargesheimer never forgot his helpers, 'who saved his life'. In 1961 he started to raise money to build a school for the native children, which was opened at the village of Ewasse, where he first met the two Australians. He was a teacher at his 'Airmen's Memorial School' for four years, and he and his wife have returned almost every year since, devoting their retirement to raising money to improve the school facilities for future generations of native children.

As the war in the Far East entered its final year, the Special Duties squadrons based in Eastern India and Ceylon found themselves in ever-increasing demand to support numerous clandestine organizations operating with anti-Japanese movements throughout South-East Asia. Only the converted Liberator bomber aircraft with auxiliary fuel tanks had sufficient range to reach many of the dropping zones, and some of the sorties flown were up to 20 hours long. For many of the crews shot down at extreme range on these operations, there was little chance of returning or evading capture. The first of very few to evade capture in Siam (Thailand) was Canadian Flying Officer Harry Smith and some of his crew.

RETURN FROM SIAM

When the Japanese entered Siam in December 1941, they allowed the Government to remain in office, confident of their cooperation. Initially, this seemed well founded when Siam declared war on Britain and the United States on 25 January 1942. However, the Siamese were less than enthusiastic about the Japanese presence, and some high-ranking government ministers held meetings which resulted in the formation of the Resistance movement 'Seri Thai' (Free Thai). The India Mission of SOE soon set up the Siam Country Section to provide support for them. However, the complexities and intrigues of Siamese politics prevented any significant support for some time.

As the war progressed, a viable and effective Siamese Resistance movement was in the interests of the Allies, and aid, supplies and SOE agents were delivered by long-range Catalina and Liberator aircraft flying from eastern India. By late 1944, the Resistance forces were starting to be effective, and by the end of the year there were large parts of the country, particularly in the north, that were in the hands of the guerrilla forces and Resistance movements. Dropping-zones and small airstrips were constructed, allowing an increasing amount of arms and supplies to be provided.

At midnight on 29 May 1945, 21-year-old, Winnipeg-born Flying Officer Harry Smith RCAF lifted his heavily laden 358 Squadron Liberator aircraft (EW 174) off the runway at Jessore, near Calcutta. He and his nine-man crew were on a Special Duties operation to drop supplies and four US military personnel over Siam. Just after dawn they were approaching the dropping-zone when nine Japanese

A supply drop over Indo-China. The photograph was taken from a Liberator flown by Flying Officer Harry Smith RCAF after he returned to his squadron following his unique evasion from Siam. (Andy Thomas collection)

'Oscar' fighters were sighted closing in on the Liberator. The fighters made a series of coordinated attacks, setting the heavy bomber on fire and killing three of the crew. All four engines were put out of action and Smith was faced with the almost impossible task of getting the stricken aircraft down. He ordered the crew to take up their crash positions as he set the aircraft down in a heavily forested area. The wings of the aircraft were ripped off and the fuselage careered through the trees for 300 yards before coming to rest. One of the crew and a passenger died in the crash.

Harry Smith was injured in the head, back and ankle, but he managed to struggle from the wreck to meet some of the crew who had also scrambled free despite being injured. Others were trapped inside the aircraft, and Smith entered the wreckage to rescue a badly injured American, Corporal Napieralski. The crew were making a stretcher for the American when they heard the sound of voices approaching and a dog barking. Believing that the Japanese were approaching, Smith decided to remain with Napieralski, and giving his revolver, kukri and escape purse to the senior American, he ordered the survivors to escape as best they could.

Shortly after the party left, Smith lapsed into unconsciousness for a while, but on coming to, he returned to the aircraft and retrieved the escape purse of the dead navigator. He also recovered some parachutes, medical supplies and survival kit, including two rifles, and he destroyed the wireless codebooks and crystals. When he returned to Napieralski, 100 heavily armed natives had assembled, but were keeping their distance. With the aid of the blood chit, he was able to make contact with the natives, who appeared friendly. They gave him some water to drink and to bathe the American. Soon afterwards, Corporal Napieralski died.

The natives took Smith to their village, about half a mile away, where he met the chief, who gave him some hot rice, but indicated that he must move on. Several natives escorted him to another village about a mile away, where he met the rest of the crew. Owing to the injuries of some of the men, including bullet wounds and burns, they had made slow progress until they heard voices, when they hid in the thick scrub. Major Gildee, one of the American agents, went forward and established contact with the natives, who proved to be friendly. They were taken to a village where they were given rice, invited to give up their arms, and made comfortable. By 11 a.m. all the survivors had been reunited in the chief's hut. The natives heated some water, and out of the meagre medical supplies they had rescued, together with strips of parachute, they were able to effect some first-aid treatment. The rest of the day and the night were spent at the chief's house.

Early the next morning a party of mounted hill police arrived, and through an English-speaking member, they were told that they were to be taken away, since the Japanese were expected at the village later in the day. They were taken on bullock carts to a lake in a forest some three miles from the village, where they remained all day. Fruit and rice were provided, and Flight Sergeant Copley spent all day sterilizing water. During the day, a Thai aircraft brought eight police officials, including the Chief of Police of the Nakaun Sawan district, who remained with them throughout the journey to his head-quarters. Late in the afternoon the police escort returned, having been to the crash site, where they had buried the five dead and salvaged a quantity of gear from the crashed aircraft. They had three bullock carts to take the party on their journey.

When news of the crash reached the Japanese, they sent out a party of 70 soldiers to search for survivors. A Japanese officer telephoned the Chief of Police at Nakaun Sawan to ask if he had any news. The police staff informed the officer that 'unfortunately the Chief was away from the office so we could tell them nothing' – he was busy escorting the survivors to safety!

After six hours' travelling on very bumpy tracks, the party stopped at midnight, when they were given a good meal of chicken and rice. Having changed the bullocks, the party set off with an escort of three horsemen. Whenever they stopped, the police were extremely thorough in clearing up all traces of the party, and giving security talks to the villagers. During the night halt, they were told that two Japanese had entered the village, but the police had shot them and buried the bodies. At midday on the third day, they stopped at a village where they were given an extremely good meal of Chinese food, and they rested until resuming their journey in the evening. No halt was made during the fourth day, when the party had to share one bottle of water and a few pineapples.

During the early hours of the fifth day they arrived at a much more prosperous village, where they received efficient medical attention from a doctor's assistant. After a meal and a short rest they were taken on covered ox carts to a river where they embarked on two 30 ft covered sampans propelled by two oarsmen. Owing to a storm, the sampans had to lie up for a few hours, but by midnight they had arrived at a large houseboat, belonging to a Chinese family, moored on the edge of a lake. The family were most hospitable and the daughter of the house dressed their wounds. After a meal, and invitations to return after the war, a captain and a lieutenant of the police arrived to escort them on the next stage of their journey. Throughout their journey, it was clear that they were expected, and arrangements for their reception had been made.

After a two-hour rest, it was time to say goodbye to the Chief of Police, who had taken charge of them from the time they had crashed. The party crossed the lake by a rowing boat before the police escorted them, one by one, across a railway line patrolled by the Japanese. They descended to the river and embarked on a police launch. It was open at each end but covered amidships, allowing the party to be reasonably well hidden from the many Japanese about. The party now consisted of the captain and lieutenant, with six other policemen, the six RAF personnel and three Americans, the launch driver, the engineer and his wife, who acted as the cook. They travelled all day and well into the following night, avoiding sampans and always crossing to the far bank when passing villages.

By early afternoon on the seventh day since the crash, they

disembarked somewhere in the Bangkok region, where they went to the local police station. They were transferred in a covered bus to a police headquarters on the outskirts of Bangkok, where medical orderlies treated their wounds, and they were given a very good supper before retiring to sleeping accommodation. During the early hours of the next morning, Smith and Major Gildee were woken by the police, and out of sight of the rest of the party were introduced to a Thai general who was the leader of the Resistance movement. He was violently anti-Japanese, and explained that he would have to tell the Japanese authorities that the Liberator had a crew of nine, that five had been killed and four would be interned in a Thai camp. He would arrange for the remainder of the party to be rescued.

Harry Smith faced an agonizing decision. Since Flight Sergeant Cyril Copley had virtually finished his tour of operations and was due to leave India, he selected him to accompany himself and the three Americans. He explained the situation to his four colleagues, and before leaving an hour later, they left all their useful belongings with them. The party then left under the cover of darkness, accompanied by the General and armed guards, for the headquarters of the local American OSS organization. They remained at the headquarters for the next four days, receiving medical attention and excellent food. On 11 June an American pilot, Major Kellogg, who had been shot down 13 months earlier, and an Australian soldier, Private Olle, who had escaped from a working party on the Burma–Siam railway, joined them.

At 1.30 a.m. on 12 June the party were issued with revolvers and machine-guns before boarding a bus with a police escort. Anticlimax followed as the bus back-fired all the way down the street before eventually grinding to a halt outside a police station. Another bus took them back to the OSS headquarters. Late that night, and with a breakdown truck proceeding them, they left in a new bus, and travelled some 80 miles in a northerly direction. They arrived at an airfield where they stayed until dawn. They were then loaded into three small communications aircraft, and taken on a two-hour flight to the airfield at Pukio, where they spent the day concealed in a bamboo basha. Later that evening a meteorological report was sent to Allied headquarters. The next morning, Smith made an inspection of the state of the 3,600 ft runway, and another report was sent.

At 9 a.m. on 14 June, a Dakota of 357 Squadron piloted by Flight Lieutenant L. G. Lewis landed at Pukio. The pilot found the short runway adequate, but the aircraft became bogged down at the end of its landing run. Within an hour it had been recovered and was airborne with the evaders on board *en route* to Rangoon, where it landed to refuel. By late afternoon, it had arrived at Alipore, near Calcutta, where Smith and his colleagues were taken to the SOE Mission and E Group headquarters for debriefings and recuperation, three weeks after they were shot down. Two months later, the Thai authorities released their four colleagues.

On 14 August 1945, the *London Gazette* announced that Flying Officer H. V. Smith RCAF had been awarded the DFC for his outstanding gallantry during the attack by the Japanese fighters. The citation concluded: 'although wounded, he successfully crash-landed the crippled aircraft and thus saved the lives of the remaining members of his crew. In the face of great odds, this officer set a fine example of coolness and bravery'. Twelve months later it was announced that the French Government had awarded Smith a Croix de Guerre in recognition of the seven long-range resupply missions that he had flown over French Indo-China.

Epilogue

THE END OF THE WAR IN EUROPE did not signal the end of MI 9's work. In addition to supporting the war in the Far East, there was much to do to seek the identities of the very many helpers in order to offer them compensation and expenses, and to identify those deserving awards. This work was carried out in close conjunction with the Americans. An awards bureau was established in the autumn of 1944 within the organization of IS 9 to vet the many claims and to establish those that were justified. At its head was Donald Darling, who had returned from Gibraltar after the liberation of France had made the escape lines through France to Spain redundant. In two years the bureau processed over 35,000 claims in Western Europe alone. Needless to say, there were some bogus claims, and as M. R. D. Foot wrote: 'Some collaborators with the enemy sought to find cover to protect themselves against irate neighbours.' But for every collaborator there were many secret and brave helpers who simply never came forward and remained anonymous. A particularly gratifying task for IS 9 (AB) was to identify and recommend many helpers for gallantry awards in recognition of their wonderful services, and some have been mentioned in previous chapters. There are many more who deserve to be mentioned, but have not been identified.

During the First World War the services of certain foreigners had been recognized by the award of a special medal. The terms for this award did not fit the circumstances of the Second World War, and so a new medal, 'The King's Medal for Courage in the Cause of Freedom', was instituted by Royal Warrant on 23 August 1945. It was awarded to men and women, both military and civilian, 'for acts of courage entailing dangerous work in hazardous circumstances, in the furtherance of the Allied cause'. Very many of the 3,200 awards were made to those who gave assistance to evading aircrew.

Certificates of thanks for helpers were designed and sent to helpers. Sadly, this was an important matter that was not well handled, particularly by the RAF. Winston Churchill agreed to sign each one personally, but the RAF insisted that an airman should sign the certificates since the majority of evaders were aircrew. Eventually, it was agreed that Air Chief Marshal Sir Arthur Tedder – the Deputy Supreme Allied Commander – would sign the certificates. Unfortunately, his signature appeared as a rubber stamp. Other theatres of war also produced certificates of gratitude to helpers, with Field Marshal Earl Alexander signing those for the Mediterranean theatre and Admiral of the Fleet Lord Mountbatten for the Far East.

To most helpers it was the gratitude of the evaders that meant the most. Very many unique friendships were established between evaders and helpers and their families, and these flourish today with reunions and regular visits. After the unfortunate handling of the helpers' certificates, the RAF more than made amends by sponsoring and financing the RAF Escaping Society (RAFES). Marshal of the Royal Air Force Viscount Portal of Hungerford, the then Chief of the Air Staff, founded the Society in 1945, and became its first President. The first Chairman was Air Chief Marshal Sir Basil Embry, himself an evader, and his drive and personal involvement ensured that the men and women who had given so much to help evaders would be given assistance when needed, and certainly they would never be forgotten.

The objects of the Society were given as:

1. To give financial support to surviving helpers and to the dependants of those who lost their lives assisting escapers and evaders of the RAF and Commonwealth Air Forces.
2. To make donations to appropriate charities in the former occupied countries as an expression of gratitude from escapers and evaders.
3. To encourage reciprocal visits between members of the Society and their helpers.
4. To assist helpers in any matters that help foster good relations with the British Commonwealth.

Branches were established in Australia and Canada, and the society flourished as a charity for 50 years. Sadly, but inevitably, numbers

This certificate is awarded to

as a token of gratitude for and appreciation of the help given to the Sailors, Soldiers and Airmen of the British Commonwealth of Nations, which enabled them to escape from, or evade capture by the enemy.

Louis Mountbatten

Supreme Allied Commander, South East Asia.

1941-1945

The certificate awarded to 'helpers' in South-East Asia and signed by Lord Mountbatten. (TNA: PRO WO 900/51) started to decline significantly in the 1990s, and it was decided that the Society should 'go out with a flourish'. It was closed officially at the Annual General Meeting on 16 September 1995, followed the next day by a moving ceremony at Lincoln Cathedral, where the Society's standard was laid up in the presence of its last president, Air Chief Marshal Sir Lewis Hodges, and the Chief of the Air Staff, Air Chief Marshal Sir Michael Graydon.

An informal Escaping Society was formed, and the former members of the RAFES and their helpers continue to keep in touch through newsletters, reunions and visits to each other. To build up an archive and research facility for all escape lines, the Escape Line Memorial Society was founded in 2002. Among its worthy objectives are 'to foster relationships between nations, and second and third generation escaper, evader and helper families', and 'to educate and inspire future generations'. As age catches up with the Second World War generation, it will be the responsibility of the new Society to perpetuate the memory of so many gallant people, and to honour the sacrifices made by those who assisted Allied escapers and evaders. In this way, Lord Portal's steadfast intention when he founded the RAFES, which became the motto of the Society, will live on into the future:

'Let us always remember those who helped us when we were in need.'

Appendix

OUTLINED BELOW IS THE LIST of subjects given to students of the RAF 'B' Intelligence Course. Each student was required to produce a lecture to be given in front of the other course members at the conclusion of the course. It provides an ideal précis of the advice given to aircrew during lectures at their OTUs and squadrons.

SUBJECTS FOR PRACTICE LECTURES

1. Introduction. Duty to escape. To bring back (a) yourself (b) information (c) to be a nuisance (d) in P/W camp to keep healthy. German report on PW camps last war. Propaganda, sabotage.
2. General conditions in France, Belgium, Holland. 90% inhabitants friendly. Coast useless. Avoid officials. German sentries can't distinguish between Frenchmen and Englishmen. Examples. Line of Demarcation. New conditions with German occupants of Vichy.
3. Evasion. Baling out. Hide parachute from road. Preliminary disguise. Belly-landing. Destruction of aircraft. German search, run, hide. First half hour all important (Examples).
4. Instructions for making first contact with helpers (Examples). Instructions for Belgium. Stay hidden with satisfactory 'host'. Watchers. Don't ask for Organization. Get civilian clothes. Don't take risks. Don't take addresses. Don't compromise inhabitants.

5. Travel in France. In civilian clothes, on foot in daytime. Curfew at night. Towns dangerous at night. Motors at night are German. Walk as though on business. Agricultural instrument. Don't steal bicycle.

6. Train travel in France and Belgium. Buying tickets. Short journeys from and to small stations. Night control at big stations. Sometimes controls on fast trains. Railway workers helpful from Holland to Barcelona. Crossing Paris (Examples).

7. Once in hands Organization, obey implicitly. Don't talk. Pas de Calais. West route over Pyrenees. Take no money to Spain. Consuls. Miranda camp dangers.

8. If captured. Wait opportunity to escape. Any ruse to avoid going to Germany. Malingering. Train jumping. Preliminary German search and interrogation. Only name, rank and number. Red Cross forms. Be careful with first letter.

9. Dulag Luft. Explicit instructions. Cherbourg. Hospitals.

10. Evasion or escape from Norway, Ireland, Italy, Spain, Portugal, Denmark.

11. Evasion Germany. German search. Hiding is main task. Water bottle. Walking through Germany. Walking on railways. Jumping goods trains. Food. Villages. Value of remaining 'at large' as long as possible. Coal trains in Frankfurt. 6,000,000 foreigners in Germany.

12. Exits from Germany. Westwards to Dutch, Belgian borders. Northern ports. Swiss frontier. Approach to Swiss frontier. Sign posts. Hitler Jugend.

13. Morale in P/W camps. S.B.O. Escaping committees. Maps, gadgets, and knowledge already in camps. Keep fit. Prepare carefully. German morale drops with defeats (Examples).

14. International Law. Geneva Convention 1929. Escaping permitted. P/W tried for offences under laws of detaining power. Conspiracy. Rights of P/W. Any disguise permitted. Invaders may change civilian clothes under certain conditions but not into German uniform. What is uniform? (Examples.) Rights to escapers in neutral countries.

Bibliography

OFFICIAL SOURCES AT THE NATIONAL ARCHIVES

ADM 199/1044	Naval Operations in the Aegean – 1943
AIR 14/354	Escape Aids
AIR 23/2146	E Group Operations – China and Formosa
AIR 23/2708	Air Jungle Rescue. Evasion Reports
AIR 23/2934	Education in Escape and Evasion
AIR 23/2937	Escape and Evasion. Rescal Summaries E Group
AIR 23/6079	Air-Sea Rescue – Desert Rescue
AIR 23/6742	Operations in Cos/Leros
AIR 27/Various	RAF Squadron Operational Record Books
AIR 40/1548–51	Evasion Reports
AIR 40/1832	Mediterranean Allied Air Force Bulletin
AIR 40/1846	Escape and Evasion
AIR 40/1874	Escape and Evasion Reports
AIR 40/2462	Escape and Evasion. Far East Reports
AIR 40/2467	Selected Escapes and Evasions
AIR 51/260	Escape Aids
CAB 44/151	History of the Long Range Desert Group
HS 7/172	MI 9 Activities in Eastern Mediterranean
WO 208/3242	Crockatt's Historical record of MI 9
WO 208/3251	Summary of MI 9 Activities in India and SEAC
WO 208/3253	Summary of MI 9 Activities in Eastern Mediterranean
WO 208/3268	MI 9 Bulletin
WO 208/3298–3327	MI 9 Evasion Reports
WO 208/3352	IS 9 (WEA) Interrogation Reports
WO 208/3424	Specimen Lecture. Far East 1945

WO 208/3428	Pre-capture Training
WO 208/3449	MI 9 Advance 'A' Headquarters in North Africa
WO 208/3494	Escapers and Evaders
WO 208/5011	Summary of MI 9 Activities in India and SEAC
ZJ 1/920–1015	*London Gazette*, 1939–46 (also available online at www.gazettes-online.co.uk)

PUBLISHED SOURCES

Brome, Vincent, *The Way Back* (Cassel, 1957)
Crawley, Aidan, *Escape from Germany* (HMSO, 1985)
Cruikshank, Charles, *SOE in the Far East* (Oxford University Press)
Darling, Donald, *Secret Sunday* (Kimber, 1975)
Deane-Drummond, Anthony, *Return Ticket* (Collins, 1957)
Derry, Sam, *The Rome Escape Line* (Harrap, 1960)
Dumais, Lucien, *The Man Who Went Back* (Leo Cooper, 1975)
Foot, M. R. D., *SOE 1940–46* (BBC, 1984)
Foot, M. R. D. and Langley, J. M., *MI 9: Escape and Evasion 1939–1945* (William Kimber, 1985)
Haestrup, Jorgen, *Europe Ablaze* (University Press, Odense, Denmark, 1978)
Haga, Arnfin, *Kystens Partisaner* (J. W. Cappellen (Norway), 1980)
Hargesheimer, Fred, *The School that Fell from the Sky* (Auburn, USA, 2002)
Howarth, David, *The Shetland Bus* (Thomas Nelson, 1951)
Hutton, C. Clayton, *Official Secret* (Four Square, 1962)
Langley, J. M., *Fight Another Day* (Collins, 1974)
Long, Helen, *Safe Houses are Dangerous* (William Kimber, 1985)
McCaig, Dennis, *From Fiji to Balkan Skies* (Woodfield, 1999)
Neave, Airey, *Saturday at MI 9* (Hodder & Stoughton, 1969)
Richards, Brooks, *Secret Flotillas* (HMSO, 1996)
Ride, Edwin, *British Army Aid Group: Hong Kong Resistance 1942–45* (Oxford, 1981)
Verity, Hugh, *We Landed by Moonlight* (Ian Allen, 1978)

PRIVATE PUBLICATIONS

Adams, Murray, *Against the Odds*
Cooper, Mike, *One of the Many*
Lacey-Johnson, Lionel, and Jeudwine, Geoffrey, *Global Warrior*
Strand, Inge, *Arbok for Beiarn*

Index

Italic page numbers refer to illustrations.